KILLERS, CROOKS AND CONS

KILLERS, CROOKS AND CONS

SCOTLAND'S CRIMES OF THE CENTURY

REG McKAY

BLACK & WHITE PUBLISHING

First published 2007
by Black & White Publishing Ltd
99 Giles Street, Edinburgh EH6 6BZ

1 3 5 7 9 10 8 6 4 2   07 08 09 10 11

ISBN 13: 978 1 84502 145 0
ISBN 10: 1 84502 145 2
Copyright © Reg McKay 2007

A CIP catalogue record for this book is
available from the British Library.

Typeset by InReach
Printed and bound by Creative Print and Design Group Ltd

To the healers

I'm grateful to the *Daily Record*
for helping me with the pictures for this book.

CONTENTS

1900 TO 1909

NEW CENTURY, OLD WAYS

The twentieth century was greeted with great celebration. The Empire Exhibition in London was renowned the world over while in Scotland, the Glasgow International Festival in Kelvingrove Park in 1901 attracted thousands of visitors. But the days of the Empire were numbered, as were those of Queen Victoria who died in 1901 after sixty-four years on the throne.

A time of great invention, it saw Marconi send the first radio signal across the Atlantic (1901), Henry Ford produce the first Model T Ford (1908) and the Bleriot make the first cross-Channel flight (1909).

Albert Einstein presented his Theory of Relativity (1905), Sigmund Freud's *The Interpretation of Dreams* was published (1900) and, for the first time, the major blood groups were identified (1907).

As usual, war raged as Britain was embroiled in the Second Boer War, revolution broke out in Russia (1905) and the stirrings of rebellion turned China into a bloody zone.

Poverty was rife among the mass of ordinary Scottish people with a low life expectancy and a high proportion of infant deaths. Those lucky enough to work in the heavy industries of the cities or down the coal mines put in seventy-hour weeks for barely enough money to survive. Medical services were private and beyond the pocket of most people.

For those who broke the law, treatment was harsh. Punishment treadmills were finally banned from our jails in 1902 though birching, hard labour and bread and water diets remained. It took till 1908 to end the capital punishment of children but the decade would end with hundreds of children being thrown into adult jails each year. Penal colonies were still used for offences as minor as stealing bread. The cops received their first ever motor vehicle (1909) but it was used for taking prisoners to jail, not preventing crime.

THE FINAL INSULT

The creak of the rusty door hinges cracked the silence causing the young man to jump with a start. He looked up at the others in shock and fear. Yet he knew fine well what was happening, had known for three long weeks. The hangman had come for him.

We meet Patrick Leggett in 1902 near the end of his tale, the end of his life. It hadn't been a good life even by the standard of those violent, poverty-ridden times.

Raised in the teeming slum tenements of downtown Partick in Glasgow, Leggett's lot was fairly ordinary. Originally a town in its own right, Partick had grown with the expansion of shipbuilding and the heavy industries that made the city one of the most powerful in the world. This was all on the back of the workers who toiled at dangerous jobs and were rewarded with only slightly more than survival wages. The masses of people were merely a tool in the creation of wealth and no one much cared how they suffered or died. That was how it was then.

Like many before him Partick Leggett fell into bad ways when he was still in short trousers and wearing the heavy hobnailed boots handed out by welfare agencies to families struggling to get by. There was no shame in that. Most of his neighbours were rigged out the same.

Very young children were required to earn money any way they could. Sweat shops, stinking tanneries, lugging barrels in breweries, they worked everywhere and, if they weren't up to the work, they were sacked on the spot with someone else taking their job from the long line of waiting kids.

Leggett did his fair share of grafting but also sought easier ways. Minor pilfering, a bit of pickpocketing, stealing from some prone dock worker who'd collapsed after too many beers on pay night or following a lucky bet with some illegal street-corner bookie. He frequently got caught, of course, and was handed out swift street justice by local beat bobbies – a sharp slap on the face or a kick up the butt. It was the way of the times.

Many other children strayed off the straight and narrow but they soon mended their ways as they grew up. Not Leggett – by the age of eleven, he had already been birched for his crimes. The birch – a thick bundle of strong, thin branches bound tightly together – was a nasty, vicious implement. It would be unleashed with the full power of a grown man on to the naked buttocks and back of a mere child. One lash was agonising. Usually several were dished out. Still it wasn't enough to deter Leggett.

When only a child, he was sent to one of Scotland's many reform schools. These brutal, violent institutions were places where staff often gave full vent to their sadistic and, all too often, child-abusing perversions with the state, if not sanctioning such behaviour, then certainly turning a blind eye to it.

By this time, another characteristic of Patrick Leggett had emerged – he had a raging temper and a capacity for the most extreme violence. Violence was a way of life for many young people back then, with street gangs comprised of thousands of members who'd be armed to the teeth. But Leggett's violence was more of a personal nature. Although perfectly capable – as he had to be – of holding his own when challenged by local heavies, Leggett turned particularly nasty when he believed he had suffered some personal slight – often a slight that only he thought had happened.

It would be many decades before psychiatry would come into its own and search out reasons for unreasonable behaviour such as

Leggett's. That he was emotionally damaged at the very least, there is no doubt yet, in that era, this was never considered.

Leggett's violence, even as a child, took him into very dangerous territory. At the end of the nineteenth century, they hanged children for a range of crimes and certainly for murder. That law would not be abolished till 1908.

Still, Leggett's troubled childhood grew into adulthood and he seemed to settle down. His big breakthrough came when he met and married Sarah Jane, an attractive young woman from a decent background. The two became inseparable – the picture of young love even in those slums. Leggett was very attentive to his wife – too attentive. If she slipped out to the shops, he'd want to know exactly where she'd been, whom she'd seen and why she'd been away for so long. To start with it felt like young love, infatuation even. Then slowly, gradually, it felt like possessiveness and then paranoia set in as he burst out into jealous rages just because he noticed the man in the corner shop smiling at her politely as he served her.

It was a short honeymoon that was ended by Leggett lashing out at his young wife. She left him and went to live with relatives, only to return on his promise that he'd never hurt her again – a promise that didn't last long.

By 1902, with Patrick Leggett thirty years old and Sarah Jane just twenty-seven, they'd lived with this violent yo-yo-ing relationship for some years. Every time she left for her own safety, she had returned, knowing fine well how often he'd broken his promise before. Things got even worse when he took to drinking heavily on a regular basis, leaving her alone at home while he boozed, only to come home drunk and accuse her of seeing someone else while he'd been out.

Despite this, she kept returning. Divorce was unheard of among poor people. A woman without her man was assumed to be a fallen woman, little better than a prostitute. Respectable working-class young women like Sarah Jane always returned to their men, no matter the violence they faced.

The jealous taunts and beatings became Sarah Jane's daily existence till eventually she left Patrick again, this time moving in with her brother where she knew she'd be safe. Thought she'd be safe.

One warm day in September Sarah Jane went out shopping with her cousin Christina and Christina's little baby. For reasons lost in time, Christina was known by the family as Teezy. When they returned to Sarah Jane's brother's home in the early evening, Sarah Jane was carrying her cousin's baby. As soon as they had stepped through the front door, Sarah Jane sensed something and called out, 'For Christ's sake, Teezy, take the wean.'

With fear gripping her heart, Christina reached out for her child and suddenly her world went blank. Perhaps it was just as well for her since what came next was too awful to behold.

Patrick Leggett had been waiting in ambush by the front door. As soon as the women got close enough, he had battered Christina on the side of the head then turned on his young wife. Sarah Jane screamed as loud and long as she could and neighbours came scurrying. Too late to help. In time to witness.

Leggett stuck a long-bladed knife into his wife's back. She continued to scream so he knifed her again. And again and again, till she went silent and, clawing at the air vainly, she used her last breath and energy to try to flee. She crumpled on the ground and he stabbed her again.

Blind fury had engulfed Patrick Leggett but now deep remorse overtook him. Taking to his heels, he sprinted to the nearby River Clyde and without stopping threw himself in. A suicide attempt? Who knows? But he was still alive some distance down the deep, fast-flowing river when the ferryman at Linthouse pulled him out.

At his trial at the old High Court in Glasgow, Leggett pled insanity. The Crown brought in two eminent doctors who found no evidence of madness. As if that wasn't bad enough he had another, bigger, problem – premeditation.

It wasn't just the neighbours who had watched the horrific killing. Others came forward – friends of Leggett sickened by the murder – to swear he had told them he planned to kill his wife. He had shown one the murder knife and told him it was for Sarah Jane only a short time before the slaying. Case closed.

It took the jury a mere five minutes to find Patrick Leggett guilty of murder. There were no hysterics, no appeal, no protest and no delay. A mere twenty-one days later on 12 November 1902, the hangman came for Patrick Leggett as he cowered in the condemned cell at Duke Street Prison.

As the time approached and the noose was placed round Leggett's neck, a large crowd outside cheered in celebration then waited in hushed silence. In those bitter, hard days his senseless murder of an innocent young woman had horrified the people. Now they waited to witness revenge delivered.

The last thing that Patrick Leggett probably heard was that cheer – a cheer celebrating his imminent death. Did he get angry and take affront at the public insult, the personal slight? Who knows? It was too late for him by then. Too late for anything.

BITTER SWEET

'POISONED! I'VE BEEN POISONED!' the woman cried, her face pale as death, arms and legs rigid and stiff. An exaggeration, the others thought, even as they ran to fetch the doctor. After all, they were feeling ill too. It would just be something they had eaten. They weren't wrong about that.

The woman who saw her life flashing in front of her eyes was Miss Grace McKerrow, a middle-aged, portly and very good housekeeper-cum-cook for widower William Lennox at his home in Woodside Cottage in New Cumnock, Ayrshire. A well-to-do businessman, he could afford a full-time housekeeper and a maid. But now all the money in the world wouldn't help.

It was 23 March 1906 and things had taken a nasty turn at Woodside Cottage. The maid had felt unwell to start with – she had a terrible bitter taste in her mouth that glass after glass of water couldn't rinse away. In fact the taste got worse. Then Grace McKerrow, the housekeeper, was overcome with nausea, dizziness, spasms in her neck and a strange stiffening of her limbs. With their boss, William Lennox, feeling ill as well, the maid staggered out of the house to fetch neighbours and the local GP, Dr Robertson.

The good doctor called promptly at Woodside Cottage. By then Miss McKerrow had been half carried, half dragged, to her own home by the maid. Probably the distressed woman just wanted to be in her own bed as most ill people do. By the time the maid had made sure Miss McKerrow was safe at home, she herself was too ill, her limbs too rigid, for her to make her own way to Woodside Cottage and she had to be fetched back.

Dr Robertson took his time examining William Lennox, forcing him to vomit and then making him as comfortable as he could. Then he gave the maid the same treatment before going on to visit Miss McKerrow. It's not recorded if the doctor regretted his actions or not. What is known is that Grace McKerrow died soon afterwards.

'Strychnine poisoning,' Dr Robertson announced that night. 'All parties are suffering from strychnine poisoning.' These days it may seem remarkable that a local, country doctor could be so sure of such a diagnosis. But it must be remembered that deadly poisons such as strychnine – as well as hard drugs such as opium – weren't subject to the same controls as they are now. Strychnine was commonly bought across the counter at chemists in order to kill vermin, particularly rats. Accidental or suicidal strychnine poisoning wasn't common but wasn't rare either.

Strychnine poisoning can lead to a slow agonising death of the first order. It causes convulsions in the neck and head which then spread to all the limbs. Increasing in intensity, the spasms never stop and the victim's backbone is permanently arched till eventually they die of asphyxiation. As well as being an awful poison, strychnine is one of the most bitter-tasting substances known to mankind.

An independent post-mortem by Professor Harvey Littlejohn confirmed that strychnine was found in the stomach, blood and liver of Miss McKerrow. The police and the doctors immediately started asking questions about the source of the strychnine. This was no accident from, say, rat poison. That might have been suspected if only one person was affected but not three as in this case. William Lennox and the maid, recovered fully, quickly pointed their suspicion at a most unexpected source – some iced shortbread.

Earlier that week, on Monday, 19 November 1906, the postman had delivered a plain wrapped tin addressed to William Lennox at Woodside Cottage. Inside the tin was the icing-covered shortbread, clearly home-baked, and a card saying, 'With happy greetings from an old friend', but, with no name and no address, there was no hint who the sender might be.

William Lennox clearly had many old friends who might send a present in this manner since he wasn't suspicious at all. It should be remembered that, even in a well-off household such as his in 1906, such a sweet treat was a generous gift indeed. The cake had been laid aside till the fateful night when a neighbour paid a visit and the cake was brought out along with other delicacies. Being a kindly boss, William Lennox ensured that the housekeeper and the maid were both given some of the short-bread. Miss McKerrow, the housekeeper, died from his kindness.

The doctors soon sussed that the icing was laced with lethal amounts of strychnine. The very sweet icing sugar would be ideal to mask the terrible bitterness of the poison, if the dosage hadn't been too high. They also noticed what everyone at William Lennox's household had noticed, that the icing was rather shoddy though the shortbread was well made. The police soon came to the view that the killer had bought the cake and then iced it none too proficiently – with added strychnine, of course. Probably a man, they reckoned. What man, apart from a baker, knows how to ice a cake? In 1906, it was a fair question.

The police were in no doubt that William Lennox had been the target of the strychnine. Why else send the laced cake to him? But who would do such a thing, especially in that quiet Ayrshire backwater? It had to be someone who hated Lennox yet he appeared to be a well-liked man with no enemies. Could it be a madman then?

One of the benefits of policing such small communities is that the populace are well known to the cops. Not just the people but also their habits, their movements and anything unusual they got up to. The cops soon arrested their prime suspect. A man who was known to have bought strychnine. To have travelled to an ironmonger's in Glasgow where they sold tins like the one containing the cake. To be a regular customer of a baker whose shortbread was known for its excellence. Just one question – why would he want to kill his best friend?

The police were in doubt that the murderer was one Thomas Brown. Not only was he William Lennox's closest friend but also a most unusual bloke. Everyone knew he was as madman. Well, so they thought.

Thomas Brown behaved strangely for sure. Once he'd been discovered walking the streets of Old Cumnock where he lived, ripping his clothes as he marched towards some woods declaring that God had called him. One time at his work, he was found in his office stark naked, on his knees praying and weeping. At all times, he was known to talk over people, often making obscure, fantastic, boastful claims of having been shot four times, of owning whole towns, having farms in South Africa and having fought in the Boer War.

Yet Thomas Brown wasn't mentally ill. He was suffering from a type of epilepsy – not the grand mal type of seizures that many assume is always present in epilepsy but temporal lobe epilepsy, a type that brings on behaviour so weird that, in the not too distant past, some cultures worshipped sufferers as saints while others burned them at the stake as witches.

His symptoms included: hallucinations – both seeing and smelling things that weren't there; blank periods where he'd continue moving and talking but be unaware of his actions; knowing what was going to happen before it happened; sleepwalking, not for minutes but for hours; seizures during sleep with vivid dreams; and talking at great length articulately about complex subjects.

Brown's doctor had diagnosed his epilepsy when he was a child. His parents were advised to send him to an institution but they refused. Instead he set about leading a normal life, being successful in business, marrying and having children. His wife was the niece of William Lennox who became Brown's best friend and mentor. The same William Lennox who was now the target of a killer.

Though his doctor knew what ailed Thomas Brown he was very limited in the treatment he could give him. Daily doses of potassium bromide was all he could prescribe to stop the convulsions. These days it is still used for that purpose – but for animals, not humans. In Brown's case, it helped a little but was almost useless. After forty years of this treatment, the few beneficial effects were wearing off and Brown's behaviour was beginning to deteriorate. It showed for, to all intents and purposes, he started behaving like a madman.

This was a time when those with mental health problems were thrown into brutal asylums if poor or, if rich, locked away at home, sometimes literally in the attic, for their entire lives. Thomas Brown walked about freely and many local people were scared. If he was capable of stripping naked at his work, what else was he capable of? Murder?

Some people believed so – especially William Lennox's next-door neighbour, David Murray, who was visiting the day after Miss McKerrow's death when Brown and his wife called by. He reported to the police that Brown didn't even ask after his best friend's welfare or commiserate with him on his housekeeper's terrible, agonising death. Instead, he prattled on about new business opportunities in the area, bullets being in his leg and other unrelated matters.

Murray claimed to the police that he'd confronted Brown, saying, 'Death by strychnine is a very painful death, Mr Brown.' But Brown had just ignored him and Murray watched as Brown hurried away.

It might not have been exactly damning but don't we make hasty judgements on people's reactions to such murderous horrors? Human nature was no different in 1906 and unfortunately then the police shared those hasty judgements.

A cop raid on Thomas Brown's house found icing sugar as well as a pestle and mortar, such as a chemist might use, covered in a film of white powder – the colour that strychnine crystals would leave. When this was added to the information that, on the day of the poisoning, Brown had travelled to Glasgow and visited an ironmonger's and baker's, it was enough to put Brown in the frame. He was duly charged with the murder of Grace McKerrow and attempting to murder William Lennox and the maid.

The Crown promptly had Brown examined by two psychiatrists though at the time that name was not yet in common usage. They declared him unfit to stand trial due to mental illness. Usually the matter would have ended there with the accused being ordered to a locked lunatic asylum. But they hadn't reckoned with Thomas Brown.

Brown had been unwell since childhood yet he had still fought on to achieve success in business and settle happily with a wife and children. With no adequate treatment for his health problems, it must have been a hellish struggle. He was a fighter, in other words, and he was also very obstinate – so obstinate that he instructed his lawyer to fight for the right to a trial, no matter that, if found guilty, he could hang. Brown's lawyer won the right for a trial.

The evidence was trotted out by the Crown and immediately gaps began to show. No strychnine had been found in Brown's house. Worse, the strychnine he was known to have purchased months earlier from the chemist to kill rats was of a different type and the crystals of a larger size than those found in the icing.

No one recognised Brown from the bakery where he was alleged to have bought the shortbread. Wouldn't a strange man like that – who would no doubt have, at the very least, been prattling in a loud voice about some obscure topic or some wild claim – have stuck in their minds? Then the bakery staff argued with each other from the witness stand. One said he was certain that the shortbread was made by their firm since it could be recognised by a pattern they made round the edge. Another said it didn't look like their pattern at all.

The ironmonger first said that the tin used for the iced shortbread had been bought from his store but that his label had been cut off. Then he changed his mind.

Two independent handwriting experts both agreed that the writing on the parcel could not be identified as belonging to

Thomas Brown. They thought it more likely that two, if not three, different people had been responsible for the writing.

Brown's own housekeeper owned up to the icing sugar found in his home and admitted using the pestle and mortar and not washing it.

The police even failed to find one person who could identify Thomas Brown as having been to Kilmarnock post office from where the parcel was sent.

Thomas Brown was right to insist on an open trial. What started as little more than circumstantial evidence was torn apart by his defence lawyer. Even the trial judge, in his address to the jury, said that the case against him, if there was any, was extremely weak. They didn't listen. By a majority, the jury found Thomas Brown guilty of murder by poison.

For most people, this would have resulted in a date with the hangman and death on the gallows within a few weeks. But the court had already heard from two eminent doctors that Brown was insane. That saved him from execution. Instead of a trip to the hanging shed, he was sent off to the equivalent of today's State Hospital, the quaintly named Criminal Lunatic Department in Perth, to be detained there at His Majesty's Pleasure.

Strictly speaking, to be detained at His Majesty's Pleasure meant to be kept locked up till sane. In practice, this was rarely considered – once mad, always mad was the belief in 1906. Thomas Brown was never free again and died a few years later in an asylum in Ayr.

In modern times, with global mass media and a strong notion of human rights, there is no doubt that a campaign would have been launched to free Thomas Brown as innocent. Then again, with our deeper knowledge of epilepsy and modern treatments, he might well never have been suspected in the first place, let alone charged.

If he had been, however, would the modern-day jury have found him innocent or guilty? That may well have been influenced on whether or not they were prejudiced against the mentally ill. Have things changed that much?

WATCHED AND DAMNED

Rank, ripe odours wafted in from the fields in that rural place. Yet even there the stench was too much. It was a different smell, coming not from the farms but from the downstairs flat. The neighbour decided to investigate. She'd find more than a stink.

It was 29 September 1907 in the small village of Lhanbryde in the north-east of Scotland, lying between Inverness and Aberdeen, slap bang in the middle of whisky and farming country with fast-running streams, low rolling hills, fields full of cows and rough pasture dotted with sheep. Life was slow there, unchanged from an earlier time, and people trusted people. Sometimes that proves fatal.

The smell had been worrying Jane McGillivray for days. Some folk would have acted sooner but, like most of her kind, she was a trusting, patient soul. Why shouldn't she be? She knew everyone in the village and they knew her. Families that had lived close by for generations. That type of long association bred respect. Then the smell got worse and her patience ran out.

The smell was coming from the house of her downstairs neighbour, one John Barclay Smith. She'd known John Smith for years and knew, like most people in the village, he left his door unlocked. What had they to fear? She could've simply gone in and checked for herself. John wouldn't mind and nor would she if the roles had been reversed. Instead, Jane McGillivray went to fetch the local bobby. Why did she do that? There was something about that smell she didn't like – something that frightened her. She wasn't wrong.

The policeman found John Smith's door locked. That was most unusual and it worried him. He too had lived in Lhanbryde for many years and knew local habits only too well. Normally he would have walked away, calling back later. But Jane McGillivray was right about that smell – something was wrong.

When he forced open a window, the stench got worse, making the bobby gag and choke. Behind him Jane McGillivray wrapped a shawl round her face and backed away from the house some distance.

Covering his mouth and nose as best he could, the policeman stepped into the tiny flat. There, naked on the bed, lay John Smith, his face and skull gone, replaced with blood and bone. The bedding was soaked through with the red of his blood and the grey, green and brown of his rotting body fluids. Next to the bed lay a heavy, bloodstained hammer. The poor man had been brutally killed and had been dead for days.

Poaching game, rustling cows, drunken brawls – those were the usual crimes in Lhanbryde and even they didn't happen often. Murder? Who would have thought it? The case promptly became a national scandal. The country was going to wrack and ruin. It had to be if you weren't safe in your own bed even in sleepy Lhanbryde.

Village life had its limitations but not when it came to murder investigations. Familiar and even nosy neighbours make very good witnesses. It didn't take the police long to ascertain that the last time anyone had seen John Smith alive was on the morning of 24 September 1907, five days earlier. It was also said that he had been in the company of a man, a stranger to Lhanbryde. That unknown face attracted a lot of silent curiosity. That's the way with villagers. Several of the witnesses gave excellent, almost identical descriptions. Better still, the description sounded familiar to the police.

Rural Scotland had another industry then aside from whisky and farming – soldiering. For generations, many young men had been tempted to take the King's or Queen's shilling and serve in the army. They made good fighting men for sure. Testament to this was the many Scottish regiments who had won battle honours in every war and campaign in the long history of the British Empire. The prospect of war was in the air again and there was no let-up on recruitment in the Scottish hills. Yet life in the British Army didn't work out for everyone.

A week earlier, the police had received a notice from the Highland Light Infantry regiment based in the barracks at Fort George that a deserter was on the loose – not an unusual occurrence in a nation with so many soldiers. This time the police could do more than help their soldier pals – in fact, it was vice versa. The deserter's description matched that of the man last seen with John Smith.

The deserter was twenty-five-year-old Joseph Rutherford from the central belt of Scotland – or so the army thought. After some enquiries, the cops came up with another name for the man, Joseph Hume. No one was sure why Rutherford had assumed another surname. Maybe he'd led a life of crime and was wanted by the police elsewhere. Maybe his family background was complex and he wasn't sure who his father was. Both situations were common then and changing names was easier than in modern times. After all, police records and birth registration weren't comprehensive or efficient. This didn't just affect the suspect. No one knew how old John Smith, the victim, was – not even Smith himself apparently.

With the police force yet to be motorised and telecommunications at a very early stage, the police did all they could do by sending out wanted notices to other police stations across the country. They particularly concentrated on the central belt, making sure their colleagues in Stirling and Falkirk were alerted. This was based on the principle that most runaways – even from prison or the army – go home. They weren't wrong.

On 24 October, one month after the murder, Joseph Hume was arrested on the streets of Stirling. He denied the killing right from the start. However, he did admit to some things – deserting from the army and passing through Lhanbryde while making his escape. The police were in trouble since there were no witnesses to Smith's murder and, in those days, there were no sound forensic tests that could match a killer to the scene. They could check for one thing though – blood.

From the description of the villagers in Lhanbryde, Hume appeared to be wearing the same clothes as on the day they spotted him. Not unusual since clothes were extremely expensive for ordinary people and ideas on hygiene called for infrequent ablutions. Smith's killing had been a brutal affair and the murderer's own body and clothes would have been soaked in the man's blood and this would have been obvious even four weeks later. When he was duly stripped, searched and examined, not one speck of dried blood was found on Hume or his clothes.

It looked as if the police had been chasing the wrong man and Hume would be released. Given the high public profile of the case and the fact that a very violent killer was on the loose, the police were understandably reluctant to let him walk away free. First, they decided to thoroughly check his account of his movements.

On 25 September, the day after Smith's murder, Hume claimed he had been in Edinburgh where he had pawned a watch. This was part of his alibi since the journey from Lhanbryde to Edinburgh in 1907, though possible in the time span, was long and arduous.

Hume couldn't recall the name or location of the pawnbroker's shop so the cops went round them all making enquiries. Eventually, one pawnbroker came forward saying that the murder suspect had pawned a watch with him on the day in question and he even produced the watch.

From the beginning, the police had suspected robbery as the motive for Smith's murder. Though the man didn't have a great deal, he would have had a few pennies lying around and was known to wear a watch on a chain. No money or watch were found in his home.

Lhanbryde locals described the watch and the police were convinced it was the one pawned by Hume in Edinburgh. Now the murder trial was on.

At the High Court in Aberdeen, on 6 February 1908, Joseph Hume continued to plead his innocence. The evidence against him was the witnesses saying he had been seen in Lhanbryde on that dreadful morning and, of course, the watch. It wasn't much of a case.

Hume had a problem with the jury though. In those days, deserters were despised by the public as cowardly, immoral and failing to do their duty. Hume admitted being a deserter.

The jury found Joseph Hume guilty on the most slender of evidence. Four weeks later, on 5 March 1908, in Inverness Prison, he was met at the gallows by the hangman, Henry Pierrepoint. As public executions go, his death was unremarkable. What we do know are his last muttered words as he was led to his death: 'But I'm innocent.'

Too late. Time had run out for Joseph Hume.

THE DISAPPEARING ACT

A murder chase that ends with a confession and a suicide would usually be considered a good result . . . usually.

The Abbey on one side and the towering cotton mill on the other acted as dull-eyed sentries over the bridge. It was known as a bridge of death and for good reason. Below, the dark waters of the River Cart ran fast and deep through Paisley. For those unlucky or desperate enough to go in, if the water didn't drown them then the sharp rocks would smash their bones for sure. Too many local citizens, legless drunk, careless or sad, would tumble from that bridge. So much so that local worthies had bought lifebelts and placed them all along the bridge. But they were no good for the latest victim of the Cart – no one had seen him.

The suicide note was written in a plain hand, in red ink and was very clear:

> I murdered Mickey Brown – AE.

> You will find my body at the foot of water nearby. I filled my pockets with stones. I bid goodbye to my mother.

> Goodbye – Alexander Edmonstone.

A novice policeman might well have accepted the letter at face value. Not so the experienced and busy coppers of the burgh who'd dealt with more suicides than they cared to remember. Usually there was a straightforward message of farewell and sometimes a reason but not a description of how the writers intended to kill themselves.

The Cart was dragged and dragged again – no body. In double quick time, the cops concluded that the murder of one Michael Brown remained unsolved and their chief suspect, Alexander Edmonstone, was still at large.

A few weeks earlier, on 19 February 1909, a young man had gone to use the facilities of the gents' public lavatory in the small village of East Wemyss, Fife. A rudimentary place with no roof, one urinal, one cubicle and basic Victorian plumbing, the place was unwelcoming and acid rank at the best of times. That day it held extra horrors.

Pushing at the cubicle door, the young man felt it thud softly against something. He pushed again. Still no movement. Desperate for the toilet, he cocked his head round the door and immediately regretted it. There, slumped on the floor, was the blood-drenched body of a teenage boy.

Turning, he fled through the door, splashing in a puddle of blood as he went. A puddle he hadn't noticed on the way in. No one had. Nor had they noticed the streaks of blood, hair and skull bone on the walls and floor. A short while earlier a man had used the urinal and heard desperate gurgling coming from the cubicle. He had ignored it, assuming it was just some kid from the local school playing a joke. It was Michael Brown's last gasps at life.

As word spread among locals, horror and outrage were the universal reaction. How could such a brutal murder happen in their little rural idyll? Later, when the press reported the killing, there would be widespread shock. Everyone knew that Scotland's cities were hard, violent places but a small town in Fife?

East Wemyss was a village where everyone knew everyone. Yet, to begin with, no one recognised the body, such were the injuries. The boy had been smashed against the brick walls and stone floor so often and ferociously that his skull was cracked wide open, splashing brains, bone and blood everywhere. A dirty white handkerchief had been tied tight round his neck and a man's cap stuffed deep into his mouth. It had been a brutal, agonising, slow death.

Eventually, managers at a local linen mill, G. & J. Johnson, approached the police concerned that their junior clerk, fifteen-year-old Michael Brown, hadn't returned from his weekly trip to the Royal Bank of Scotland in Buckhaven, a mile-long tram ride away, to collect the wages. The local bobby showed one of the mill owners the body found in the toilet but, ashen faced and gagging back vomit, he didn't identify the boy. He couldn't, so bad were the boy's injuries. When shown a tram ticket and a pencil found on the dead lad, the mill owner immediately recognised both as likely to have been in Michael Brown's possession.

East Wemyss was the kind of place where people left their doors open. Where crime was rare and usually petty. Now there was murder. Why? It didn't take the cops long to reach a conclusion.

Eyewitnesses soon confirmed that Michael had been to the bank, drawn the mill's wages of £85 – a massive sum then – and left to return to work with the cash in a sturdy leather case. Along with the young clerk's silver watch, the cash and the case were missing.

Young Michael went to the bank at the same time on the same day every week to fetch the firm's wages. It must have been common knowledge in that small community. Reckless? No – trusting. Who in that community would want to rob the young lad, let alone murder him? The police weren't long in finding out.

Many sightings had been made of one man either next to Michael or nearby him – he had been seen in Buckhaven, near the bank, sitting next to him on the tram ride home and in East Wemyss heading in the direction of the public lavatory – and that man was twenty-three-year-old Alexander Edmonstone.

Locals spotted Edmonstone easily. He and his family had recently moved into the area and newcomers always stuck out in that tight-knit community. Then there was his appearance – bright ginger hair, a black hole in the front of his mouth where teeth had been knocked out, scruffy clothes and a rough tattoo on his arm of AE, his initials. He shouldn't be hard to catch – or so the cops thought.

The police didn't hesitate in bringing in sniffer dogs and tracked all the area around East Wemyss with every able-bodied local also volunteering. No luck. Then they had a wanted poster made up from an artist's impression, a common device in those days when there was little technology available and newspapers were the main form of mass media. To start with, the posters were circulated in the East Wemyss area, then the whole of Scotland, then Britain. All with good reason – the wanted man had fled fast.

Later it would emerge that he had headed out of East Wemyss immediately. After at a stop-off at the village of Strathmiglo, twelve miles from East Wemyss, where he bought a whole new outfit of clothes, he caught a train to Perth where he booked in to St John's Temperance Hotel, a high-class, expensive place. The next morning he caught another train to the big smoke of Glasgow and took lodgings at 113 Renfield Street in the city centre.

If Edmonstone thought he could simply lose himself in the second city of the Empire, he was soon to have his mind changed. He hadn't reckoned on the public outcry over young Michael's murder or that wanted poster turning up everywhere. After a few days, he paid for the room and left in a hurry. So much of a hurry he was to make a crucial mistake.

In going to clean the room after Edmonstone departed, the Glasgow landlady discovered he had left two parcels. Curiosity soon took a grip and she untied the string, probably hoping for a small windfall. She got a lot more than she bargained for – two bundles of stinking, blood-soaked clothes.

By the time the landlady had rushed to the Glasgow police, Edmonstone's faked suicide note had been found in Paisley and the River Cart was being dragged. By the end of the day, the cops concluded that the murder suspect had given them the slip and moved on elsewhere. They did all they could do – issued yet another wanted poster to all corners of Britain offering a reward of the then massive sum of £100 and gave reports to as many newspapers as would print the story. Most did.

Alexander Edmonstone had slipped south, to Chorlton-cum-Hardy, a small, gentle town a few miles from the outskirts of the sprawling industrial city of Manchester. In 1909, ordinary people would rarely travel such distances. Edmonstone must have considered himself far beyond the reach of the Scottish police.

Settling into a boarding house at 12 Brunswick Street, he now called himself Albert Edwards, using his own initials in case anyone spotted his tattoo. To start with, he felt safe, then he noticed something – the wanted posters were in Manchester.

His landlady would later recall his strong Scottish accent she struggled to understand, his tendency to drink a lot and splash around his money. The other thing she noticed was that he didn't sleep well. She could tell by hearing him pacing the floor of his room most nights. A bad conscience? Nightmares about his terrible deed? Fear of being caught? Maybe all of those things but what would also transpire was that Edmonstone had suffered from very bad headaches for some years and they had got worse – blindingly bad.

If the landlady didn't notice anything sinister about Edmonstone, one of her other lodgers did. Jack Atherton's lot was far from happy. Like his father before him, he scraped a living by selling cheap goods on the street or going from door to door, selling or offering to sharpen kitchen knives. He was a grafter but still barely earned enough to support himself. Now there was the £100 reward on offer for information leading to Edmonstone's capture . . . that would transform his life.

Atherton wasn't alone in studying the wanted poster, something he took extra time over in the police station in Manchester where he was applying for a hawker's licence. The sum of £100 was a fortune to most ordinary folk in 1909. But he had an advantage over the others – he thought he recognised the man.

One night in March, Atherton allowed the man he knew as Albert Edwards to take him for a drink. The man was always looking for company and wouldn't let anyone else put their hands in their pockets and, true to form, Edwards bought all the drinks that night.

A few hours into the boozy session, Atherton asked his companion the time. Obliging as ever, the man whisked out a silver watch and told him the time. Alexander Edmonstone aka Albert Edwards had just signed his own death warrant.

The next day a team of forty policemen stormed the boarding house at Brunswick Street and arrested Alexander Edmonstone for the murder of young Michael Brown. As the handcuffed prisoner was led away to the police wagon, Jack Atherton congratulated himself on his powers of observation that were about to make him a rich man. The night before, when he'd asked the time, Edmonstone had read it from a silver watch, a fancy watch with delicate inscribed detail. It matched the description on the wanted poster exactly – Michael Brown's silver watch.

Edmonstone immediately confessed to the police as being the murderer of Michael Brown but claimed he had blanked out at the time. He claimed he didn't know the boy and had no idea how he had ended up in that public lavatory with him let alone why he had killed him. But did he know him?

When Michael Brown was last seen alive he was walking towards the toilet, away from the mill where he was expected with the wages. It appeared to witnesses that he was going to the public lavatory and the same witnesses reported Edmonstone walking a discreet distance behind him. Cottaging, they call it these days – gay men meeting in lavatories for illicit, quick sex – but it's not a modern creation. Ever since public toilets were introduced late in the 1800s, gay men had been using them for sexual encounters. In 1909, homosexuality was still illegal. It was punishable by imprisonment and discovery resulted in being cast out socially. If two men had been meeting for sex, it would be the most closely guarded of secrets.

Then there was that bogus suicide note in which Edmonstone called his victim 'Mickey', a familiar term his mates knew him by. A slip of the pen? Or a revelation? This wasn't even examined by the High Court in Perth at the murder trial. The only time such august institutions considered gay men was when they were prosecuting them. Besides, they didn't need motive when they had a confession.

Edmonstone's lawyers filed an insanity plea. Certainly there seemed to be some evidence to support that. His grandfather had died in a lunatic asylum after years of incarceration there. Edmonstone himself had been treated for those constant blinding headaches and for sunstroke and fevers – all of which we now know were frequently misdiagnosed then, instead of being seen as symptoms of serious mental illness.

Was Alexander Edmonstone mad? We'll never know. On 6 July 1909, convicted of the murder of young Michael Brown, Edmonstone kept an appointment with hangman John Ellis in Perth Prison. Ellis, a Rochdale barber, was an official executioner for twenty-three years. In his career he would see off 203 souls from the gallows, including some of the most infamous killers Britain has known. After the Easter Rising in Dublin, he hanged six rebels in one day.

He was a nervous, fussy man and each and every execution got to him. Later, after retirement, he'd try to kill himself and fail and, a short while afterwards, he finally succeeded, cutting his own throat in front of his family. Some say that it was the ghosts of all the people he killed, especially the women, that drove Ellis to despair. Others that he lived with such high standards at each and every execution that the strain eventually drove him over the edge.

In 1909, those years of anguish were a long time away for John Ellis. That year, in Perth Prison, he was taking great care with every measurement, every piece of equipment. Some said that if you had to be hanged, it was better that John Ellis hanged you than some sloppy executioner.

Was that how Alexander Edmonstone felt that day as he took the long short walk in Perth Prison – lucky? Or was he a madman killed for actions he couldn't prevent?

1910 TO 1919

WAR AND REVOLUTION

The world was changing fast. The Union of South Africa was formed and apartheid was on its way (1910), Mao was a foot soldier in the revolution in China (1911), the Irish Rebellion raged (1916–21) and the war to end all wars, World War I, began and ended with at least thirty-two million souls killed (1914–18).

Tragedies abounded: almost 1,500 passengers and crew died in the sinking of the *Titanic* (1912); a train crash near Gretna killed 227 people (1915); and the HMS *Natal* blew up on the Cromarty Firth killing 350 souls (1915). As if the war wasn't bad enough, the dreaded Spanish flu wiped out another forty million (1918–19), killing more people in a single year than the bubonic plague had in four years.

On the bright side, Charlie Chaplin made his first film (1914), modern transport was on its way with the first flight across the Atlantic (1919) and a cure was found for syphilis (1910).

In politics women over thirty were given the right to vote for the first time (1918), Parliament rejected Scottish Home Rule (1913), Lady Astor was voted the first female MP (1919) and Hitler joined the National Socialist German Workers' Party (1919). In Scotland, inspired by Marxist John MacLean, 100,000 strikers demonstrated in George Square in support of a forty-hour week. The government called it a Bolshevik Uprising and drafted in 12,000 English troops armed with machine guns and tanks to take over the city (1919).

Criminals in Glasgow felt under pressure when the number of cops was increased to 4,000 and they got their first motor vehicle

(1914). Due to so many men being away at the war, Emily Miller was appointed Scotland's first female cop (1915).

During the war years the government ordered that there be no reporting of serious crime in an effort to keep up the morale of the population. Crime in Scotland continued just the same.

AVARICE AND ARSENIC

Crystal glasses clinked and sang as the man rose to his feet. 'Ladies and gentlemen – a toast. Please raise your glasses to the happiest couple I know – Mr and Mrs Charles Hutchison.'

Around the sumptuous dining room, eighteen guests stood and toasted their hosts on the celebration of their twentieth wedding anniversary that day, 3 February 1911. As well they should to such good and respected friends. A splendid evening was coming to a close. Or was it?

The toastmaster was Alfred Corrie, who had more reason than most to celebrate the Hutchisons' silver wedding. His daughter was engaged to their only son, twenty-four-year-old John, and soon their families would be joined together. But would it be in the way they thought?

The guests left the table, the men to light a cigar and take a brandy while their hostess, Mrs Hutchison, poured the coffee as the maid tidied up. This was a family with wealth and respect but they also had a reputation as warm people, fair to everyone including their servants. People always enjoyed a pleasant evening at the Hutchisons' home, quaintly called The Neuk, which stood in its own grounds at the edge of Dalkeith. And that's when the scream rang out.

A female guest had remarked to her husband that she didn't feel well then screamed in agony. As other guests rushed to her side another woman groaned and fell to the floor. Then a man and another man.

One of the women clutched her stomach and vomited over someone trying to help her. Guests rushed out into the gardens, breathing deeply, trying to get fresh air. Others lay down on the lawn, gripping their bellies, groaning, racked in agony.

Soon even most of the helpers had become ill and incapacitated. Only two were unaffected, one of whom was the Hutchisons' son, John, and he took control of the situation. He was very good, quickly fetching a mustard mixture designed to make people sick though many of the guests couldn't face even that in spite of their pain. The other unaffected guest went to fetch two local doctors, Blackstock and Mitchell.

When the physicians appeared on the scene they immediately took over and moved all the stricken people into the house next door and it became a mini hospital. The two doctors quickly suspected that the victims had somehow swallowed some poisonous substance – an accident surely in that respectable home.

Their concerns became deadly serious when Charles Hutchison and his friend Alec Clapperton, a local grocer, both died. It was now a tragedy that needed swift investigation.

The police were called in and promptly contacted a Dr Lovell Gulland in Edinburgh who was an expert on poisons. The doctor was swiftly at the scene, in time to help the local physicians care for the sick. Some were recovering quite quickly while others lingered on, their very lives hanging by a thread. One or two were gravely ill including the hostess of the evening. She would survive, thankfully, only to face the terrible news of her husband's death.

Dr Gulland didn't just care for the sick, he asked them questions. Very quickly suspicion pointed firmly at the after-dinner coffee. Everyone had noticed that it had a strange, mildly unpleasant taste. Those who had taken ill had done so immediately after drinking the coffee. Those who recovered quickest had only taken the slightest of sips. The two who had not been ill hadn't taken any. Charles Hutchison and Alec Clapperton had both downed a whole cup and died as a result.

Everything about the coffee was thoroughly tested but it threw up no clues. The police and the medics were going to have to look elsewhere.

Meanwhile, a few days after the incident, the funerals of the two men took place and they were attended by thousands of mourners. No wonder – Alec Clapperton was well respected by the public and in business alike and Charles Hutchison, if anything, was more prominent, working as he did for the Duke of Buccleuch and being a high-ranking member of the Freemasons.

The tragic incident wasn't just big news around Dalkeith – it also made waves farther afield. In Scotland at that time, as in the whole developed world, there was still a great concern about eating safely, keeping nasty stuff off the menu and killing germs. This was before effective disinfectants had been developed and it would be some time before the likes of penicillin were discovered. If eminent people like Charles Hutchison could die in such a way in his own home, was anyone safe?

Shortly after the funerals the medics made their first big breakthrough. Arsenic had killed the two men. Known as the poison of kings, arsenic had been a favourite of murderers for years since it was deadly effective yet had little taste. Adding it to strong-tasting coffee further concealed its presence and it had been used in this way several times by murderers in France and Italy. Though arsenic was used in a number of domestic applications and in medicines for treating syphilis, it was unlikely to have been carelessly left lying around the Hutchisons' house. When arsenic was present, the cops always suspected murder.

Keeping this information to themselves, the police quietly continued their work in The Neuk though now their minds weren't concentrated on possible domestic accidents – they were searching for clues in what looked like a double killing.

The Neuk didn't throw up any more clues so the police turned their attention to local chemist shops where they would store arsenic. They started with the one where John Hutchison worked as a dispenser and, sure enough, the logs showed that a bottle of arsenic was missing. By the time the police went looking for John Hutchison, he had fled. Knowing about the cops' visit to his employers, he had told friends he was going south for the day. John Hutchison had no intention of coming back.

Hutchison was a bit of a playboy, unlike his very sober-minded parents. He wore the best suits, attended the wildest balls with landed gentry, gambled on the horses – as gentlemen did back then – and always drove brand-new fast cars, frequently exchanging them for bigger, sleeker models when he got bored. Given his father's standing in society, no one had thought anything of this – till now.

As the majority of local police spread the net as wide as possible looking for John Hutchison, others were quietly prying into his private affairs. His fiancée knew nothing – which was just as well for her. Hutchison, it seems, wasn't too regular in his personal life and was in the habit of going out with several women at the same time, most of them of looser sexual scruples than his well-bred wife-to-be. In fact, one had become pregnant and Hutchison was forced to support her. Yet that was just a hint at his financial problems.

John Hutchison's playboy lifestyle was well beyond his means and he paid for it the only way he knew how – by borrowing. At that time, it was a social disgrace for an ordinary working man to borrow but, among the middle classes, it was quite acceptable. That kind of double standard suited John Hutchison dandy at the beginning – but now it had run out of control.

After just a few days' inquiries, the cops soon ascertained that Hutchison was in debt to several people to the tune of at least £10,000, a massive fortune in 1911 and one he couldn't hope to repay on his wages as a dispenser in a chemist shop. If, on the other hand, his parents died, he would inherit over £4,000 in insurance as well as their house and entire estate – more than enough to clear his debt and set him up well with his new wife and even his mistresses.

Better than that, at the anniversary party that fateful night was a man he owed £1,000 to. This was none other than Alfred Corrie, his fiancée's father. Such transactions between gentlemen involved no contract, no record, just a shake of the hand. If Corrie died, Hutchison's debt to him would die too.

The police soon concluded that John Hutchison didn't care who he killed that night – the more the merrier and the better the outcome for him. The arsenic in the coffee could have wiped out eighteen souls. His parents, his fiancée, his future in-laws, people who had bounced him on their knee when he was a babe. This was one dangerous man.

Hutchison had used his fast car to get away from Dalkeith at top speed and put many miles between him and his pursuers. The police did all they could do and released photographs to the national press and spread wanted posters up and down Britain and even in Ireland. What had started as a significant tragedy suddenly turned into national outrage. A man who would slaughter innocent men and women – and a toff to boot. The working people liked it when the better-off folk got caught out. The people of Britain paid full attention.

The wanted posters worked. From cities in England, various reports of Hutchison having been seen came in, only for him to flee farther away before the police arrived. The man seemed to be heading south by degrees so it came as no surprise when he was traced to a hotel in The Strand, London.

From Scotland, a local cop, Detective Inspector John Laing, was sent south. Laing was a top copper and, better, he knew Hutchison, not only from his dealings with the case but through local knowledge. Given the high profile the case was getting in the newspapers, Laing's brief was straightforward – don't come back without Hutchison, whatever it takes.

Hutchison had fled from the hotel in The Strand the day before Laing arrived. He'd been using a false name, as he had since the day he fled Dalkeith, but the hotel staff recognised him from the posters and newspapers. Laing settled in. He wasn't for budging till the next sighting came in. He didn't have long to wait.

'I've seen him,' said the man, his voice full of excitement and edged with fear.

'Who have you seen, sir?' asked the desk sergeant in the London police station.

'The Dalkeith Poisoner,' gasped the man. 'Look – him!' He held up a newspaper showing a picture of John Hutchison.

The day before the man had been on Guernsey in the Channel Islands waiting for a ferry when he spotted a man who had just arrived on the island. There was something familiar about the bloke but what? The man had bought a newspaper, flicked it open and walked away fast, looking sickened, worried.

'It was him looking at his own photograph,' the man almost shouted. 'It was Hutchison!'

London cops didn't know that Detective Inspector Laing was still in their city or maybe they didn't care. The publicity surrounding the case would bring a great deal of kudos to the force that finally caught the poisoner who had killed his own father. A London police sergeant was dispatched to Guernsey at top speed.

It was 20 February 1911, seventeen days after the double murder in Dalkeith. It had been a long seventeen days as the police desperately tried to catch a man who callously planned to murder as many as eighteen people. But now they were closing in on him – or so they hoped.

Armed with a photograph of Hutchison, the London sergeant started checking out the many hotels and boarding houses on Guernsey. He prepared himself for a long haul – unnecessarily, as it happened.

On visiting only the second boarding house the cop was told that the man in the picture was indeed there and was even in at the time. The landlady took the policeman directly to the individual who was clearly the elusive John Hutchison.

Denial was Hutchison's first response, of course, but confronted with the photograph he soon conceded and agreed to go quietly. For reasons only known to him the police sergeant decided not to place handcuffs on his prisoner. Maybe it was because he came across as such a gentleman, such a toff. Big mistake.

When they had reached the front door, Hutchison suddenly broke off and ran back inside the house. The police sergeant caught up with him just in time to see the murder suspect swallowing the contents of a small glass phial. John Hutchison slumped to the floor, a dead man.

The phial had contained a massive dose of deadly prussic acid – enough to kill twenty people. Death was instantaneous and almost pain-free.

The Dalkeith Poisoner was dead. But was it justice? At that time, many people didn't think so. A swift death was too good for the son who had killed his father and his friend, causing them to die in great agony. A painless death was a let-off for the man who would have killed eighteen people including his own mother and fiancée.

The Dalkeith Poisoner was dead but had he escaped justice?

TWO FOR TEA

The room was set for high tea – china crockery, crystal glasses, linen napkins and the second-best silver cutlery. In the centre of the table, a large meat pie, like everything else, lay untouched. All was ready for the two diners. One problem – feet away lay the body of the hostess.

The room might well have been set for tea but it smelled rank. Not only was the meat pie off but the homeowner, sixty-five-year-old Jean Milne, had also lain dead for weeks.

It was no surprise that an earlier alarm hadn't been raised. Miss Milne lived on her own in her massive home, Elmgrove House, in Broughty Ferry. It was so large that ten of the rooms were permanently sealed and she comfortably lived in the rest – a woman of means living on her own.

The postman had raised the alarm. On 3 November 1912, he had noticed her postbox was filled to overflowing. This wasn't like Jean Milne, a very neat, organised woman. The local police knew her well. Her family had been big shots in the tobacco manufacturing business in nearby Dundee – a wealthy, highly respected family.

When the cops broke down her front door they didn't have far to search. There at the bottom of the stairs lay Miss Milne, dead.

In death, Jean Milne was fully clothed, almost tidy, covered in a sheet. But she had died a violent death. Blood stained the floor, the walls and the banister. When the cops pulled back the sheet they found the woman's ankles tied together with a curtain cord. It was murder all right.

Black, dry blood crusted over the victim's skull where she had been smashed several times. Nearby they found a hefty iron poker broken in two. The murder weapon they assumed.

Investigating cops also assumed Jean Milne had been killed in the course of a robbery. After all, she was wealthy and she lived alone – an easy target. Then they discovered that nothing had been stolen from the house. Nothing at all – not even the valuable rings gracing her fingers and her other jewellery. The police had just encountered their first problem but it wasn't going to be their last.

Elmgrove House showed no sign of a break-in. The dining table had been set for high tea for two and lay untouched. She had obviously been expecting someone. Had she been killed by a friend?

Jean Milne had a lot of friends who would often visit for tea or dinner. But those friends were of her own social class – upright, responsible citizens, involved in their local churches and supporting good causes. Not the usual suspects for murder, especially such a brutal murder of a woman.

Most of her friends in the local community were women of her own age. Even hard-bitten, experienced rozzers in 1912 couldn't imagine that any of them could be the killer. Yet a post-mortem revealed that Miss Milne had suffered no single injury leading to her death. Rather, the killer had struck her numerous times on the head and body with a heavy object, probably the poker. And it seemed like the killer didn't have great physical power and had had to strike her repeatedly. Most men would have the strength to kill the slightly-built victim with one or two blows to the skull.

A local man collecting for charity had called at Elmgrove House a few days after Jean Milne was thought to have been killed. Receiving no reply when he knocked on the door, he departed but, as he did so, he looked up. He later swore to the cops that he saw the outline of a woman looking down from an upstairs room. Yet Jean Milne was dead by that time. Could the killer have been a woman?

That was how the matter was left – with the local cops chasing a possible female suspect. From the dates of letters in Miss Milne's stuffed postbox and various sightings, they were certain that she had been killed between 15 and 16 October and, because there had been no sign of a break-in, they believed it had been by someone she knew – possibly the person she was expecting for high tea – and that that someone was a female. Yet every line of inquiry met a blank. Most cops would simply leave the matter at that but this murder was too outrageous – the public and many powerful people were angry about the crime. They had to do something. So they called in a national hero.

In those days, the exploits of soldiers, sailors, explorers and policemen were very much in the public eye. Detective Lieutenant John Trench of Glasgow Police had a reputation second to none. He was the real-life Sherlock Holmes as far as the public were concerned. Dundee cops applied to Glasgow to borrow Trench to crack this case.

Like all good cops, the first thing Trench did was to visit the scene of the crime. There, in the ashes of a fire, he found a cigar butt – Jean Milne had been visited by a man in the recent past. The Dundee cops had missed that clue but they had spotted something else – a two-pronged carving fork stuck under a unit in the hall rather than being in the dining area. They simply dismissed it as irrelevant but not Trench.

When he examined the clothes Miss Milne had been wearing when she was killed, he found they were pockmarked with holes matching the fork's dimensions. Her body must have had the same pattern of wounds but there was no mention of this in the post-mortem. Trench immediately applied for Jean Milne's body to be exhumed but his request was refused. Then, as now, exhumation was taken very seriously. That the doctors had overlooked some minor wounds wasn't seen as a good enough reason to disturb Jean Milne's grave.

With no alternative, Trench turned to good old-fashioned policing. A reward of £100 was offered for information and he began asking people questions. That's when he discovered there was more to the victim than her socially respectable public face.

A well-built, fair-haired man with a foreign accent – possibly German but no one was quite sure – had been seen in and around her house about the time of her death, according to neighbours and a taxi driver. That became the identity of the police's number one suspect.

Then a dustbin man came forward to say that on 16 October – the day Miss Milne might have been killed or already lay dead – he had seen a man in the gardens of Elmgrove House. This wiry, pale-faced bloke was wearing a bowler hat and he'd hidden behind a bush when he spotted the dustbin man. The local police seem to have just noted this rather sinister encounter, preferring instead to concentrate on the description given by the majority of people of the heavily built, blond-haired man with a foreign accent. One thing they were now sure of – the killer was a man.

Jean Milne wasn't indiscreet but she did confide in some very close friends. There was a young man she had taken with her on a holiday touring the north of Scotland. Also, not long before her death, she had been excited about some handsome American she'd met in London.

Contacting Scotland Yard in London to see if they knew of any American man matching the description they had, the Scottish cops were in luck. One Charles Warner was in police custody in Kent for not paying a restaurant bill. Sure enough, he was of a build that matched the description and he was fair-haired and Canadian – close enough to being American for the police.

Shown a photograph of Warner that had been sent up from London, the local witnesses swore it was the man they had seen at her house – murder mystery solved as far as the Dundee cops were concerned. John Trench, on the other hand, was still keeping an open mind.

It was Trench who travelled to London to arrest Warner. As they travelled back to Dundee – a slow, long journey in 1912 – the experienced detective interviewed the accused man. Warner swore he was innocent. That wasn't good enough for Trench, of course, and he set about grilling him.

Warner claimed he didn't know Jean Milne and hadn't even arrived in London till 18 October, two days after Jean Milne was thought to have been murdered. But he was broke, homeless, often sleeping rough and other times booking into hotels under fake names so he could slip away undetected without paying the bill. There was no way he could prove his arrival in London. Then again, he knew where he had been on 16 October – in Antwerp, where he had pawned a waistcoat for money to buy food. By good fortune, he still had the ticket.

Once Trench had deposited Warner in police custody in Dundee, he immediately set off for Antwerp. This should not be taken lightly. It wasn't just a case of jumping on to an airplane or modern, luxurious ferry like in modern times. The journey was hell and most cops would have given it a miss, especially on such slender claims of alibi. The pawn ticket wasn't good enough on its own. Warner could have stolen it or found it. Would the pawnbroker remember a man who pawned a mere waistcoat weeks before? Remember what he looked like?

As it happens, the pawn ticket matched the dates in the shop's records. Better still the pawnbroker recalled the young Canadian. Back in Dundee, Trench was greeted with a wide smile from Charles Warner. It was the only warm greeting waiting for him. Local cops threw him sour looks. They had their man. With all the witnesses, they would have gained a conviction and the plaudits of the public as well but now, thanks to John Trench, they had no accused, no suspect, no chance of solving Jean Milne's murder. That's how the murder remained – unsolved.

Sad as that was, John Trench was going to face bigger trouble. He had made some enemies in Dundee by proving a man innocent. Later he would discover he had enemies in much higher places (see 'Stabbed in the Back'). The question was, what price would he pay?

AS POOR AS DEATH

No one went near that water. Even the kids knew that. Monsters lived down there. You could die in those waters.

The local myth in Linlithgow frightened kids away from the disused Hopetoun Quarry. It was a dangerous place right enough with no one sure how deep the pool was or exactly what lurked down there. But two men were about to discover the real horrors of Hopetoun Quarry.

Although it was a bright, sunny day in June 1913, the quarry, with its still, dark pool, looked menacing – but not so menacing as to worry two local men, ploughman Thomas Duncan and his pal, James Thompson. That was about to change.

Walking past the quarry, as they had done regularly throughout their lives, Thomas Duncan thought he spotted something in the water. A dead sheep maybe? If only.

When the two men moved closer their blood froze. Two young boys lay there, their bodies tied together and their lifeless eyes staring up at the two men.

The two children were some way out and the water was too deep for the men to wade in. Fetching a long branch Duncan carefully eased the tiny corpses towards dry ground but when they had almost reached the bank the branch snapped. Another effort brought one child towards them but the other floated free. One poor wee boy flopped lifeless at their feet as another floated away, dead eyes staring at the men.

Duncan and Thompson were hardy, farming types but this game of deadly fishing was just too much for them. They fetched the local bobbies. An hour later, the two bodies lay on dry ground. They were bloated and covered in algae and, here and there, their flesh had been nibbled by pond life. Yet the freezing, cold water had done the cops a favour in preserving the corpses very well.

Good-looking boys, they had been aged around six and four and, even in death, they were recognisable as brothers. Unaccustomed to major crime as they were, even the local police knew it was murder. Unless they had been playing some deadly game, that rope trying them together was a bit of a giveaway.

It didn't take the police long to suss out that only two kids – the two Higgins boys – had moved from the area in the past few months. Or had they? According to some friends and neighbours of their father, they had gone to stay with a relative in Canada. Others were told they were with an aunt in Edinburgh and some heard they had died in an accident. Maybe, if Patrick Higgins had stuck to one story about his sons, he would have avoided suspicion or maybe not. Either way, he was arrested and charged with the murder of William, aged six, and John, aged four.

Those who knew Higgins were shocked. They saw him as a decent enough man who had simply fallen on bad times. Having been in the army and seen active service in India, he was discharged and returned to civvies but his health wasn't good. He'd complained to his doctor of having no concentration, being forgetful and suffering frequent headaches. The doctor was sympathetic but could do little to help. There just wasn't the medical knowledge let alone the treatment then for Higgins' maladies. Patrick Higgins, like so many of that time, just had to grin and bear it – make the best of a bad lot. Then disaster struck.

In 1910, his wife had died. With no extended family to help care for the young children, Patrick Higgins was in a real fix. The welfare state had not been conceived of, let alone introduced. He would just have to struggle on.

Higgins was a labourer and had to travel around the Linlithgow area searching for work. If he didn't work, they didn't eat. In those dark days, his two boys had no choice but to go with him.

The measly daily wages he managed to earn couldn't feed the three of them properly, never mind provide a decent home. They often slept rough under hedges or in barns and ate stolen potatoes roasted in open campfires. At one point, someone reported Patrick Higgins to the police and he was charged with child neglect. The laws protecting children had been passed only a short time before and it was still rare for adults to face such charges. That Patrick Higgins was charged reflects the severity of his sons' neglect. The boys were taken into care and placed with a woman in Broxburn. But, back then, the parent – even a neglectful, poverty-stricken one – had to pay for their children's keep.

This was an era when people still starved to death in Scotland and, struggling to earn enough to feed himself, Higgins fell behind with the payments. His sons' foster mother couldn't have that and promptly delivered them back to their father – as you do. The ghost of Jessie King, the murderous baby farmer from Edinburgh's Stockbridge, lived on in Scotland's foster parents.

Nobody paid any attention to the fact that the two young boys were again being cared for by a man who had been judged incapable of looking after them. By turning a blind eye, they were signing the boys' death warrant.

Loneliness, the constant struggle to earn a crust and now caring for two needy young boys had driven Patrick Higgins to booze which, of course, just made his problems worse.

It all got too much for him. One rainy night in November 1911, Higgins was out walking with his two boys. Locals were well used to the bedraggled threesome trailing the streets and paid no attention. This time, he wasn't desperately looking for a shelter for the night – Higgins knew exactly where he was going.

Down by Hopetoun Quarry he took a rope from his coat pocket and tied the two youngsters together. They may have been ne-glected boys but they were well behaved. They cried and asked their father what he was doing. He told them to be good and they were – good boys obeying their dad. Then the father picked his sons up and threw them as far as he could into the murky water.

Did Higgins feel a pang of remorse? It is now impossible to say. But what we do know is that, after killing his boys, he went immediately to a pub in nearby Winchburgh – to drown his sorrows?

Higgins pled not guilty to the murders. Not that he denied killing his sons but he claimed to have been insane at the time. He blamed his health problems and Scotland's most eminent neurosurgeon was called to assess if he had epilepsy.

It didn't wash with the judge, Lord Johnston, who declared that the accused man's 'callousness, cold-bloodedness and deliberate cruelty were not insanity'.

Higgins was unanimously found guilty of the murders but the jury took a most unusual step. In spite of needing less than two hours to decide on his guilt, they felt some sympathy for Higgins. Most ordinary people in Scotland had known hardship. Most feared that they were only one step away from the impoverished state Patrick Higgins had found himself in. The good jury asked for mercy. The judge sympathised but couldn't help. Given the gravity of the offences, the law compelled him to sentence Higgins to death.

Lord Johnston pronounced the death penalty but, on this rare occasion, he did not don the customary black cap. A symbolic statement of his unhappiness at events and Higgins' fate? It seems so.

The judge wasn't finished. From the bench, he slated the lack of care and professionalism of those paid to protect the two children.

Wee William and John would have still been alive if those officials had done their job when the foster parent gave them up. His words echo many a modern childcare tragedy yet he was speaking back in 1913.

It wasn't just the judge and jury who'd been moved by this trial. When the murders of the wee boys first became public, the people of Scotland rose up in arms at the horror slaying. Gradually, some began to see the innocent victims and their killer as victims of ill health and poverty – both rife among working Scots at that time.

A larger crowd than usual gathered outside Edinburgh's Calton Jail on 2 October 1913. The good mood and the drunkenness and frivolity that normally accompanied public hangings were not as evident as they usually were. Many held a silent vigil and prayed in groups around bonfires all night.

When the black flag was hoisted inside the jail telling the world that Higgins was dead, no cheer went up as it usually would have. Instead there were some final prayers and much quiet weeping as the crowd dispersed.

Was this the start of many things changing in Scotland? A public mood in favour of taking more care of our vulnerable? A swing against every murder being punished by death?

Maybe the sad lives and sadder deaths of wee William and John Higgins were not in vain. Maybe the hanging of their father had a greater purpose than punishment.

Were all of them the victims of dark, uncaring days?

STABBED IN THE BACK

It was a terrible murder. An elderly, frail woman battered to death in her own home. Worse, she could have been saved and she wouldn't be the only one to pay the price.

The Adams family were worried by the strange noises coming from the flat upstairs in the well-to-do tenement they lived in on Glasgow's West Princes Street. The flat owner was a quiet, elderly spinster who kept herself to herself. For hours, the family debated what was going on upstairs till finally the woman's live-in maid returned home and they followed her into the flat.

Quietly opening the front door, they edged from room to room till finally they pushed the door of the dining room open. To their horror, there lay their neighbour, covered by a curtain and surrounded by a blood-soaked floor – her blood.

Marion Gilchrist died before the doctor arrived. She gave no clue as to what had happened – no clue as to who had murdered her.

After different descriptions were given of a man seen briefly in the hall that night, police suspicion fell on one Oscar Slater, a German Jewish immigrant who'd settled in Glasgow.

This now-famous murder is given excellent treatment elsewhere so, in this book, we'll touch on another story, another victim. It's the least he deserves.

Oscar Slater was, of course, eventually convicted of Marion Gilchrist's murder. Scottish cops even pursued him to America where he had moved. In fact, Slater was so sure of his innocence,

46

he returned voluntarily to face trial. Still, Slater was sentenced to hang for the murder but, instead, was reprieved at the last minute and sent to Peterhead Prison for life. In his case, life meant just that – his entire life. Hell on earth. Peterhead Jail was a penal colony. So many of the Scots convicts sentenced to be dispatched to Australia had escaped on the route through England, creating havoc in the shires, that parliament decided it was safer and cheaper to build a penal colony closer to home.

It was hard labour every day, with the inmates hacking granite from nearby quarries. Rations were minimal and the guards carried cutlasses and rifles and they weren't slow to use them. Any indiscipline from the inmates was rewarded by severe lashings with a cat-o-nine-tails. Hell on earth.

The trouble was that some people believed Oscar Slater had been wrongly convicted – including one Detective Lieutenant John Trench of Glasgow police who we've met before in the case of Jean Milne (see 'Two for Tea'). Trench had been involved in the Marion Gilchrist case in 1908, though not as the lead officer. Even as the cops secured Slater's conviction in 1909, Trench had doubts about the validity of it – doubts he held on to as he went about his business solving other cases.

Around 1913, he met up with a Glasgow lawyer, David Cook, and a journalist called William Park. It was a private meeting since coppers had to be careful that they weren't seen to be working against their colleagues in any way. This meeting finally convinced Trench that Oscar Slater was innocent. To a man like Trench, that was as bad as a guilty man walking free yet first he sought to protect his job. He asked for a meeting with the Police Commission that oversaw the work of all police forces in Scotland on behalf of the Secretary of State for Scotland – the most powerful government minister in the country.

Presenting his evidence to members of the Commission in 1914, he so convinced them of Slater's innocence that they ordered an enquiry and asked Trench to submit his evidence in full. It was to be his undoing.

Trench could prove that police officers deliberately lied and forced witnesses to give false testimony in order to convict Slater – this was information that no police force or government minister would want revealed. It must also be remembered that hostilities with Germany had been festering for some time, with German spies being arrested in Britain – one as early as 1912 in Central Station, Glasgow. Anti-Semitism was also rife among Scots so Slater suffered on both accounts. If you add to that Slater's live-in relationship with a high-class call girl in Glasgow that the cops knew all about and his success as an entrepreneur, complete with fancy suits and fat cigars, it's easy to see that he faced a collection of prejudices from the investigating officers.

Before the enquiry was heard, John Trench was arrested and charged with sharing information outside the police force without permission. What was being referred to was the report on Oscar Slater that he'd been asked to submit to the Police Commission on behalf of the Secretary of State for Scotland. Remarkably the charges stood and, on 14 September 1914, Glasgow Magistrates' Court found Trench guilty and dismissed him from the police.

The career of the one of the brightest, most capable detectives in Scotland had just been sacrificed. Oscar Slater, meanwhile, continued to labour in Peterhead Prison.

Trench's tribulations were far from over. With World War I now declared, he volunteered for the army, becoming a drill instructor with the Royal Scots Fusiliers. The night before he was due to set sail with his regiment for the front, he was arrested and charged with handling stolen property – as was the solicitor, David Cook. The charges came from one of Trench's many great successes in solving crimes. A large theft had occurred and, through excellent detective work, he managed not only to catch the thieves but to get a large amount of the stolen goods returned. At the time, he was praised by everyone involved – including the Chief Constable. Now that same force was accusing him of an offence for the same actions that once made him a hero.

The trial judge saw through the ploy and dismissed the case as inappropriate, thereby saving the two men from possible jail sentences. But the tactics did work in another way. Never again did David Cook or John Trench speak out about Oscar Slater. Though he was publicly declared innocent, the case ruined David Cook as a solicitor and broke him as man. He died less than two years after the trial.

John Trench was made of harder stuff. He went on to serve in the army, being promoted several times. In that most bloody of wars, he served at the front for years and survived. Demobbed in October 1918, he returned to civvies and an empty life. The police force had meant everything to him. The war had provided him with an alternative. Now . . . now he had nothing. Six months later, on 13 May 1919, John Trench died a sad and lonely man. Was he bitter and angry at the betrayal by his beloved police force? Who knows? He never spoke out again.

Against all the odds, Oscar Slater had survived in Peterhead penal colony. Although the state had silenced David Cook and John Trench, they didn't silence the likes of Sherlock Holmes' creator Sir Arthur Conan Doyle, a figure known and respected throughout the world, or William Roughead, a Scot pioneering the science of criminology.

Gradually, public opinion and, more importantly, that of the press began to swing behind Slater. There was one problem, though – laws to allow him to appeal had been introduced to England twenty years earlier but Westminster hadn't seen fit to pass the same laws in Scotland. Faced with growing public unhappiness, the politicians passed emergency legislation that would allow Slater to appeal.

In 1927, eighteen years after being sentenced, Slater won his appeal and was freed. Slater would go on to marry and lead a happy and full life. He'd survive till well into his seventies and died peacefully in 1948.

Throughout those decades, many people would claim credit for supporting Slater's claim of innocence. What did the man himself think of all that? Did he believe those folk? Or did he spare a thought for the man who sacrificed his career to get him of jail? That good and honest cop – Detective Lieutenant John Trench.

DEAF TO DEATH

Screams and sobs rang out from that flat every day, every night. Even in that brutal, harsh place they were recognised as the sounds of terror. The neighbours heard but never said a word. Why should they? Their lives were bad enough without prying into the business of others. Many women wanted to but didn't. Their own men were heavy handed and too many of them were so often drunk and brutal that frequently it was their screams filling the night air. No one bothered to help them. Why should they? Wasn't it the same for everyone?

And the streets, with their tenements packed so close together that they blotted out the sky, were just as violent as the homes. Thick smog hugged the walls most days as men on the street corners talked and watched. In the unlit rat traps of dark closes, anyone or anything could be waiting for you. To the outsider, it might seem hell – for them, it was home.

Why should they complain? There were worse places to be. For three years, World War I had been raging. It had been going on long enough for men to come home from the front. Men with broken bodies and, too often, broken minds. Men with stories – living nightmares – about pals who'd been blown to smithereens right next to them, their faces getting splattered with the flesh and blood of their friends. The whistle of shells coming their way, always fearing that their name was on the next one. Legs and brains numbed with terror as they stepped up and into no-man's-land. Sleeping upright in water-filled trenches with rats everywhere, gnawing their flesh. The mist heading their way – was it mist or deadly mustard gas coming to sear their skin and boil their lungs? The men, boys really, who cracked, wept and fled only to be caught and killed by a firing squad comprised of their own comrades. The ones praying to be shot – a good one, enough to need medical care back home but not so much as to stop them leading a life. Maybe a leg or an arm off – that would do. Conditions so bad, they were praying to lose an arm or a leg.

Yes, there were worse places to be than Govan.

The Govan area of Glasgow was thriving, according to those who didn't live there. Ships were the present and the future face of world transport and, in 1917, the capital of shipbuilding was Govan.

Blackburn Street was like most other streets in the area though more rundown than most – especially number 101 where Thomas McGuiness lived with his live-in lover, Isobel Imlach, and Alexander Imlach, known as Alick, her five-year-old son from another relationship. The family were recent newcomers – not an unusual thing in those war years when people flitted in search of work. Govan had more work than most places.

They were a quiet family. Thomas McGuiness was a quiet, stern-looking man. Even at his work, he didn't have much to do with the other men and, in the pub, he'd usually stand on his own drinking his beer. Young Alick was shy, pale faced and a wee bit thin but he was a nice young boy who was always polite to his elders. Isobel was an attractive woman, pretty and younger than her man. She was the most sociable one of the family and she'd stand for a chat with her neighbours whenever she got a chance. But she'd only speak about the weather, news from the front or some gossip about what some woman had been up to when the woman's man was away at the war. She never spoke much about herself or her background, neighbours noticed. But then having a child out of wedlock wasn't exactly socially acceptable in 1917. They thought maybe she was embarrassed. Isobel wasn't embarrassed – she was ashamed.

She had met Thomas only the year before up north in her native Aberdeen. They had courted for a few months when he told her that he was going to move to Dundee and she was welcome to join him along with wee Alick. After the move, the three became a family unit, living together for the first time. It was the honeymoon from hell.

Almost immediately, the gentle man she had taken Thomas McGuiness to be disappeared and he was replaced by a bully who became violent towards both her and Alick. After a couple of months, she'd had enough and she took Alick away to live in Edinburgh. That should have been the end of the matter but, a couple of weeks later, McGuiness turned up in Edinburgh and begged Isobel to give him another chance. As is too often the way of things with domestic violence, she believed his promises that he'd change and agreed to move with him to Glasgow, to a single end in Baltic Street.

Things instantly got worse. McGuiness now seemed to turn his aggression more on wee Alick and his furious outbursts grew into calm cruelty. He would grip and twist the skin of the boy's wrists giving him friction burns. He'd hold him upside down and swing his head into furniture. He'd light cigarettes and, while sitting on the child, stick the lit ends into his flesh, making patterns. When Isobel tried to stop these horrors, she was beaten to a pulp and, just for good measure, McGuiness threw Alick down a set of stairs when she was too battered and helpless to stop him.

Isobel, so protective of her wee boy, now seems to have fallen into the trap of the abused woman – hating being there yet unable to leave. It's a state you can only really understand if you've experienced it – a state of hell.

On McGuiness's insistence, the family moved yet again. This time it was to Glasgow's Springfield Road where they stayed for a short time before moving to 101 Blackburn Street in Govan. A change of place can often change people – as it did this time but it was to be a change for the worse. Now, he turned on Isobel in a different way. No matter how much he earned, he gave her only three shillings per week to feed the family and pay the rent. The equivalent of fifteen pence today, the money had much greater value in 1917, of course, but was it enough to house, feed, clothe and heat three people? Nowhere near it.

None of the family's neighbours knew about this, of course. They were a quiet family – apart from the screams of terror.

As most mothers would, Isobel Imlach was reduced to doing anything to feed her child, even selling her body on the streets for a few pennies. Her child starving to death or her dignity? It was an easy decision.

On 8 March 1917, she went out in the morning in search of some money for food, leaving Alick asleep in his bed but in the care of Thomas McGuiness. No doubt it wasn't a situation she liked but what choice did she have? When she returned, only fifteen minutes later, she saw McGuiness sitting with Alick on his knee. It was immediately obvious the boy was gravely ill – or gravely damaged.

'Alick has taken a fit,' McGuiness said, looking her straight in the eye.

'Taken a fit?' She knew that look. It was a threatening look that promised violence on her unless she simply agreed. Isobel Imlach took one look at her child and immediately forgot about any threat.

Alick was gasping for air. His face was blue down one side and his top lip was obscenely swollen. Snatching Alick from McGuiness's lap, Isobel ran with him to a neighbour for help. Looking at the stricken child and his mess of bruises old and new, the neighbour heard echoes of the screams coming from that house.

'We'll need to get a doctor urgently,' the neighbour said. 'But we'll have to call the police as well.'

Behind them, McGuiness called out that he'd go and fetch a doctor and went running down the close. The doctor never arrived. Young Alick died.

When the police arrived along with a medic, they immediately concluded that the child had been battered and strangled to death.

Under his pyjamas fresh bruises and welts glowered. The cops immediately launched a search party for Thomas McGuiness and found him later that day on a street in Springburn.

At the High Court in Glasgow on 24 April 1917, McGuiness stood trial for Alick Imlach's murder. The evidence for him having repeatedly and seriously assaulted the wee boy, including having attacked him on the day of his death, was so overwhelming his defence team didn't even try to counter it. Instead they presented an argument of insanity and brought forward his mother and sister to support such. As the women stood in the witness box and spoke about his alleged strange behaviour, McGuiness put on a show for the court. He mumbled, grimaced and wobbled from side to side as if he would collapse any minute. Would the court believe him?

Lord Justice Johnston, the presiding judge, wasn't known as a particularly fierce judge but he wasn't known as a soft touch either. He ordered that McGuiness be taken to the cells below and that a doctor attend to him. The next day McGuiness was seemingly well and back in the dock to hear that the jury had returned a majority verdict of guilty.

Three weeks later, on 16 May 1917, a large angry crowd waited silently outside the gates of Duke Street Prison, all their eyes focusing in the same direction. Behind the walls, a prison officer stepped up to a short flagpole and raised a flag to half mast. Suddenly the silence broke and the crowed bayed and cheered.

McGuiness was one of the few civilians to be hanged during World War I years – officially, at least. The government's view was that the morale of the people had to be sustained – their anger and energy directed at the enemy, not each other. Yet, when confronted with the brutal torture and murder of a young innocent child, there seemed to be no option. After all, then as now, young Alick Imlach's demise horrified all decent citizens.

Thomas McGuiness was dead. The child killer had received his just deserts.

Artist's impressions of Helen Harkness and her husband William. In 1922, the couple were charged with the murder of young Elizabeth Benjamin. Elizabeth collected payments in the Whiteinch area of Glasgow for her brother who ran a draper's credit business.

A scene from the Harknesses' murder trial. The court heard how Elizabeth had been killed for the £2 she had taken on the evening of her death. Both were found guilty and sentenced to death. Helen's sentence was, however, commuted to life in prison but William was hanged.
('Twenty-Four Pieces of Silver')

A newspaper image showing how the IRA tried to free one of their own from a prison van. In 1921, Frank Carty was being taken to Glasgow's Duke Street Prison when the ambush happened.

Detective-Sergt. George Stirton, D.C.M., M.S.M., who, although wounded, made a gallant stand against the assailants.

Inspector Robert Johnstone, shot dead by Sinn Fein gunmen in Glasgow, yesterday.

As the van approached the prison, gun-toting IRA men attacked it from three sides. They tried blasting the door off the van to get Carty out but failed. Bullet holes can still be seen in the prison walls today.

('Blood Red Rotten Row')

John Johnston,
the little boy who was murdered.

John Newell is seen here with the police, leaving Haddington where he gave himself up after reading a description in a newspaper of the man they were seeking in connection with young John Johnston's death and recognised himself.

Only Susan Newell was found guilty of murdering John Johnston at her home in Coatbridge. Susan Newell loaded the body on to a cart with the intention of taking it to Glasgow to get rid of it. Ironically, the place she chose to dump the body was Duke Street, not far from the prison where she was hanged. ('The Long Short Walk')

In 1920, Albert Fraser (left) and James Rollins were found guilty of the murder of Henry Senior (below, right) in Glasgow's Queen's Park. For some time, the pair had been mugging men in the park, using two young women, Elizabeth Stewart and Helen White, as bait.

Along with Albert Fraser and James Rollins, Elizabeth Stewart (left) and Helen White were picked up in Belfast where they'd fled after the killing of Henry Senior. Both women turned King's evidence and Fraser and Rollins were hanged for murder.

Crowds of folk unable to get in to Glasgow's packed High Court wait for the verdict on Fraser and Rollins. ('Honeytraps and Killer Bs')

HELEN PRIESTLY,
Victim of Murder.

MRS. JEANNIE DONALD
Sentenced to Death.

Jeannie Donald's death sentence for the murder of eight-year-old Helen Priestly in Aberdeen in the 1930s was commuted to life in prison. Helen's body was found in the lobby of the tenement where she and Mrs Donald both stayed. She appeared to have been sexually assaulted. ('Bread and Blood')

Street trader Nathoo Mohammed (left) was terrified local extortionists would take their revenge on him for not paying them protection money. During a siege by an angry mob, headed by John Keen (right), at a house in Port Dundas in 1925, Nathoo's countryman, Noorh Mohammed, also a street trader, was stabbed to death. ('The Colour of Hate')

Dr Buck Ruxton and his common-law wife, Isabella. Ruxton murdered her and their children's nursemaid. He chopped the victims up, wrapped the mutilated body parts in paper and flung them in a stream near Moffat in Dumfriesshire.

In 1936, after one of the first trials to rely heavily on forensic evidence, Ruxton was found guilty of double murder. Here excited crowds turned out on the day of Ruxton's execution at Strangeways Prison.
('The Scalpel Blade Duel')

Courtesy of University of Glasgow Archive Services

Saughton Prison in Edinburgh where Allen Wales was hanged. Wales killed his wife in broad daylight on the streets of Leith in 1928 by cutting her throat, almost completely severing her head. Today, his mental limitations would have been recognised but, in the late 1920s, they were not and he was sentenced to death for murder. ('Wasted Warnings')

Professor John Glaister of Glasgow University. A world-renowned forensic scientist, his evidence was instrumental in the conviction of Buck Ruxton ('The Scalpel Blade Duel'). He also gave evidence at the trials of Peter Queen ('Deadly Disgrace') and Stanislaw Myszka ('Old Allies, New Foes'), both of whom were found guilty of murder.

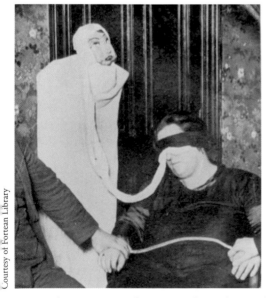

Courtesy of Fortean Library

Courtesy of Scotsman Publications Ltd

Helen Duncan, a famous medium during the 1940s. She toured the country, conducting séances and producing 'materialisations' of dead relatives of members of the audience. One such materialisation during wartime, however, led to her being arrested and charged under ancient witchcraft laws. ('Damned and Damned')

Billy Fullerton, leader of the Billy Boys, one of Glasgow's most notorious razor gangs. During the 1930s and 1940s, gangs like the Billy Boys had hundreds of members and brutal inter-gang warfare was rife. ('The Fiend')

Billy Fullerton and his gang caused the cops many a headache but this man, Patrick Carraher, was in a different league. Known as 'The Fiend of the Gorbals', his appetite for bloody violence knew no bounds. ('The Fiend')

Sir Percy Sillitoe, the man tasked with ending the gang fights on Glasgow's streets. One of his solutions was to match like with like by recruiting as many hard-men bobbies as he could. ('The Fiend')

Originally rejected by the police because of his lack of height, William Merrilees went on to have one of the most distinguished careers of his generation. One of his trademarks was his use of disguises. He loved detective work and gained a reputation for cracking difficult cases. ('A Lonely Place')

1920 TO 1929

DEADLY DEPRESSION

This was a decade of great poverty. The General Strike saw the collapse of British industry and troops on the street in every major city (1926). The economic crisis spread worldwide and, in the USA, it resulted in the Wall Street Crash (1929).

The USSR was created (1922), Lenin died (1924) and Hitler published his vision of the future, *Mein Kampf* (1925).

Talkie films were introduced (1927) and Mickey Mouse made his entrance (1928). The BBC made its first radio broadcasts (1922) and John Logie Baird demonstrated TV (1926). They said it would never catch on. Crime-writer Agatha Christie disappeared only to be found in The Swann, Harrogate, claiming to have lost her memory (1924). Tutankhamen's tomb was discovered, unleashing a deadly curse on the explorers (1923). Scotland had a new sporting hero when Eric Liddell won the 400m Olympic Gold Medal (1924). The country also had a cause célèbre when Oscar Slater was freed after eighteen years' wrongful imprisonment (1927).

Mass unemployment hit Scotland as heavy industries closed down. The first old-age pension was introduced at the rate of ten shillings (fifty pence) a week (1928). Fleming discovered penicillin (1928) but it wasn't yet available to the public.

Scottish cops changed their uniforms but kept their Dixon-of-Dock-Green-style helmets. By the end of the decade, Glasgow had ten policewomen and Edinburgh's new police boxes with phone lines were hailed as an end to all crime.

TWENTY-FOUR
PIECES OF SILVER

Washday blues, they used to call it when doing the laundry was a heavy, steaming, terrible task. Some days turned out worse than others.

It was 5 November 1921 but, more importantly to Margaret Baird, it was a Saturday and washday. Though she wasn't looking forward to it, she knew she was luckier than most. After all, there was a communal washhouse for her flat in George Street in the Whiteinch area of Glasgow. All she needed was the key.

Her neighbour Helen Harkness had used the washhouse last and she handed over the key with a little social chat. Helen and her man, William, had moved in only a short time before but they had settled in well. All the neighbours liked them. Margaret Baird liked them and could have stayed chatting for longer but she had a big wash to see to.

An hour later, the washhouse was filled with steam as Margaret moved bundles of dripping laundry from one zinc sink to another. She was a hard worker and, as she allowed one wash to soak for a while to get the soap out, she found herself with a few minutes to spare. She stood gazing out of the window on to the back green and, not being someone given to fancies, she had to look away and shake her head. She just didn't believe her eyes. She looked back again and, sure enough, there it was or rather there she was – a trussed up woman lying in the grass.

Margaret flew down the road to fetch the local police. When they arrived on the scene, it was clear that the woman was dead.

She had been battered on the skull, her hands had been tied together with a rope and a coat belt was tied tightly round her mouth. It was also clear that she had been lying there for some time. The windows of the surrounding houses didn't overlook the green where she lay so the cops weren't surprised that no one noticed her sooner.

Word of the poor woman's demise spread round the Whiteinch area fast. When Maxwell Benjamin called on one of his customers, he got more than he bargained for. He ran a credit draper's business from which people could buy clothes and pay for them over time. All he was looking for was his week's money but he got some shocking news. The gossiping customer was quick to tell him the tale of the woman's body found on the green at the back of 67 George Street. Benjamin turned and sprinted from the house.

A uniformed constable stopped him before he reached the crime scene. Benjamin blurted out his story. His young sister worked with him and had gone out on her rounds to collect payments on the Monday before, 31 October. She had not returned. He had reported her to the police as missing. It wasn't like her. She was young, just fourteen, didn't have a boyfriend and she was a good girl. A very good girl. The poor man was frantic.

Once Benjamin had calmed down, the police took him to see the body. With one look, he burst into sobs. It would be long, painful minutes before he regained enough composure to confirm that the dead girl was indeed his sister, Elizabeth.

The police had a corpse, a name and now they had a motive. Elizabeth Benjamin had no money on her.

Interviewing all of Elizabeth's customers, the police soon ascertained that, on the previous Monday, she had told one of them that she had just changed £2 for shillings – a shilling is equivalent to a mere five pence nowadays but each one was seen as a valuable coin in 1921. Her brother, who knew the business well, told the police that would be about right – that her takings that night would be just over £2 or forty silver shillings.

Elizabeth had one more visit to make on her rounds and the police made their way to that address. Before they reached their destination they were stopped by Margaret Baird, the washer-woman who had spotted Elizabeth's body. Margaret was pale faced and shaking, her fingers fidgeting with the buttons of her coat as she spoke. 'I think I can help you with that poor lassie,' she said tears filling her eyes.

The police held their breath. Even by 1921, they had learned to treat certain parties as prime suspects in murders – people like the husbands, wives or partners of the victims and people like those who discovered the body. Were they about to get a confession?

'There's a stain,' she went on, 'I think it might be blood.'

No confession from Margaret Baird but a vital clue. When she had gone to Helen Harkness's flat to collect the washhouse key, she had noticed a red stain running up to the door. At the time, it had meant nothing to her but now there was a murder, now it might be important.

The police thanked Margaret Baird for her information and left her with one of their number to make a statement. But they weren't going to change their plans. They'd still go and see the last family on Elizabeth's rounds that night – William and Helen Harkness. Sure enough there was blood-like stain running in a long line to the Harknesses' door. Sure enough William and Helen Harkness denied knowing anything about the stain or having seen Elizabeth on the night she died. Someone must have killed her on the way to their house, they suggested to the police. But not all the family took that line.

John Harkness was William's brother and, under police interrogation, he soon blurted out the truth. He had been visiting his mother-in-law when Helen Harkness turned up, asking to speak with him. She said that William needed to see him urgently so John went straight away.

In the Harknesses' home in George Street, William had con-fessed to John that he had hit a woman on the head with a hammer that day. He said that he and Helen had trussed her up and dragged her to the washhouse. But she was too heavy for Helen and he needed John's help get the woman to the canal or the River Clyde nearby.

Reluctantly, John Harkness had agreed. But, when he and William had lifted the woman out of the washhouse, they had only got as far as the green when he'd taken fright. He felt sick and he dropped her there, refusing to go any farther. His statement was enough to see William and Helen Harkness charged with murder.

At their trial in Glasgow High Court on 30 January 1922, police confirmed that bloodstains had been found in the Harknesses' home and in the passage leading from it. Their house had been the murder scene.

The most disturbing evidence came from the post-mortem which revealed that the blow on the head hadn't been enough to kill young Elizabeth Benjamin. A dirty handkerchief stuffed into her mouth then secured by a coat belt had slowly choked her to death. With her hands tied up with a rope, poor Elizabeth was helpless and had died a slow, lonely death.

The trial lasted a mere two days and the jury took only minutes to reach their decision. Both William and Helen Harkness were found guilty of murder and sentenced to be hanged by the neck till dead. The date of execution was set for 21 February 1922 at Duke Street Prison and the pair were moved into separate condemned cells to await their fate. Three days before the planned execution, the prison governor paid Helen Harkness a visit in her cell. She had been reprieved and instead would serve life in prison.

It may have been William not Helen who had struck the fatal blow in order to rob young Elizabeth of her purse full of silver yet she had helped her man tie up the young girl and might well have stuffed that fatal gag in her mouth. Wasn't she as guilty as he was?

Many of the public thought so and some gathered to protest outside the jail. Women were campaigning for the vote and equal rights so the view was that they should face the might of justice as well. But it was all to no avail and William Harkness alone dropped to his death on 21 February 1922. The fate of his wife is not known.

BLOOD RED ROTTEN ROW

The hill was a killer. At least of cars. But, one day, someone else had more sinister plans afoot. It wasn't personal – it was politics.

The Black Maria spluttered and spat as it neared the top of the hill. The driver changed down a gear and revved harder. The weary motor was going to be the least of his worries.

It was Wednesday, 4 May 1921 – just another day in Glasgow. The cop wagon with the worn-out engine was ferrying prisoners from the old Central Police Court in St Andrew's Square to Duke Street Prison – like cop wagons did five days a week or even six days if the streets had been active. No one paid any heed. Well, almost no one.

The back of the van was split into what, with good reason, they called 'dog boxes'. Still known by this name today, they are small metal compartments, a yard square, stretching from the floor to the roof. Each one housed a prisoner, separated from all the others. They were too cramped for their occupants to get up to much badness was the theory.

Cramped as he was, Frank J. Carty might well have been pleased that he was separated from the only other con being transported that day. The bloke stank and he didn't shut his trap but that wasn't it. He was a small-time lowlife facing charges of indecent assault – not the kind of company a commandant of the Sligo Branch of the Irish Republican Army chose to keep. And that's what Frank Carty was. Also known sometimes as Frank Somers among other names, he had played an active part in the IRA's battle to free Ireland from British rule.

This was 1921 – only five years after the Easter Rising, which saw the Republicans take over the main post office in Dublin in a bloody shoot-out with the British Army. That day had ended with victory for the British Army and a good few rebels paid the ultimate price at the end of a rope. Hangman John Ellis had led six men to the drop in one day alone. The British thought they were teaching the rebels a lesson – thought that would be the end of it – but all they had done was to create martyrs. They came off best in the battle that day but the war was far from won.

These were dangerous days and Frank Carty was a dangerous man. Having escaped from two of the Irish authorities' jails in the previous two years, he was also a man they couldn't hold. Now he had fallen into the Glasgow cops' hands on minor charges. That morning he had appeared at court and been bound over till the next weekend. It was enough time to ship him back to Ireland but would they be able to?

The Scottish cops had been warned there was going to be an attempt to free Carty during the journey to and from the court. These days there would be helicopters hovering above, a convoy of cop cars, an armoured and bulletproof wagon for the prisoner, motorcycle outriders and more semi-automatic shooters than you could count. In 1921, there were three escort cops in the front of the van squeezed in beside the driver and each of the escorts had a handgun. That was top security back in 1921.

It wasn't much and the cops knew it. They were nervous, tense and tight-lipped but they were almost there at Duke Street Prison. They turned off the High Street and started along the prison walls. The end was in sight. They were beginning to relax. That's when the bullets started flying.

Scores of attackers came streaming at them from three sides – out of Cathedral Street, Rotten Row and a nearby lane. Bullets smashed into the van and the windscreen was shattered. Early on, one slug hit Detective Inspector Robert Johnstone, ripping off a chunk of his skull. The police officer fell from the open door of the van, tried desperately to get up and then collapsed there on the street. His colleagues, Detective Sergeant George Stirton and Constable Murdoch McDonald, were out after their gaffer in a flash, guns in hands. Standing over Johnstone's blood-splattered body, they traded shots with the IRA.

The ambush had been planned perfectly. The cop wagon was now stuck between the walls of Duke Street Prison and a water pumping station – all walls, no windows, no witnesses.

Gunmen surrounded the cops, pinning them down with heavy fire at the front of the Black Maria, and they were moving in. Stirton was wounded in the wrist but he kept firing. Even the unarmed police driver, Thomas Ross, was doing his best, fighting hand-to-hand with the gun-toting attackers.

As all that action was happening at the front of the van, the IRA ambushers at the rear were trying to free their comrade but they'd hit a problem. The door was locked, of course, and none of the uniforms were about to assist with the key. One man shoved the barrel of his heavy-duty pistol right at the lock and blasted. In the movies the metal doors would have just swung open. But this wasn't the movies. This was the streets of Glasgow. The door stayed shut.

Swearing loudly, the gunman fired again – and again. Inside the van, the bullets pinged off one wall to another and ricocheted again, almost blasting the head off IRA man John Carty. Still the doors wouldn't budge. In fury, the ambushers yanked at the doors and booted the locks – all with no result.

Realising what was happening, DS Stirton, now splattered in blood and with his gun arm wounded, headed towards the ambush party, pointing his pistol at them. The IRA group turned to deal with him and he stood there, face-to-face with them only feet away. He lifted his gun in an arm shaking with pain and promptly dropped it. His arm was too badly injured even to pull the trigger. Now he was a sitting duck, a dead man for sure, but suddenly one of the gang gave out a signal and they were off. Attack over.

The IRA team knew what they were doing. They broke up into small groups and headed away in many different directions down the different lanes and closes that honeycombed the street, slipping their hot-barrelled pistols into their coats as they moved away from the scene and headed into the city-centre crowds. Again they had chosen the location well.

Three minutes and it was all over. Or was it? DS Stirton gave chase but soon wearied due to the loss of blood from his wounds. As other cops arrived on the scene and medics took care of DI Johnstone, Ross managed to get the bullet-riddled Black Maria started and finally drove it limping, with its engine howling, into Duke Street Prison.

Prison staff had been alerted about the ambush. They didn't need much of a warning, having heard the noise of the gun battle from the other side of the walls. They knew what they had to do – get Carty locked up in a secure, solitary cell in the dungeon of the jail and fast. It was the IRA they were up against. God knows what they might try next.

The back doors of the old wagon had stuck. They were jammed tight and that was why the IRA gang couldn't open them. It took several hours and some specialist equipment to free Carty and the other prisoner who was now weeping hysterically and feeling very sorry for himself. Carty? He didn't bat an eyelid.

Back at the scene of the ambush, cops were questioning bystanders. Although the IRA team had disappeared into Cathedral Square and, from there, dispersed in all directions, the police knew where to start looking – or so they thought.

By night-time, Glasgow cops had raided numerous houses in Abercrombie Street in the Gallowgate, where they believed Republican sympathisers lived. But word of the street battle had quickly spread through the city and crowds were congregating at the ambush scene and all through the east end.

In 1921, feuding based on religious divisions was rife in the city. Only a few decades earlier, thousands of Irish immigrants had been forced to move to Glasgow to escape famine back home. Much as we might look back on that romantically now, it was a different matter at the time. The mainly Roman Catholic Irish newcomers believed, with some justification, that the authorities were biased against them. It was impossible to get some types of work if you were Roman Catholic and a broad Irish accent was assumed to be a giveaway. In those hard times, if you didn't work, you didn't eat so it was no wonder they were angry.

Massive gangs like the Roman Catholic Norman Conks and the mainly Protestant Billy Boys had been formed and they took sectarian violence on to the streets – although their weapons of choice were razors and coshes, not guns. The gangs were the organised face of day-to-day life of Glasgow's sectarian streets.

The IRA ambush to try to free Carty was just one step further down that line and the police were desperate to stamp their authority and nab the culprits. In doing so, they arrested as many people as they could till the mob decided to interfere in their plans.

The arrest of a priest is thought to have been one step too far. When the cops came out of a house in the Gallowgate, they were met by a screaming mob, looking for blood. Later that same day, an even larger group chased a team of police who tried to arrest five young men who were well known in the area for their Republican sympathies.

By evening, an estimated 2,000 rioters were milling around the Gallowgate, turning it into a no-go area for the police. The mob chanted, threw stones, smashed up shops and attacked trams. That night, they lit bonfires on the street and continued their rampage, looting, robbing and assaulting anyone in a uniform or whom they suspected to be on the side of the police.

Only two years before, a bloody battle had raged between 100,000 strikers and cops all through the city centre. The next day, Winston Churchill had sent English troops and tanks into the city to restore control. Now the people assumed to be IRA supporters were taking over the streets.

Glasgow had turned in to a lawless city. Detective Inspector Robert Johnstone had died. Detective Sergeant Stirton was in a critical state. The police were armed and moved through the streets in convoy, determined to get the suspects. The army moved into a central location in the city and waited for orders to act.

In the houses the cops raided, they didn't just find suspects but illegal weapons and explosives. They recovered over fifty hand-guns, tens of rifles and boxes of ammo, gelignite and blades – at the time, it was the biggest haul ever found in Scotland. Glasgow was a sectarian tinderbox and it was ready to explode.

The riot raged all that night and rumbled on for days but gradually peace was restored and the smoke cleared. Only twelve people were arrested for rioting – a mark of how much the mob and not the cops had ruled the streets – but thirty-four suspects were arrested in connection with the ambush. Those arrested were possibly facing charges of the murder of DI Johnstone and the attempted murder of Constables Ross and McDonald as well as DS Stirton who had survived his wounds. It was 1921 and these were hanging offences.

Days after the ambush, Carty was secretly and quietly transported to Dublin. A short while later, the funeral of DI Robert Johnstone was held and Glasgow witnessed one of the biggest funeral processions the city had ever seen. Now it was the turn of citizens to mourn a cop they thought of as a hero.

Eventually, thirteen men appeared at Edinburgh High Court in August 1921 charged with murder, attempted murder and conspiring to free a prisoner. DS Stirton, not yet fully recovered, had positively identified nine of the accused. All the men pled not guilty and their skilled defence produced alibis for each and every one of them. Now it was down to the jury to decide who to believe – the police officer who had almost died in the line of duty or the accused, their friends and relatives.

On 6 August 1921, the jury was out and Scotland held its collective breath. Would anyone be punished for the biggest riot Glasgow had seen in those troubled times?

Six of the accused were found not guilty and the cases against the other seven were not proven. The jury had chosen to believe the accused not the cop hero. Someone had murdered a policeman in Glasgow and walked away free. Someone had tried to murder another cop and would never be brought to justice. Many people and politicians didn't like that one bit and the controversy raged for months. Then, as all controversies do, it petered out, to be consigned to dusty history books.

Eighty-six years later no one else has been brought to trial. Yet, unless we forget, the evidence is still with us in the form of bullet holes high up on the old prison walls – a fitting memorial to the day Glasgow's streets ran red.

THE LONG SHORT WALK

No one else noticed except the woman standing in her living room peeking out the side of her curtains. She was suspicious but was she right?

It was night-time and Duke Street was heaving with people, carts and motors on that day of 20 June 1923. Many industries were based there, it was a main route out to the east of Glasgow and row after row of tenements was packed to the gunnels with humankind. It was so busy that people didn't notice much – well, that's what someone hoped.

Helen Elliot was known locally as a curtain twitcher – a wee bit nosy but harmless enough. Home entertainment was in its infancy then and few working folk were able to afford a wind-up record player or big box wireless. Helen's entertainment was what she could see through her window out there on the street and something was worrying her.

A lorry had pulled up to the kerb and the driver was helping a youngish woman lift a cart down from the back. Most folk would have thought, so what? It was common to hitch a lift from lorries back then. But, as the cart was lifted down, was that a human foot Helen had seen flop over the edge? She couldn't ignore that, could she?

The lorry driver, Thomas Dickson, was a good soul. When he had passed the woman pushing the cart with a young child perched on top, he pulled in immediately. It was just outside Coatbridge and he guessed rightly that the woman was walking

67

all the way into the east end of Glasgow. That was some walk – especially with the heavily laden cart and the kid.

The woman was thirty-year-old Susan Newell, the child her eight-year-old daughter from an earlier marriage, Janet McLeod, and they were in luck. They were heading to Duke Street and the driver was going exactly that way.

As he helped the woman down with the cart on Duke Street, Thomas thought for the second time that it weighed a ton. But it would've been nosy to ask what was in the cart and Thomas Dickson wasn't that – unlike Helen Elliot.

Helen ran and got her sister, telling her, in a voice shaking with fear, what she'd seen. They went out and followed the woman with the cart and the child till she turned and headed into the close at 650 Duke Street. Now they needed help so Helen blurted out her story to two men, Robert Foote and James Campbell, who agreed to help. Foote carefully sidled through the close at 650 Duke Street while Campbell quietly edged into the close next door at 652 Duke Street.

Foote arrived in time to see the woman clamber over the wall adjoining the two back greens. Campbell caught her dropping down the other side. Her behaviour was just too suspicious so the men grabbed Susan Newell and sent someone for the police.

While they were waiting for the cops Newell blurted out that in the cart wrapped in a red quilt was the body of a teenage boy. That she'd come to Duke Street to dump the body. She didn't explain why she'd chosen Duke Street but, to those who knew the area, it was obvious. The place was so busy and so built-up that no one would find the body in a hurry. The area was also infamous for violence so, when the corpse was discovered, people would assume it was some deadly deed carried out by a local and not someone from her hometown of Coatbridge. Susan Newell's plan was sound and might well have succeeded if only that foot hadn't slipped out while Helen Elliot was watching.

The dead boy was thirteen-year-old paperboy John Johnston. Both Susan Newell and her husband, John, were charged with his murder.

At their trial, the jury heard from neighbours of the Newells at their home in 2 Newlands Street, Coatbridge, that young John Johnston had been seen going up to the Newells' flat at around 7 p.m. on 20 June 1923. A short while later, loud thumps were heard and an adult voice screamed, 'Shut that fucking door!' and then there was silence.

More damning evidence came from the mouth of a babe. Susan Newell's own daughter, Janet, told how she had returned to the house that evening to find her mother with Johnston's corpse lying on the floor. For reasons Janet didn't understand, her mother had been angry with her, telling her to get inside right away and stay quiet. It was a big mistake. The tiny witness hadn't seen the killing and was never told how it had happened but she was there to detail what had occurred next. According to Janet, her mother wrapped the corpse in a red quilt, dumped it in the cart and with her sitting on top set off to Glasgow. When they had just left Coatbridge on the Glasgow road, a wheel of the cart had developed a problem and it became difficult to push. That's when the kind lorry driver had spotted them and stopped to give them a lift.

The evidence against Susan Newell was damning and her insistence of her innocence was looking thinner and thinner. But what of her husband?

John Newell produced a line-up of witnesses, mostly his relatives, who swore that he was with them that day at a family funeral in Edinburgh and had stayed over. There were those, not just the police, who believed John Newell was lying. He had a reputation for having a wild temper and being quick to use his fists. Then there was how the young lad had died.

Medical evidence found that John Johnston had been killed in a most brutal way. He had been throttled so viciously his windpipe had burst. And he'd been battered about the head so hard that sections of his skull were smashed in. Finally he had suffered extensive burns when still alive as if someone had deliberately and cruelly held him into the grate of the house fire.

Would a woman – even a young, fit woman – have the strength to inflict those injuries by herself? As Lord Kinross for the prosecution wondered this aloud at the trial, he echoed what many others were thinking. And what of that shout 'Shut that fucking door!' that the neighbours had heard? Had it been a man's voice? Two adults talking to each other? The neighbours weren't sure. They couldn't say yes or no. Maybe it had been a man's voice.

Wily Kinross tried hard to have wife and husband convicted. Despite using every legal trick in his repertoire, he failed. After only thirty-seven minutes of deliberation, the jury found John Newell not guilty and Susan Newell guilty of murder.

Susan Newell appealed and several public petitions pled for clemency. There was just one problem with that – she still protested her innocence. While the state didn't like to hang women, it would also show no mercy to someone who showed no remorse. If she was going to escape the noose, she had to admit her guilt. She refused.

A few weeks after the trial, on 10 October 1923, she made history by being the last woman to be hanged in Scotland. The place of her death? Duke Street Prison, only a very short walk away from where she had tried to hide the evidence that dark night.

HONEYTRAPS AND KILLER Bs

It was a dangerous thing to do and his mother knew that.

'You're not taking all that money with you?' she'd said as she watched him getting ready to go out and slipping £10 into his coat pocket. The equivalent of many weeks' wages in those days, it would tempt any thief – worth killing for, even.

Mrs Senior knew her son Henry would be meeting his lady friend in the usual place – Queen's Park near their home at 50 Robson Street in Glasgow's southside. Like many other locals, she worried about that park and its history of violence. She was right to.

Ten years before, an older man had been beaten to death there. Rumour was he had gone to the park looking for sex. For years, no one walked alone there at any time or at night even in a group. The same type of thing had happened there many times before. Now, in 1920, young lovers were back using Queen's Park as a meeting place. Even though he was grown man, she worried for her son, as mothers do. With all that money in his pocket, she'd be frantic.

Henry smiled at her and put most of his cash back, taking only £2. That was still a lot of money in 1920 but she knew how he liked to show off a bit as well as treat his girlfriend to a good time. He was generous that way.

Henry ruffled his mother's hair with a grin, said a gruff goodbye to his brother and was off out the door – away to meet his woman, a happy man.

They found him the next day in Queen's Park, lying behind some bushes, battered, bloody, dead. The police didn't know it was thirty-five-year-old Henry Senior for very good reasons. The corpse had no wallet on it, wore no coat or even shoes, never mind having any papers identifying him. All they could do was release a description to the local newspapers.

Two days later, Henry's mother and brother, frantic because he hadn't returned home, read the description in the newspapers and dreaded the worst. After identifying the body, the brother went on to describe what was missing from Henry's possessions – his good coat, his shoes and, of course, the money.

Glasgow cops had been concerned about the number of violent muggings there had been recently, particularly in and around Queen's Park. By talking to the many people – always men – who had been beaten and robbed but survived, they managed to garner good descriptions of two men.

They then did what Glasgow cops could do in those days. They circulated the IDs with a description of Henry's coat and shoes to their best helpers – the drivers of trams, buses, trains and taxis. These days some gangsters call taxi drivers 'the Second Force' because of the help they give the police. It has always been thus.

The violent muggings and now murder had attracted a great deal of press coverage. There had also been a number of rapes, not in Queen's Park but nearby. The folk of Glasgow, especially in the southside, were scared to even venture out on their own. No wonder the response to the cops' cry for help was spectacular.

Before long, they could trace the men's movements from the southside of Glasgow to a hotel, a bar and then on to the Belfast Boat Train at Glasgow Central Station. What was more, two young, attractive women had often been seen with them and good descriptions had also been provided of them.

Then names were suggested. If the descriptions were right, the cops were looking for a James Rollins, twenty-two, and Albert Fraser, twenty-four. Their young female companions were Elizabeth Stewart and Helen White. As is the tradition with ladies, their ages weren't known. But, as would become clear, these were no ladies.

The frightened public had been very cooperative. As many experienced detectives admit, a helpful public is the best weapon in their armoury in solving cases.

Glasgow cop, Detective Superintendent Keith was sent on the chase to Belfast. With the help of local police, he scoured rough areas where there were cheap lodgings and pubs. Wherever he went, he showed descriptions of the four suspects, leaving copies with pub landlords and landladies of the boarding houses. Keith's methods might seem slow and old-fashioned. His job was made even more difficult because Belfast was affected by the kind of sectarian violence that had flared up in 1916 in Dublin and was burning still. It meant that people were suspicious of outsiders – particularly those with English or Scottish accents who could be British spies. It didn't look promising for the cop.

Yet, in less than two days in that sprawling, troubled city, he found the men, though not the women. Rollins and Fraser were immediately arrested and taken to a local police station. In interview, they were sullen and uncommunicative, denying any involvement in the murder. So it was just as well the police had the right to search them. A large bloodstain was found on the cuff of Fraser's jacket. Whoever had killed Henry Senior would have been splattered with blood. Some of the witnesses who reported seeing the men carrying the coat and the shoes also said they had blood-smeared clothes, hands and faces.

At that time, before the vast development of forensic science, one bloodstain wasn't enough to convict. But the biggest breakthrough was about to happen. In Rollins' pocket, they discovered an address written on a small slip of paper. Cops were dispatched there immediately and, as had been hoped, they found the two young women.

Helen White and Elizabeth Stewart were good looking, right enough, and even younger than the men. They had also been sickened by the attack on Senior and it had frightened them – or so they said.

DS Keith explained to the young women how much trouble they were in – their victim was dead and, if they were found guilty, they'd swing by their necks. Within twenty minutes of talking to the cops, the women agreed to turn King's evidence and told the whole story of Henry Senior's demise.

True to their word, the women repeated the same evidence when they appeared as witnesses at Rollins' and Fraser's trial for murder on 20 May 1920 at Glasgow High Court.

Helen White's evidence was most important. For some time, the foursome had been setting honeytrap robberies using the women as bait. Usually they operated in the north and east of Glasgow but they had been a bit too busy there and the cops were on the lookout for them. That day, 3 February 1920, White had been told that she was to be the bait and they travelled across the city to Queen's Park, knowing it was a place where couples met and lone men looked for illicit sex.

Helen White had watched Henry Senior from a little distance off. He was obviously dressed up and waiting for someone – a woman no doubt – and she was late. Strolling past him, Helen stared him in the eye, winked slowly and grinned. Henry loved the ladies and, in a flash, he was by her side and the two had started chatting. It was a routine she had worked time and time before – she'd let the target think he was charming her while, all the time, she was the one in control. She might well have been very young but Helen White knew men very well.

After a few minutes, James Rollins emerged from some bushes. 'What the fuck are you doing?' he demanded.

'Just walking my girl,' replied a startled Henry.

Usually, at this stage, Rollins would claim that Helen was his girl, get all upset and angry and threaten to bash the victim if he didn't apologise and cough up some cash. Instead, he grabbed Henry round the throat from behind and yanked. At that, Albert Fraser ran from bushes and started whipping Henry's face and skull with a revolver, not stopping till he was a mess of blood and bone, quite still – already dying, in fact.

All through this, if she was to be believed, Helen White was weeping and calling for the men to stop. However upset she was, she still ran off with the men and Elizabeth after they had callously stripped Henry's body of his coat, shoes and money. Later she was sent to pawn the coat and received seventeen shillings for it – 85p in today's money but worth a lot more then.

Elizabeth Stewart took the stand and gave evidence supporting Helen's in every detail of the murder. They were attractive, tearful and convincing witnesses. It took the jury a mere twenty minutes to find both Rollins and Fraser guilty.

The judge, Lord Justice Sands, donned the black cap and pronounced the death sentence on both men. Meantime, all over Scotland, men and women were avoiding meeting in the isolated splendour of our city parks. The killing of Henry Senior had reminded Scots just what dangerous places they could be. By late afternoon every day, parks, and Queen's Park in particular, would be devoid of people. That's how they would stay for years until folk drifted back to them – even to Queen's Park whose future would turn out to be just as bloody as its past.

On 26 May 1920, Rollins' and Fraser's hangman, John Ellis, kept his date with them at Duke Street Prison, Glasgow. Helen White and Elizabeth Stewart, the honey in the trap, were free to get on with their lives. It's a good bet neither of them set foot in Queen's Park again.

THE COLOUR OF HATE

Street life in Glasgow has always been hard but to be poor and black on those streets? That could be deadly.

Nathoo Mohammed was in trouble. He had moved away from the crippling poverty of India to make a new life. Back home, disease and poverty stalked the streets. If those didn't get you, local gangsters would take your money and squeeze you back to that line one short step away from death. He had to get out or perish. He had pinned all his hopes on Glasgow – a fine city, he had heard – and moved there. The trouble was that some people were intent on ruining his life.

It was 1925 and India was in turmoil. Many thousands of people starved to death every year and many more died of disease. His homeland was rife with racial and religious groups using bloody violence to settle differences. All he wanted was a more peaceful life. Was it too much to ask?

With no trade and little English, Mohammed couldn't apply for a job in the shipyards or other heavy industries that Glasgow thrived on. Besides, it was the worst of times for anyone trying to get a job. By 1925, the worldwide economic depression was picking up speed and closing down industries, factories and shops daily. The dole queues got longer and folk became more desperate – never more so than in Glasgow.

Nathoo Mohammed had got married not long after arriving in Scotland and he and his wife Louie weren't going to give up without a fight. They were used to hard times and hard graft so they decided to work at the only thing they knew – as shopkeepers selling clothes. Back home Nathoo's family specialised in brightly coloured, light silk clothes. But one short night in Scotland's harsh climate was long enough to convince him that would never do in Scotland. Instead, they'd sell jumpers and scarves. With no money to rent or buy a shop, they joined the legion of Glasgow's street traders.

Life was difficult for the young couple. The city was jam-packed with recently arrived immigrants all trying to scratch a living. The biggest group was the Irish and they were particularly concentrated towards the east of the city where Mohammed and Louie ran their stall. Many Jewish families who'd escaped slaughter in the pogroms of Europe settled in numbers in the Gorbals. At one time, the biggest group was the Chinese, many of whom had escaped starvation and sometimes slavery to centre round Garnethill. But those from India and Pakistan were still few and, unlike the Chinese, they were not concentrated in any one area but scattered all over the city. With no strength in numbers, fitting in was even more difficult for them.

Some of the Chinese families and many more of the Jewish folk sold textiles and clothes, many of the latter group from the east end of the city. They slashed their prices to the bone, minimising profits in an effort to undercut competitors. Survival was the name of the game.

Mohammed understood all that. It was just business, after all, and he would do the same given half a chance. Yet it was more difficult for him as a recent arrival because he'd had no chance to build up regular trade or save a nest egg. There were also very few people from his homeland in Scotland and the few there were all suffered from the same difficulties of the newcomer. So they made do with less income and trusted that hard work would get them by. It was working just fine – till the protection racketeers came calling.

A couple of young guys appeared at the stall demanding a few shillings. To start with Mohammed couldn't understand what they

77

meant. It wasn't just his lack of English and the men's strong accents. He'd eventually worked out what they were saying but what did it mean? If he gave them money, what would he get in return? So he sent them away, politely but firmly. They left with curses and threats.

A short while later, they came back with a few mates, kicked lumps out of Mohammed, terrified Louie and stole some scarves. Now Mohammed understood only too well what the game was. India had its protection rackets too.

Nathoo Mohammed needed some help or he would be left unable to earn enough money to feed himself and his wife. In those days, there were very few places they could go for help. It was well known that some of the beat bobbies got regular payments to turn a blind eye to the shenanigans of some street players. Complain to them and they'd make things worse for you.

Besides, Mohammed and Louie didn't want to complain to the authorities. He hadn't been in Scotland long and they wanted to be seen as peaceful, trouble-free citizens. They suspected that, if they were seen as troublemakers, he might get sent back home – a suspicion that was well founded.

He couldn't go to the white folk around them. Indians weren't that common in Glasgow then and there was a great deal of low-level racism. People would go on about them being out to steal their jobs and speak about the smell of their cooking or say that they were dirty. It was plain to Mohammed and Louie that they weren't accepted by Glaswegians – even the law-abiding ones.

There was only one place he could go – to that small group of Indian traders in the city. Mohammed spent a few days scouring the city targeting the areas where he knew there were Indian markets and stalls. Spotting a compatriot, he'd introduce himself, apologise for interrupting business and ask if they had a few minutes to talk. He was a polite man and wasn't about to throw away his manners just because there was some trouble.

Most greeted him warmly and revealed that they had been suffering problems similar to his own. From the description of the men making the threats, it sounded as if the same group had been targeting all the Indians. Mohammed wasn't surprised. That's how they worked in India too.

At a meeting in one of their homes one night it became absolutely clear that all the Indian traders were being harassed by the same protection gang. Some of the traders had been paying up. Others had moved their stalls to different streets but the gang soon found them again. All felt the same way – angry and used. They agreed that they weren't going to pay up. From then on, they stuck together, spent time in each other's houses, set up their stalls close to one another and went running to each other's aid if there was trouble. They had to be constantly on their guard but the group action was working – working so well, in fact, that the protection gangsters decided to up the pressure.

One of the racketeers, John Keen, shared a plan with a few friends in a pub one night. By last orders, Keen, Robert Fletcher and John McCormack were at work. It didn't take much for the three men to stir up hatred of the Indians among local white folk. Poverty was rife, many people were almost starving to death, most couldn't afford medical care, more and more were thrown out of their homes for rent arrears, the poorhouses were full and the queues for the soup kitchens grew longer every day. In such awful conditions, prejudice could easily flourish – just blame the Indians for all the woes of the time.

Soon life had got worse for Nathoo Mohammed, his wife and their friends. It was difficult enough dealing with a team of roughneck gangsters but the whole population? The ordinary people of Glasgow had turned against them – that's how it felt. Still, the Indians refused to pay the protection gangs and they stayed even more alert and stuck together.

It all came to a head on 6 May 1925. Nathoo Mohammed and Louie had congregated with other friends at the house of Sundi Din at 56 Water Street, Port Dundas, Glasgow. They knew that a bloodthirsty mob was walking the streets dishing out grief wherever they went. Such street violence and mob rule was becoming a regular feature of Glasgow. Usually it was reaction against the police or heavy-handed landlords but this time it was different.

In the north and east of the city centre, the mob trashed homes and looted shops belonging to anyone they suspected of being foreign – especially if they were black. Terror stalked the streets but there was one person they were hunting in particular – Nathoo Mohammed. He was the first one to stand up to the protection gang and they in turn had stirred up racial hatred towards him. They knew where he lived in Clyde Street and went there but he and his wife had flown. The city of Glasgow was, in many ways, a village and they knew where Mohammed's friends lived.

Sitting nervously comforting each other in Sundi Din's house in Water Street, Nathoo and the others heard the mob coming. A hard core of around 200 heavies soon filled the street and were baying for blood outside Sundi Din's house. The Indians had to do something. If they just sat there, the rioters would come in through the door and windows – maybe torch the place.

In the street, the crowd was growing every minute, swollen by men staggering out of local pubs and women and children running from their homes, eager to join the fun. Someone started chanting, 'Hang the niggers, hang the niggers!' It had turned into a massive lynch mob and they were moving in.

Nathoo Mohammed knew he was their number-one target. As the race rioters started to smash into the front door, trying to break it down, he knew it wouldn't be long before they succeeded and were in the house attacking everyone, even the women. Louie begged Nathoo to leave Sundi Din's house before it was too late and, going out a back way, he made it to safety. Some of his friends thought Nathoo had gone to fetch the police but one, Noorh Mohammed, wasn't so sure. As the mob smashed the windows, Noorh Mohammed picked up a broom handle and, without a word to his friends, he charged out amongst the throng. He was a brave man but had he acted too soon?

Nathoo Mohammed hadn't gone for the police but someone had. Local lad John Stirling hadn't liked what was going on and had rushed to Canal Street to fetch the cops who immediately sent for reinforcements and, at the very time Noorh had gone out into the street, they were sprinting to the scene. If Noorh Mohammed had only waited another five minutes.

In the heart of the mob, Noorh Mohammed hit out right and left to defend himself. A small man unused to street fighting, he was quickly overpowered and fell to the road with a knife plunged deep into his heart. His weeping friends rushed out and grabbed him, carrying him inside and upstairs to a bed. Within half an hour, he had died. Noorh Mohammed had become Scotland's first fatal victim of race hate.

John Keen, Robert Fletcher and John McCormack, well known to the cops for other crimes, had been spotted by them as the riot ringleaders. All were charged with Mohammed's murder.

At their trial at the High Court, Glasgow on 1 September 1925, Keen freely admitted the knife was his but claimed someone else had taken it from his pocket and killed the man. In the days before effective fingerprinting, never mind DNA testing, the police needed to prove otherwise the hard way. Normally it would have been difficult for the cops to get witnesses to stand against small-time gangsters like John Keen – but not this time. Maybe something in the way Mohammed had put his own life on the line to save friends had moved the ordinary people of Glasgow. Whatever the reason was, John Keen was in big trouble.

One Richard Stephen came forward to swear he'd seen Keen after the killing sporting a badly cut hand – the kind of wound you might suffer if using a knife in violence. Another man, Robert Purdon, who was actually a pal of Keen, took the stand to say Keen had passed him the knife but only after the murder. He in turn had passed it to a man called Joseph McCall to hide. Later, Robert Purdon and his brother admitted approaching McCall to ask him to return the knife which he promptly did. Purdon then handed the blade in to the police station.

Charges against McCormack were dropped. Fletcher was found guilty of the lesser crime of culpable homicide and sentenced to seven years in jail. But John Keen was found guilty of murder, the first person in Scotland to be convicted of a racial killing. Decency had prevailed – and justice too.

Sentenced to death, Keen took the long short walk with the hangman, Thomas Pierrepoint – brother of more famous hangman Albert – at Duke Street Prison on 24 September 1925.

Noorh Mohammed's friends mourned his death. They had learned a bitter lesson that their quest for a new life and a new homeland would be hazardous and take longer than they thought.

Fear and prejudice between ethnic groups can run deadly deep and we are still trying to conquer those fears and prejudices more than eighty years later.

JUST ANOTHER MAN

'Kitty's got another victim!' The woman's voice rang out strong and clear, ripe with sarcasm. Around her, women cackled while others pursed their lips at the antics of the local lady of the night. In a short while, they'd find out just how right their outspoken friend was.

The target of the sneers was Catherine Donaghue, better known as Kate Donaghue or Katie Rose when she was trying to be fancy. A handsome woman with bright eyes, Kate Donaghue used her looks to good effect, being skilled in getting men to do her bidding – and very skilled she was too.

Kate Donaghue was an unashamed prostitute who liked to drink a great deal. Both tastes she had developed after her husband deserted her. At least she thought that he had. They married in 1914, the year World War I broke out. As an enlisted soldier he had gone off to fight and never returned. Maybe he lay dead and unidentified in some foreign field as so many did. The government of the time weren't keen to admit that was the case. They would rather have hearts broken back home than acknowledge the daily slaughter and chaos of the Somme.

Kate Donaghue healed her broken heart by drinking whisky and sleeping with strangers, usually for money. It was a life that had hardened and shaped her into a brazen working girl by 23 June 1923, when we meet her taking another stranger back to her home at 40 Jamaica Street in Edinburgh.

The local women could sneer all they wanted. Kate Donaghue didn't care. She knew their men said one thing to their wives' faces and acted another way down the pub – buying her drinks, feeling her arse. Some of them even paid her for a quick good time in one of the closes or lanes down at her favourite drinking area, Rose Street.

That's where she had been that day, in a pub in Rose Street, and she had come home with a man – even better, he was a man with money and a carry-out of booze.

Her company was a highly respectable bloke by the name of William Cree, thirty years old and from Dunfermline. Cree had been a war hero in the Black Watch, seeing active duty in France for the years of the war, always returning to the front in spite of being wounded three times.

Back in civvies he got a job on the railways as a peewee man – the almost sweet term for the hard labour of checking the train tracks. In those days when the railways were the kings of transport, it was important work. It was also regular work with a guaranteed future, even during the bleak economic depression that was beginning to hit hard. The main tools of Cree's trade were a heavy hammer and an industrial-sized shovel. It took a strong man to do that work and he was all that – big, muscular and powerful. No doubt Kate Donaghue thought she was in for a good time as well as a lucrative time.

William Cree was football daft. Most Saturdays he would travel from Dunfermline to Edinburgh to watch a match – though whether he supported Heart of Midlothian or Hibernian isn't known. It doesn't matter – they were both top teams in Britain. Usually he'd watch the game then travel home but not that day. That day he lingered on in the pub in Rose Street and paired up with Kate Donaghue. What he didn't know was that she had a man at home.

Donaghue had been living with thirty-year-old Philip Murray for a couple of years. They had a few things in common – sex, alcohol and money, her money from prostitution. Murray knew all about Donaghue's lifestyle and lived with it at peace – or so the neighbours thought. The couple had their rows, their shouting matches, for sure but no more or less than anyone else on the street. That was about to change.

A few minutes after Kate Donaghue and William Cree went into her house, it started.

'Oh don't!' cried out a man's voice in terror and then there was the sound of splintering wood.

The women on the pavement looked up at Donaghue's windows, nodding at each other. Glass smashed and suddenly William Cree was hanging out of that window. The terrified man's arms flapped in the air and reached back, grabbing at someone behind him. That same person was hitting and thumping at Cree, pushing him out the window.

'Help me,' Cree pleaded with the women below.

Not one budged. Men had come running from nearby houses to see what the commotion was about.

'Please help me,' screamed William Cree.

Not one of the men budged either. Why would they help Kate Donaghue? Or anyone else to do with her? They could all rot in hell as far as they were concerned. That's when the window frame fell out and William Cree came hurtling through the window.

CRUNCH. The sound was sickening as he landed at their feet, face down. Later one person would say he gave a moan then lay still. No one else heard him utter a noise. What wasn't in dispute was that William Cree had died right there on the pavement.

The women weren't sneering now. They were howling and sobbing. Two beat bobbies nearby heard the row and wandered over to do a nosy. Leaning over Cree, they checked for signs of life and found none. The coppers weren't surprised to hear that he had fallen from Kate Donaghue's window – was pushed out the window? They knew Donaghue well. She was bad news and something like this was bound to happen sooner rather than later, they reckoned.

The cops rushed up the stairs and kicked in Donaghue's door. She and Murray came away easily enough though all the way

Kate never let up. She talked and gibbered, saying how the man had fallen out. She didn't even know William Cree's surname nor had she ever intended to find out. That was her way, the nature of her life. The cops were left to find out from the dead man's wallet.

Witnesses lined up to say that Cree had been pushed from the window while pleading for his life. Donaghue and Murray were going to be charged with murder – but not if Katie Rose had anything to do with it.

At the High Court in Edinburgh on 9 October 1923, there was a surprise witness. Kate Donaghue had turned King's evidence in return for all charges being dropped. Philip Murray alone was in the dock for murder. Donaghue and Murray's versions agreed to an extent. Both admitted that she had brought Cree to their home. Murray had been asleep in their bed, drunk and fully clothed, when he woke to find the strange man there. For reasons he never explained, this angered Murray who was no stranger to his partner's profession. There was a fight between the men. This was as far as their agreement went.

Donaghue said that Murray somehow got the strapping Cree to the window and, after a struggle, threw him to his death. Murray said that they fought and Cree fell backwards through the window, hurtling to the ground. If that had been all that was said, the jury would have had to decide who to believe – man or woman, neither of whom was of impeccable character – but there was more.

Some of the witnesses had caught a severe dose of memory loss and claimed not to recall anything, even though, in their statements to the police, they'd had more to tell – a lot more.

Several eyewitnesses swore that there were two people behind Cree, punching, thumping and pushing him out of that window – Philip Murray and Kate Donaghue. That would explain how the powerfully built Cree was forced out of the window. It would take some doing no matter how drunk he was. Besides, the unfit, long-term boozer Murray was so drunk he had fallen asleep. It's not easy to push anyone out of a window but two people against one? That might do it.

Then again, it was well known that Kate Donaghue's neighbours hated her. Was this not so much a case of veracity as spiteful vengeance?

It took the jury less than half an hour to decide it believed Kate Donaghue. After all, the police had accepted her evidence and they couldn't be wrong, could they?

Even as he was sentenced to death, Philip Murray quietly and calmly made a statement of his innocence then added, 'I am fully prepared to meet my God.'

On 30 October 1923, Philip Murray walked to the gallows to meet his god without murmur or complaint. For a man who had misspent much of his life he met his death with dignity.

Soon after the trial, Kate Donaghue was back at her old haunts in the pubs of Rose Street having a good time as if nothing had happened. In some times and places, life is cheap for some people.

WASTED WARNINGS

Young, attractive and certain she knew what was right for her, she was so typical of young people in any era. In her case, it was to be her downfall.

Isabella Hain was only eighteen years old. A popular girl, she was keen to fall in love, marry and have babies. It was the 'dream life' pushed at every young woman in the 1920s and she had bought it all.

She was a good girl and good girls didn't go out with a lot of boys. Maybe that was the problem. When Allen Wales came along and courted her, innocent and naive Isabella fell for him big time.

Allen Wales was young too, just a couple of years older than her. But, in the 1920s, a man aged twenty and a woman of eighteen years were seen as fully adult and they would have been expected to earn a living since the age of fourteen. It was a different, harder time when people lived shorter and harsher lives, when childbirth and child-rearing were best tackled by young, fit women and strong young men who could bring in a wage.

The problem was that Isabella's family didn't approve. They weren't stuffy or over-protective but there was something about Allen Wales they didn't like. Something worried them though they weren't sure what.

The young man was keen and attentive to their girl. He was always the gentleman. He told them of his ambitions to take good care of her and the children they planned. But still the parents felt there was something not quite right with him.

In age-old tradition, the parents said 'black' and the daughter said 'white' and that's how it stayed till on 2 December 1926 Isabella married Allen Wales near her Leith home. She might as well have been on the dark side of the moon as far as her parents were concerned. They weren't invited to the wedding and wouldn't have attended if they had been.

For the next eleven weeks, Isabella didn't see her family at all – not the best way for a loving daughter to embark on a new life but sometimes these things happened. During that time, Allen and Isabella, now also Wales, moved from lodgings to digs. It was step down and perilously close to homelessness. Getting money wasn't easy for young couples in those difficult days and Allen Wales struggled more than most.

When Isabella swallowed her pride and started visiting her family again, she complained that Allen rowed with her constantly and had started beating her. A patchwork quilt of bruises on her body was evidence she was telling the truth.

Nevertheless, she stayed with Wales and gave birth to his son on 2 October 1927, less than a year after they were wed. For many young couples, the birth of a baby smoothes out their problems by setting their priorities – not so for the Waleses. Allen continued to row with his young wife violently and carried on beating her.

Isabella stayed with her husband even though her life was hell. In those days women were expected to stick with their legally married husbands no matter how bad life was. This expectation cost many women dear. Men, in turn, were still expected to be the breadwinners and provide for their wives and children. In those days of economic blight, money was hard to come by in many families – something that could add pressure and cause rows even in the most caring of relationships.

Neighbours and friends thought that Allen and Isabella were just another example of a couple who'd turned the pressures of poverty in on themselves but Isabella's family still thought there was something else wrong with Allen Wales.

In June 1928, Isabella was out with her mother when they accidentally met Allen Wales at Kirkgate. He immediately launched into a verbal assault on his wife, accusing her of being a bad mother, seeing other men and a list of other misdemeanours. By all accounts, none of them were true.

Finally, the family decided they should get between husband and wife and suggested to Isabella she and her wee son move away from Allen Wales. Now in despair, Isabella agreed.

Just another sad tale of two people who'd got married too young? Sad enough as that is, if only it had stayed that way.

Over the next few weeks Wales in turn begged and threatened his wife to return to him. Isabella refused.

On 5 June 1928, he turned up at Isabella's family's house at 17 Pirniefield Place, Leith, with his own mother to plead his case. He was calm and sensible, treating Isabella with respect for a change.

Again Isabella refused to go back to him. She had celebrated her twenty-first birthday only the day before. In 1928 that was still a coming of age, of adulthood, a proper start in life. Strong willed as ever, she had set her mind on making a new life for her and her son. Allen Wales and his mother left Isabella's family's house quietly but it wouldn't stay quiet for long.

Half an hour later, Wales was back. He burst into the home, shouting, swearing and waving a long-bladed knife. Grabbing Isabella by the hair, he dragged her into the street. The terrified family, including her mother and her young female cousin, rushed out behind Wales and Isabella, begging him to let her go. In the street, he continued shouting and bawling at his wife, calling her every dirty name under the sun. The noise brought curious neighbours – mainly women and kids – out on to Pirniefield Place.

Isabella was popular with the neighbours, many of whom knew about her marital problems. They begged and reasoned with Allen Wales to let the young woman go but Wales wasn't listening. With the long-bladed knife in one hand, he held his young wife with an arm around her throat, yanking her from side to side as he shouted and swore.

'You were asking for this, you bitch,' he roared, 'and now you're getting it.'

Wales brought the knife blade across Isabella's throat. Then again. And again. He stood there hacking at the young woman's gullet as women and kids looked on petrified with shock and fear. Isabella went limp but he held her up and continue stabbing and cutting her throat.

In those days, street violence in Leith was commonplace and, with its high crime rates, the place crawled with rozzers on the beat. Two were on the scene in minutes and disarmed Allen Wales none too gently. But the police were too late. Young Isabella lay dead on the street, her head almost severed from her body.

It wasn't the manner of Allen Wales and Isabella's lives that shocked Scotland – their problems were only too common in those difficult days. It was the manner of Isabella's death – a brutal, pointless, tortured death in front of her family and friends – that rocked the country.

If the public execution of Isabella Wales had horrified the Scottish public, it actually helped at Allen Wales's trial for her murder at Edinburgh High Court on 23 July 1928. Witness after witness came forward to relate the terrible details of the killing. Of those there was no doubt but, given the nature of the murder, the court wanted to see if they could understand why Wales had acted in such an extreme way that day. Judges, police and lawyers were at last becoming more enlightened about human behaviour and the possibility of mental illness.

Doctors W. M. McAllister and Dodds Fairbairn were asked to examine the accused independently. Unusually for those times, they agreed with each other in their assessments. Allen Wales had a mental and emotional age of ten years and was of such low IQ they termed him 'feeble-minded'. Wales shouldn't have been on the street, free to go about his life and marry young Isabella. He should have been receiving long-term hospital care, possibly for the rest of his life.

In an era when people were struggling to buy bread, many people with Wales's problems were simply left to their own devices. Probably because he was capable of holding a social conversation, no one spotted Allen Wales's disabilities – apart, that is, from Isabella's family when they warned their daughter that there was something wrong with the young man – seriously wrong. They had been right.

These days, it is likely that Allen Wales would have been imprisoned for many years in the State Hospital, Carstairs, where he'd have been helped to cope with his limitations. In 1928, he was kept in a cold, bare cell in Saughton Prison, Edinburgh, for two weeks till, on 13 August, the hangman came to fetch him.

1930 TO 1939

WAR ON THE STREETS

Prohibition was the killjoy in the USA and the likes of Al Capone prospered till the law governing it was repealed (1933). Hitler became Chancellor of Germany (1933) and was soon testing his troops in the Spanish Civil War (1936).

Amy Johnson flew from Britain to Australia (1930). The *Hindenburg* zeppelin was destroyed by fire with the loss of many lives (1937) and the new talkie movies captured the disaster.

Polythene was first used commercially (1933) and nylon was invented (1935).

Driving tests were introduced in Britain (1935) and Leslie Mitchell became the first TV star as a regular announcer (1936). The Marx Brothers were packing the cinemas with *Duck Soup* (1933).

In Glasgow, the *Queen Mary* was launched to international acclaim (1934). Detective Sergeant Bertie Hammond, a fingerprint expert from Sheffield City Police, transferred to Glasgow and established a fingerprint and photographic department, the first in Scotland (1931).

Razor gangs like the Billy Boys and Norman Conks ran the streets and Glasgow responded by appointing Percy J. Sillitoe as chief constable. Sillitoe introduced new uniforms including the caps with black-and-white checks known as Sillitoe tartan (1932). The first police patrol car was introduced to Scotland (1936).

World War II was declared (1939). Lord Beaverbrook, owner of the *Daily Express*, the highest selling newspaper in Britain, was appointed to the Cabinet. In his unofficial role as minister for propaganda, Beaverbrook advised Churchill to order a ban on the reporting of major crime. Churchill agreed.

DEADLY DISGRACE

The crowds were there early. In their mufflers and coats, they were stamping their feet against the cold, munching sandwiches and drinking tea from vendors who knew a good opportunity when they saw one. All wanted a seat at Glasgow's entertainment high spot of the year – a hanging trial.

It was more than that, for the man in the dock wasn't just an ordinary soul. He was Peter Queen, the thirty-one-year-old son of top Glasgow bookmaker, Thomas Queen. In 1932, bookies were big celebrities and so were their families. Now one faced the drop – top entertainment for the masses.

There was more to the case than it merely featuring a well-known figure – there were sex and booze. What more could the people ask for?

Though thin and nervous, Peter Queen was a handsome, sallow-faced man. Agitated at the best of times, he had good reason, it seems.

In 1918, he had married but it hadn't lasted long. His wife almost immediately took to drink and got so bad she was permanently cared for in a private hospital after only two years. Little more was revealed about this woman but it seems likely that alcohol was only part of her trouble, the underlying cause probably being some form of mental illness. What is known is that she survived in medical care and was still alive in 1932 when her still legally married husband went on trial for the murder of his lover, Chrissie Gall.

Chrissie was four years younger than Peter and they had first met when she worked as live-in nanny for his younger brothers and sisters. When she left the employ of his parents to return home to care for her sick mother, the pair stayed in touch and eventually became lovers. Now there was scandal.

Because of his religious convictions and, no doubt, family and social pressure, Peter Queen couldn't divorce his hospitalised wife. There is no doubt that he soon fell in love with Chrissie Gall yet still he couldn't free himself to marry her. That was the core of the problems.

If anything, Chrissie's religious beliefs and the need for conformity to social expectations were even stronger than Queen's – so much so that she kept the true nature of their relationship secret from her family, especially when the pair moved in together. Everyone who knew her felt sure it was the pressure of the secrecy and the religious hypocrisy that had driven Chrissie to booze big time – in fact, Queen believed this too.

From all accounts, Peter Queen had had two women in his life and both had turned to drink. And this was at a time when respectable, middle-class women in Scotland were only meant to partake of the very occasional sherry. It got worse – if Queen's wife had perhaps suffered from mental illness, there's no doubt that Chrissie Gall did. The booze made her depressed and suicidal.

Many of her family and friends knew the extent of Chrissie's boozing and made repeated efforts to get her off the bottle. They also knew how it drove her to threaten self-destruction. 'Peter will come in one night and find me behind the door' and 'I'm going to make a hole in the Clyde' were just a couple of the comments she made to people over a few years. She also made apparent efforts at suicide, once hanging herself from a hook on the back of a door and, on at least two other occasions, leaving highly toxic gas rushing from the unlit cooker. But was she just seeking attention or was she serious? The High Court in Glasgow was going to decide.

Late at night on 20 November 1931, Peter Queen staggered into Partick Police Station in Glasgow's west end obviously in an agitated, nervous state. 'My wife is dead in my flat,' he blurted out to the desk officer. That much was clear. When asked by the police what had happened, Queen later claimed to have said, 'Don't think that I've killed her.'

Two cops later claimed he said, 'I think I have killed her.'

The different versions of the statements – so close but so far apart – would become part of a crucial debate in court. But on that night, Queen had sought the help of the police and they went at top speed to his home – a cramped, dingy tenement flat at 539 Dumbarton Road.

Lying on the one bed in the single end was Chrissie Gall, a rope tied tightly around her neck. One look at her face and even the beat bobbies could tell that she was dead. Her cheeks were blotched red, blue and white, her neck where the rope had cut in was blood crimson and her bloated tongue stuck from her mouth. The one saving grace for any squeamish copper was that her eyes were shut, not staring that accusatory glower of the dead.

A more careful analysis of the scene would later reveal the rope had been hacked from a pulley used to hang up wet clothes. More intriguingly, the blankets were up to her chin and covering one arm. Many people making such a discovery will automatically try to give comfort so had Peter Queen, in an attempt to do this, moved her after death? No, was his answer. He had walked in on Chrissie and found her in that state. So what had he done right away? Loosened the rope? No. Called a doctor? No. Felt for a pulse or sign of life? No. Then what?

Queen wasn't sure. Maybe he had passed out. He didn't know but, with these vague responses, the cops were now sure. They had already reached the opinion that Chrissie Gall could not have put the rope around her neck and pulled till she was dead. It just didn't seem feasible. They charged Peter Queen with Chrissie Gall's murder.

At his trial at the High Court in Glasgow, the post-mortem results added further damning evidence. The rope had been pulled so tight that some bone and gristle were shattered. That would require substantial force. How could anyone – let alone a slightly build woman – do that to herself without passing out long before death arrived? Impossible, said the doctor.

The Crown put an ace card into the witness stand – Professor John Glaister of the recently created Department of Forensic Medicine at Glasgow University. Glaister was one of the founding pioneers of forensics and he had a world-renowned reputation. When he spoke, juries listened.

Glaister's view was that Chrissie would have been found lying quite differently had she strangled herself. Both arms would have been free from the blankets. Added to that was the considerable damage to her neck. He believed she would have passed out long before she could have killed herself.

Knowing the Crown planned to pull Glaister in as an expert witness, Queen's defence team found a world authority of their own. Sir Bernard Spilsbury was a star of the English courts and world renowned himself. In that time-honoured fashion of expert witnesses, Spilsbury argued that Chrissie Gall had killed herself. There was no sign of a struggle in the room and her fingers and neck showed no sign of a desperate clawing at the rope that would be expected if someone else had been attacking her.

So the great men jousted for almost a day – men of science examining the same evidence and coming up with exactly opposing views. The packed public gallery loved it but they were in for an even bigger treat. Peter Queen took the stand.

Many lawyers would be reluctant to lay the accused open to cross-examination in such a case, for fear they'd be tripped up by the Crown and made to look guilty. Yet the case against Queen suggested that Chrissie's drinking, depressions and suicide attempts had eventually driven him to despair and murder. There was only one person who could counter that – Peter Queen.

His evidence lasted five hours – a lifetime in the witness box for an accused person. Even thinner by then and more agitated than ever, he still managed to speak in a calm, clear voice about his relationship with Chrissie Gall. Queen didn't hide from his lover's problems or how difficult life was for him much of the time. But he spoke of something else – his undying love for her, his frustration at their lack of marriage, his dreams that one day they could be man and wife in the eyes of the world. Would the jury believe him?

The trial had gone on all week and spilled over to Saturday morning, making it one of the longest trials in living memory. The judge addressed the jury and they went out to consider their verdict. With all those opposing expert views, they faced a task from hell.

Two hours later they were back. Two of the women jurors were in tears. The lady foreperson stood up to announce the verdict and immediately burst into sobs. Eventually a male member took to his feet and declared, 'Guilty, My Lord.'

Peter Queen was to hang for the murder of the very woman he had told the world he loved more than life itself. Now he would pay with his life.

Before the judge, Lord Alness, could don his black cap and pronounce the sentence, a juror stood up and declared that the verdict had been reached only by a majority vote. But all jurors did agree that they should ask the judge to show Peter Queen mercy. Behind his wig and formal regalia the judge's face had turned ashen pale. He thanked the jury for their consideration but the law allowed him no alternative. Peter Queen would hang at Duke Street Prison on 30 January 1932.

Glasgow courts were infamous for being packed with mobs keen to witness a hanging sentence being handed down. Not that day – the commotion that immediately broke out was one of howls of protest at the sentence. Queen may have lost the trial but he had won the hearts and souls of ordinary people – and not just them as it turned out.

While Peter Queen's lawyers raised and lost an appeal and a new death date was set for 13 February 1932, a petition was circulating. When it was submitted, it had the names of 400 prominent businessmen, politicians and dignitaries on it, all pleading for clemency. Justice is said to be blind but perhaps it isn't deaf for, three days before his planned execution, Peter Queen's sentence was commuted to life in prison. While the news was greeted with great public relief, there were still many who felt he shouldn't have been found guilty at all. Maybe they were right.

Only years after Queen had started his prison sentence did it emerge that, for most of his adult life, he had been being treated with bromide – a well-known medicine used to control epilepsy and related conditions. This might have explained what he had done on discovering Chrissie's body – a time he couldn't explain. It is known that great trauma and shock can bring on seizures. We also know that, when the person regains consciousness, they are often in a half-awake dream state for some time – a time they often can't remember, just as Queen had described it.

Why didn't Queen's defence use this information? A fear of prejudice in the jury against those with epilepsy? Or because Peter Queen and his family didn't want the social disgrace of revealing his condition? Just as they couldn't stand the disgrace of him divorcing his wife? The same stance that made Chrissie Gall miserable and drove her to drink.

Fear of disgrace – was that what killed Chrissie Gall?

BREAD AND BLOOD

Missing! It's a word that strikes terror into every parent, causing sleepless nightmares and waking dreams of the worst kind. Especially when the missing one is your young daughter – a good wee girl.

Little Helen Priestly was eight years old and had been sent to the shops by her mum at lunchtime to buy a loaf of bread, as she was most days. Except on that day, 21 April 1934, she never returned.

The shop was near to her home at 61 Urquhart Road, Aberdeen. Tall, fair-haired, bright Helen was well known in neighbourhood and, while she was a wee bit shy, she was a confident enough girl. How could she have gone missing?

Helen's mother, father, friends and neighbours all feared the worst. Helen hadn't wandered off – she had been taken.

Within a few hours the police had been notified and hundreds of local people volunteered to search every nook and cranny of the area. The biggest search in Aberdeen's history went on all night till around 2 a.m., when Helen's exhausted father was eventually – though reluctantly – persuaded to go home for a few hours' sleep. A neighbour, Alexander Parker, promised the man that he'd go to his house and waken him again at 5 a.m. to resume the search.

Parker didn't sleep much either. What concerned adult could when a wee lassie they knew had disappeared? Keeping his word, Parker entered the Priestlys' close around 5 a.m. and was surprised to see a large, blue hessian bag lying against a wall. He'd been in and out of that close several times in the previous twelve hours and hadn't noticed that bag before. Curious, he pulled the bag open and promptly dropped it again, acid disgust rushing into his gullet and his mouth, burning his nose till he turned and spewed.

Helen Priestly's dead eyes looked up at him.

Searchers, friends, family and the police had been up and down that close repeatedly since Helen had gone missing. Her own father had walked in wearily at 2 a.m. and there had been no bag. Someone had placed Helen there between 2 a.m. and 5 a.m. It could only have been the killer.

Why? Why there? They were the first of many questions that needed to be answered in the search for Helen Priestly's murderer.

Helen Priestly had been murdered all right – strangled, to be exact – but there was more. The wee lassie had deep bruises on her upper thighs and her vagina was ripped and bloody. A sex killer was on the loose.

Word of Helen's injuries leaked to the public. Soon those who had been searching for her were joined by even more folk in vigilante groups patrolling the area with pick handles and handmade clubs, on the lookout for a man or men who might be preying on their children. Outsiders passing through the neighbourhood were challenged. What were they doing there? Two who gave abrupt, terse answers ended up on the blunt end of a gang beating and had to be rushed to the local hospital. They were just outsiders passing through.

The police were fast losing control of Aberdeen's streets and prayed that they found the murderer before the mobs did. On the other hand, such groups on the streets milling around night and day were likely to ensure the killer didn't easily strike again.

The police methodically carried out door-to-door interviews in one of the biggest operations the city had seen to that date. It wasn't a waste of their time.

One neighbour reported hearing a scream coming from a house in the Priestly close around lunchtime. Later, a roof slater from outside the area, who had been working in the back close that day, also reported hearing a 'screech' around the same time.

Then there was the blue hessian bag. It bore distinctive marks and a fading Canadian export stamp. With a few enquiries the cops ascertained that it was used for transporting flour and there weren't many such outlets in Scotland, let alone Aberdeen. But there was one – a bakery close to Helen's house.

There a baker remembered that a woman had come in asking for a bag some time before and he'd given her one of the blue Canadian bags. He provided a rough description of the woman but not enough to pinpoint the person. Well, he was just a baker doing a kindness. Why would he remember how she looked?

The police were making progress though not enough to make an arrest. Then they looked closer to home.

The Priestlys and Helen were popular with everyone in the neighbourhood . . . well, almost everyone. There was bad blood between them and a family in the same close – the Donalds. It had all started over such trivial, piffling matters that the Priestlys couldn't remember what they were. But they did describe how Jeannie Donald in particular seemed to keep the bad blood flowing.

Jeannie Donald was the woman of her house and she had even picked on young Helen by scowling at her on the street and chasing her from playing in the close. Her husband was a barber and they had a daughter, also Jeannie, who was around Helen's age – a child who was to prove her mother's downfall.

Young Jeannie Donald told the cops how on the day Helen went missing she noticed that the bread in her home was different from the type they usually had. Sure enough, the local baker confirmed that the loaf young Jeannie described was the very type Helen bought for her mother every day.

That was enough for the cops, who were desperate to get a result. Jeannie Donald and her husband were arrested. But, before the police could escort them down the stairs to the waiting police van, an angry crowd had surrounded the building baying for blood. When they eventually arrived at the police station, another mob was waiting for them there. The whole city was united in fury at the killers of Helen Priestly – so much so that the wee victim herself had to be buried quietly in a secret ceremony to prevent huge crowds taking over.

If the lynch mobs had got hold of Jeannie Donald's man that night, they would have been making a big mistake. Within a day, various colleagues and customers at the barbershop where he worked confirmed he had been there throughout the day in question and he was released. Even then the man had to take his daughter and move out of the area in fear for their lives. At least he was in the clear. His wife, on the other hand, was a different matter altogether.

Jeannie Donald was tried at Edinburgh High Court on Monday, 16 July 1934. It wasn't just in Aberdeen that the death of wee Helen had moved people. The cobbled yard outside the court was thronged with angry people, who'd been waiting since before dawn. These were furious people determined on revenge even before guilt – or innocence – had been decided. Lines of uniformed police were brought in to keep them back but more and more were needed as the mob swelled.

The folk outside the court calling for Jeannie Donald's blood saw her as a callous sex killer though few had ideas on how a woman could rape a girl. It was a good question and one the Crown intended to prove.

The lawyers for the Crown had worked hard and declared that they intended to use 164 witnesses and hundreds of productions. Jeannie Donald pled not guilty but that would be her only defence – no witnesses, no productions, no alibi . . . nothing.

Aside from the witnesses talking about hearing screams, young Jeannie Donald's evidence about the bread and so on, the Crown were about to make some Scottish legal history by their reliance on forensic evidence. Key to this was Professor John Glaister of Glasgow University. He had been quietly studying hair, of all things, and could prove that hairs found on Helen's corpse matched hair found on a brush used by the accused in jail. Hair inside the blue hessian sack was Jeannie Donald's as well. This might seem old hat to modern followers of forensic science but, in 1934, it seemed like magic – the magic of science.

Other forensic bods found fibres from the sack in the Donalds' home and bacterial growth inside the sack matched that in their house. This was all damning expert evidence, but their trump card was yet to be played. Jeannie Donald's defence was entirely reliant on discrediting the Crown's case. So, they'd argue, how could she, as a woman, have raped Helen in such a way as to cause the injuries to her vagina? It was a good point but one made by a legal mind, not a scientific mind.

It was not rape, said three pathologists who had all independently examined Helen's body. The injuries hadn't been caused by human intercourse at all but by an object such as the shaft of a hammer or a broom handle. Why would anyone – any woman – want to do such a thing? The defence lawyers were doing their best. In order to make it appear as if the girl had been raped and killed by a man, was the reply from each pathologist in turn.

It was the most damning evidence of all. If the jury believed the forensic experts, they would be declaring that Jeannie Donald not only killed young Helen but then callously disfigured and abused her corpse to cover her tracks. It was as bad as premeditation – just as damning – and the notion of a woman disfiguring the genitals of a wee girl would have a powerful impact on the jurors.

It took the jury a short eighteen minutes to find Jeannie Donald guilty of murder. She was one of the first people in the world to be convicted on the basis of a range of evidence from forensic witnesses. Her trial set a precedent that was soon to become the norm.

Or was it simply the loaf of bread that did for her? Why didn't she dispose of it? It was a different time. Bread was a staple and essential part of working folk's diet. Some days they had little else but bread and tea. Throwing a loaf away would be seen as the greatest waste. Maybe Jeannie Donald thought of the bread as she would on a day-to-day basis and not as a murderer trying to conceal her crime. If so, it would be her most expensive loaf of bread – it was almost to cost her her life.

As outside the court an angry mob howled for Jeannie Donald's blood, inside it was a different scene altogether. Eyewitnesses reported how the judge, Lord Aitchison, was visibly moved, reduced to tears. He had never had to wear the black cap before and now here he was sentencing a woman to death. But, still, in a quaking voice, he did his duty and pronounced the death sentence.

Jeannie Donald was driven off through the screaming crowds and away back up north to Craiginches Prison, Aberdeen, to wait out her last few days.

On 3 August 1934, her lawyers lodged an appeal but, in truth, they couldn't have been hopeful. The next day, 4 August, the Lord Provost of Aberdeen had his summer holiday interrupted by a letter from the Secretary of State. Promptly he rushed to Craiginches Prison to break the news. Jeannie Donald was not to hang but she would spend the rest of her life in jail.

A couple of weeks later she was secretly transferred to the women's jail in Duke Street, Glasgow. There Jeannie Donald was given special treatment by the female governor who would often go for walks with her infamous prisoner and bring her in little luxuries and items of clothing. As prison life went in the 1930s, Jeannie Donald's was an easy term.

It's not recorded how Helen Priestly's parents felt about the reprieve of a woman the Scottish public wanted to lynch – nor what they thought when, only ten years later, Jeannie Donald was set free.

Jeannie Donald died in obscurity never having admitted her guilt or explaining how and why Helen Priestly was killed. Or why she kept that loaf of bread that almost sent her on her way to the gallows.

THE SCALPEL BLADE DUEL

A wee holiday in the country was the idea and it was suiting the young woman just fine. As she went for a walk by the stream, little did she know she was about to stumble on horrors that would make investigative forensic history.

Near Moffat, standing on a bridge over a stream called Gardenholme Linn, young Susan Johnson didn't have a care in the world. She came from a good family in Lenzie and she had plenty of friends. She also had enough money that she could even afford a holiday. What did she have to worry about? That's when she saw the package in the water and, sticking out of it, a human arm. Suddenly, the day turned cold.

Susan ran all the way to a nearby hotel to raise the alarm. She must have had a strong stomach since rather than getting word to the local constabulary, she fetched her brother and returned to the spot under the bridge to investigate further.

Her brother pulled the package up the bank and, as he did so, the soaked wrapping tore a bit, revealing more of the contents. It was like a large, mixed package from the butcher with one difference – all the meat was human.

Local police were horrified. In that package was a strange list of body parts – three female breasts, one leg, a skinned hand, one eye, a torso, an eye socket and much more. There had been heavy rain in the area a week before and those with knowledge of the geography said that the package must have been dumped farther up stream. It was then carried down in the swollen waters and exposed when the river levels fell again. A wide expanse of the terrain would have to be searched in a quest for other clues. It would prove not to be a futile search.

The accounts of the number of different body parts discovered in the area range from forty-three to seventy-two. No matter which version you believe, the cops were left with a horrifying collection and one they couldn't make sense of – the only thing they did know for sure was that someone had been up to bloody murder. They needed help – expert help – and it wasn't too far away.

Under the careful supervision of Professor J. C. Brash, the body parts were transferred to Edinburgh University's Anatomy Department. There, for the first time in forensic history, a highly specialised and gifted team were brought together: Professor Sydney Smith, of the Forensic Medicine Department at Edinburgh University; Dr Arthur Hutchison of Edinburgh Dental School; Dr Gilbert Miller, a lecturer in pathology at Edinburgh University's School of Medicine; and, the most famous of them all, Professor John Glaister from Glasgow University's Department of Forensic Medicine. It was the top forensic team in the world and they all lived and worked in Scotland within fifty miles of each other.

But even that group of forensic experts were up against it. The mess of body parts gave no easy clues as to how many people had been killed or whether they were male or female, children or adults, young or old – or, indeed, how they had died. Although the mess of torsos, skulls, feet and arms was confusing, it soon became apparent to the team that someone had deliberately chopped and sliced the bodies – scalping, skinning and gouging as they went. But for what reason? The police thought they knew.

Several other mutilated bodies had been found in London and Brighton some weeks before. In both areas, the bodies had been sliced, chopped and mutilated. Was there a sadistic sexual killer on the loose? Had he turned his attention on Scotland?

As cop forces throughout Scotland went on alert and the public held its collective breath, the forensic team beavered away. It appeared as if one of the victims was male and they concluded that the cuts had been administered by deadly sharp tools – as sharp as scalpel blades – for sexual gratification. One eye was a Cyclops eye – an accident of birth led to it appearing in the middle of a forehead. Was the mutilator someone with access to a medical school where odd human parts were stored for study?

All wrong, they later discovered. All misleading. It became clear that, skilled as they were, the traditional methods weren't enough in this case. They would have to use the new developments. It was 1935, after all, and things had moved on. The range of new procedures developed in recent times and now available to them included blood sampling, X-raying bones for age, X-raying skulls for facial appearance, dental aging and scientific measuring of torsos to give an accurate image of the whole body. They deployed all of these methods and more, even inventing new techniques, to full effect.

Before long, Glaister's team knew a great deal more about who they had on their slabs. Two were women – one aged around twenty, the other about forty. At around five foot, one of the women was small while the other was taller and one had not had children while the other had. As it would transpire, their accuracy was chilling.

At the time, discovering so much from a mess of mutilated body parts was a major breakthrough and the methodology used would soon become common in every country in the world. But that's not all the men of science had discovered. They were now certain that the mutilator had deliberately removed identifying features. Eyes and hair had been removed, certain teeth, the flesh of a limb carefully sliced off and so on. Although there had been a concerted effort to conceal the women's identities, the mutilator had been sloppy in another way – in wrapping of the body parts. A newspaper, the *Sunday Graphic*, had been used and it was a limited edition that was sold only in and around Lancaster in England. Before the Scottish police started panicking about a sadistic killer on the loose on their patch, they should have talked to the forensic team – something modern cops do as a matter of course.

The newspaper meant that now the police knew the correct area to look. Sure enough, over three weeks before, a young woman from Lancaster, Mary Jane Rogerson, had been reported missing by her parents. It was a start but the Dumfries cops were looking for two missing females. Lancaster police could help there. Mary Jane worked for a local doctor's family as a nursemaid and he had just reported his wife missing too.

Police in Lancaster already knew about the two women disappearing and hadn't been surprised. Local whisperers had been predicting for a long time that the doctor's marriage was going to break up – that his wife, Isabella, would eventually take no more of his jealous tempers and flee. Why shouldn't she take young Mary Jane with her? All fine and well as far as gossip went but now there was a possible murder the police had to take a more serious look at the situation – starting with the doctor. And a curious man he turned out to be.

Dr Buck Ruxton is what he called himself but that wasn't his real name. Bakhtyar Rustomji Ruttonju Hakim was too much of a mouthful for the average Brit, he reckoned. So, after he'd moved from his home town of Bombay, he had changed his name a number of times before settling on Buck Ruxton. There was nothing suspicious in that. Many immigrants to Britain did exactly the same in an effort to help them be accepted, to integrate.

Dr Ruxton was well qualified with degrees in medicine from two universities – a bright man and no doubt – but he had wanted to be a surgeon, having gained a bachelor of surgery degree in Bombay then trying but failing to enter the Royal College of Surgeons in Edinburgh. Here was a man who knew how to dissect a cadaver for sure. But having the skill didn't make him a murderer. But the green-eyed monster? Now, that was a different matter.

Ruxton referred to Isabella as his wife but they weren't married. They had met in Edinburgh while he had been working there years before and set up home together. On moving to Lancaster, they continued to share a home and produced three children. They were all but married and local folk believed them to be but Ruxton had a wife back in India and he had simply not sent for her. Also, as a Parsee, his religion forbade him from marrying out of the faith. The Ruxtons lived a sham life but it was a harmless one.

However, if locals didn't know the truth about their marriage, they certainly knew about their relationship. Ruxton was insanely jealous and he and Isabella would have frequent, fierce and very public rows. Later, he'd tell any witnesses with glee that, after they rowed, they always made passionate love – a very candid revelation for 1935 Lancaster. No wonder people talked about the exotic doctor and his wife. Good sex life or not, the fights continued and worsened in their violence. Plenty of locals were happy to tell the police about times Ruxton had threatened to kill Isabella in their hearing and sometimes to their faces.

A few weeks before, Isabella had gone off for a weekend in Edinburgh with family friends. Ruxton secretly tailed them there and noted that they all stayed in a hotel, contrary to their original plans. He drove back to Lancaster furious, telling everyone and anyone that Isabella was having an affair with the young man of the family and that, one day, he'd make sure she never came back.

On 14 September 1935, Isabella had gone to Blackpool to see the Christmas illuminations being switched on as she did every year. Mary Jane Rogerson had escorted her. As far as the young nursemaid's parents were concerned, that was the day she disappeared. Now, weeks later, Lancaster folk were only too happy to tell the cops that they hadn't seen Isabella Ruxton since that day either and that Dr Ruxton had told them different tales as to his wife's whereabouts – from saying she was spending some time in Edinburgh with relatives to declaring that she'd run off with some young man. It was the kind of inconsistency that spelled G U I L T Y to the cops. But it was actually a consistency discovered by the Scottish forensic team that would finally nab Ruxton.

Obtaining full descriptions of Isabella and Mary Jane, Glaister's team compared them with their findings on the body parts. Disfigured toes, a scarred hand, thick ankles and calves – those and many more marks that would identify the two women had been carefully removed by the mutilator. As the forensic team had already concluded, the bodies had been systematically sliced and chopped but not to satisfy some sexual sadism.

The skin had been carefully peeled from all the fingers. Whoever had done this knew about the recent development of fingerprint identification but he didn't know enough. Prints also lie underneath the outer layer of skin. In spite of the flesh of the body parts now being badly rotted, a fingerprint officer finally got one satisfactory print. It belonged to Mary Jane.

All clues were pointing to Dr Buck Ruxton but still the cops needed something else. They were to get it from a most unlikely source – Ruxton's cleaner, Agnes Oxley. Ruxton had given Agnes Oxley a suit of clothes and a carpet he said he was replacing. He later changed his mind and asked for their return but not before she realised they were coated in dried blood.

At Ruxton's home, he had asked her to try and remove a stain from the hall carpet. When she washed it, the water ran red. Other carpets had been removed and he had scattered straw on the floor. Two rooms were locked – most unusual in that house – and Mrs Oxley had noticed straw sticking out under the doors. When she went to clean a sink she noticed dark stains like blood. When she asked Ruxton he said he had cut his hand opening a can of peaches. Worst of all, she said, was the 'stink' – a terrible rank smell filled the place.

Dr Buck Ruxton was arrested and charged with double murder. At his trial in Manchester on 2 March 1936, the forensic team was in full flow. The forensic team's evidence had got even stronger since Ruxton's arrest. Allowed access to his home, they found substantial human bloodstains in three rooms, the hall and the bathroom. His explanation, repeated in court, that he had cut his hand opening a tin of peaches was inadequate to say the least.

Supported by all the forensic evidence, the prosecution went to town. They accused Ruxton of killing his wife, Isabella, in a jealous rage and did a good job of painting a picture to the jury of him being seen by the young nursemaid, Mary Jane, and killing her too.

The trial was rough on the jury. It was bad enough that they had to listen to the details of brutal murder but hearing of the itemised bloody disposal of the bodies was even more gruesome. Such detail was a new experience in trials and it was all thanks to the developments of forensic science. If the eleven-day trial had been an ordeal for the jury, reaching their decision was easy. After only one hour, they announced a guilty verdict against Dr Buck Ruxton. He was sentenced to hang in Strangeways Prison on 12 May 1936 but that wasn't the end of the tale.

People are strange – always have been. After one of the most horrific trials of the time, over 6,000 people signed a petition pleading that Ruxton be reprieved. In this case, the powers that be paid no heed.

A few days after Ruxton swung by his neck, never having admitted his guilt, the *News of the World* printed a sensational article. Before his execution, he had passed them a signed note confessing to the double murder. Immediately, rumours circulated that the newspaper had paid several thousand pounds for the confession – one of the earliest allegations of cheque book journalism. Other rumours abounded suggesting that the note was a forgery. Whether these rumours were spread by envious reporters from other newspapers isn't known though journalism was certainly a dirty, rough business in the 1930s. All we know is that, eventually, the controversy died down with none of the rumours ever being proven correct.

What is beyond doubt, however, is Dr Buck Ruxton's guilt. He became the first murderer ever to be caught by what we now take for granted – the combined might of the forensic detectives. Murder investigations had changed forever.

GOOD FOR THE SOUL?

'I killed a woman last night.'

The police sergeant looked at the confessor across the desk. Was he just another crazy craving attention? But confessing to what? The cops didn't know of any murder.

'I killed a woman last night in Ormelie . . .' The man was now speaking rapidly, appearing desperate to cleanse himself of the evil memories. 'The body is in the ground.'

The unsolicited confession was beginning to make a little more sense to the cops at the Torphichen Street Police Station in Edinburgh's west end. Ormelie was a large house on Corstorphine Road owned by Sir William Thomson. So at least now the cops had a scene. The question was: Did they have a crime?

Lonely and mixed-up members of the public have always wasted the cops' time-some so seriously that they have ruined or delayed investigations. These days cops are much more adept at spotting the time-wasters but in 1938 they did two things – grill the confessor and visit the alleged scene. These days there would be teams of detectives, forensic folk and cops with cameras sent to the scene but only after the police had been convinced there was a murder. In 1938 they sent two cops to do a nosy.

The house was locked and empty, backing up the confessor's information that Sir William was away. The confessor said his name was James Kirkwood and claimed he was the full-time gardener at the house. Maybe he was telling the truth. Then again maybe, as most people were, he was aware that, even in those pre-World War II days, the titled and moneyed classes could still afford to shut up house for the whole summer and go away on holiday.

The cops walked round the substantial, well-tended garden looking for signs of recent digging. Walking through a garage to the rear of the property, they noticed scuff marks on some paving, as if something heavy and awkward had been dragged along. Nearby, neat rows of potatoes seemed to have been disturbed and, at one point, the green stalks were almost covered in earth. That's where the cops started digging with a spade borrowed from the house's tool shed.

Fast progress was made in the soft earth and soon they had discovered a woman's stocking. As they carefully scraped away the soil a white, naked, shapely leg gradually appeared and, before long, an entire female corpse lay there in that hole. She was nude aside from a watch that had stopped at 5.22 and her head was battered and bloody.

Back at the police station, James Kirkwood had repeated his confession though he hadn't provided many more details or a motive.

The dead woman was found to be Jean Powell, a dairymaid who lived in lodgings nearby at 10 Roseburn Place. She had left her work that day as usual, gone back to her digs to change then left again saying she had an appointment to meet someone at Roseburn Terrace. When she didn't turn up at her digs that night, the landlady simply assumed she had gone on to see her sister and had stayed overnight.

According to Jean's family and the landlady, she was a very respectable woman who lived a steady life. She had been engaged once but, since that had been broken off, she'd had no boyfriends. She didn't socialise much and never frequented places like pubs. A very respectable woman even by 1938 standards – or was she?

Heavy bloodstains clearly indicated that Jean Powell had been murdered inside Ormelie on a sofa. Her clothes had been bundled up and hidden in a cover from that sofa but they weren't drenched in blood as they would have been had Jean Powell been wearing them when she was killed with such incredible force and brutality. How had she come to be lying naked on that sofa?

She had been held roughly by the throat and her head battered repeatedly with a hammer that the cops had found. Fragments of her skull and hairs from her head were all over the murder weapon, the couch and surrounding carpet in spite of someone's efforts to wash and clean the area.

Police inquiries in the area soon led to a clue. At around 2 p.m. on the day of the killing, James Kirkwood and a man called John Fraser had been in a pub in Roseburn Terrace, according to a barman there. A short while later, a woman came in whom the barman didn't recognise but she was later identified as Jean Powell, the dead woman.

So did Jean Powell have a secret life of men and pubs? What led to her being naked that day in Ormelie?

James Kirkwood had already confessed to murder. Surely he would oblige the cops by filling in the details? But there were problems – he wasn't talking and he wasn't well.

It transpired that James Kirkwood was an ill and disturbed man. Now aged thirty, he had suffered from serious epileptic seizures and related complaints since his teens. During the seizures, he developed incredible strength and became extremely violent. Then there were the other symptoms. He would go blank and silent in the middle of conversations, later starting up again exactly where he had left off. One time he went missing for days and was found in Port Glasgow many miles away from his home, clueless as to how he had got there or what he had been doing.

Kirkwood also had an obsession with deadly arsenic. Discovered with a large container of it one time, he claimed it was for killing weeds. His parents were so worried they went to the police who discovered that the gardener hadn't used it as he said but had hidden it in a riverbank. For what purpose? He never revealed.

Later, while he was attending Glasgow Royal Infirmary for treatment on other matters, doctors discovered that he had so much arsenic in his body that they had no doubt he was trying to kill himself. But was he? Did he have some other crazy notion about arsenic? A mad notion? Who knows? He never said.

All this was presented at Kirkwood's trial where he pled guilty to the murder of Jean Powell. His unsolicited confession, together with other factors – his shirt was splattered in the victim's blood and he had a key to Ormelie – meant the case against him was foolproof. All that Kirkwood's lawyer could do was to hope that expert witnesses would find him insane. Not that long before, people with epilepsy were treated as if they were mentally ill. But progress had been made in neurology and, by 1938, it was clearly identified as a physical not mental condition.

Media and public interest was fierce. Here was a man whose physical condition meant that, at times, he acted without knowing what he was doing and did so with super strength and tremendous violence yet he was allowed to walk freely in society to kill. The public didn't care too much about the difference between mental and physical conditions – they just didn't want to be living close to a man like Kirkwood. The trial would go some way to continuing the public's fear and prejudice against epilepsy, a prejudice that festers with us still.

James Kirkwood was found to be sane though not entirely in control of his actions due to epilepsy. Nevertheless, he was deemed sane and found guilty of a brutal murder that he never explained.

Ten years before, he would have been sent to the gallows and no doubt but, instead, he was sentenced to life in a penal colony. Was the judge taking pity on his physical condition? Or following the secret government line to avoid high-profile criminal cases and hangings? Why might he do this? There was a serious public morale, not moral, issue to be addressed. War with Germany was in the air. Inevitable. Public anger and hate would have to be directed towards the enemy not their own folk no matter how brutal they were.

World War II would start a year after James Kirkwood's trial. Soon the details would be forgotten about as a much bigger threat prevailed.

A world at war but also war on the streets.

1940 TO 1949

THE DEATH OF INNOCENCE

This decade was dominated by World War II (1939–45), during which there was an estimated worldwide casualty rate of sixty-one million. British cities were bombarded from the air and civilians swelled the ranks of the dead. Blackouts were imposed to counter air raids but they also served another purpose well – the commission of street crime.

As war raged, life went on. The government asked women to wear shorter skirts to save cloth – many obliged (1941). Orson Welles made his classic film *Citizen Kane* (1941) and Humphrey Bogart's film *Casablanca* hit the silver screen (1942). With paper rationed, few books were produced. Alexander Fleming won the Nobel Prize for Physiology (1945).

Peace brought a slow return to normal life and the first episode of *The Archers* (1949).

Chief Constable Percy Sillitoe was awarded a knighthood (1942) and moved to the top job in Kent. Special Constables had to be recruited because so many Scottish coppers had signed up for the armed forces. Billy Fullerton, leader of the Billy Boys razor gang, joined the navy along with scores of his men. He served with distinction in the Far East and survived the war.

Clydebank, Glasgow, Edinburgh, Dundee and Aberdeen suffered horrendous bombing and destruction and there was strict rationing of food and goods. In the midst of this, street players took to the black market. Some would get rich on the proceeds and move on to a legitimate life after the war.

DAMNED AND DAMNED

'Are you there?' The woman's Scottish accent rang out through the hall. The place was crowded, jam-packed, but not a soul said a word. They knew something special was going to happen. A dead soul was about to appear.

It was Portsmouth, a key naval town now but more so in 1943 in the heat of World War II. The Master Temple Psychic Centre wasn't in the main thoroughfare of the town but half hidden above a chemist shop. Yet that didn't stop the government keeping a close on eye on the place and especially its star performer.

Helen Duncan had known she had gifts from her young days in Callander, Perthshire. By the age of forty-four, she was based in Edinburgh but she was sought after by folk from all over Britain to demonstrate those very gifts. Materialisations. Séances would be held and, when Helen was present, they were never boring – especially not dead boring. Apparitions would appear and talk and walk and make sense to whoever was in the room. It sounds like the typical smoke-and-mirrors act that fakes have been using to wheedle money out of the desperate and lonely for many years but there was just one difference – even the psychic detectives concluded that Helen Duncan was the real deal.

Duncan would turn up at a hall in some backwater far away from where she lived, sit down in a séance and produce a materialisation of a close relative of someone she'd never met before that night and had had no time to investigate. When she had finished her work, she'd depart just as quickly as she had arrived.

There has always been a strong following for paranormal phenomena in Britain – never more so than when war broke out and so many families suffered the loss of loved ones. The mainstream churches offered little more than sympathy and comfort. Spiritualists offered that plus the hope of contact with their loved ones. Well, the gifted psychics like Helen Duncan did.

On that night in Portsmouth in 1943, an apparition appeared. A young sailor seeking his mother. Clear as day to all who were there. So clear they could read his cap badge – HMS *Barham*. Duncan didn't know it but her world was about to turn upside down.

In the room was a government spy. This we now know wasn't unusual. A country at war has to watch its people. But a spy at a psychic show? He was there because someone close to the War Cabinet had decided Helen Duncan was a risk. That night proved him right.

A country at war also controls public information. Positive propaganda abounds and bad news is held back till the time is right. One thing being held back was that HMS *Barham* had been sunk by German U-boats two weeks before with great loss of life. Helen Duncan revealed all that before anyone was meant to know. How did she know?

Soon afterwards she was arrested and charged under ancient witchcraft laws – Section 4 of the Witchcraft Act 1735 to be precise – laws that hadn't been used since they burned so-called witches at the stake. For good measure they charged her with other offences – causing money to be paid by false pretences – conning folk, in other words. She either admitted being a witch or admitted being a fraudster. Damned if she did, damned if she didn't.

The Old Bailey – the most senior criminal court in London and Britain – was the scene of her trial in February 1944. Appearing there at the best of times was enough to scare the most court-hardened gangster but for an inexperienced woman like Helen Duncan – during wartime, being driven through all the anti-aircraft guns, the security lights, the troops and the tanks – it must have been terrifying.

Duncan's lawyers went to town describing the witchcraft charges as 'nonsense', 'ridiculous' and 'a sham'. They won that battle but lost the war as the judge promptly found her guilty of the dishonesty charges and sent her to jail for nine months.

There was a huge public outcry – or at least as much as would be allowed during wartime. But Helen Duncan was supported by a great many believers, not least of whom was a friend of well-known psychic sceptic, Sir Arthur Conan Doyle, and a reporter for *The Scotsman*, James Herries. Herries was just one of forty-four witnesses swearing that Duncan's psychic powers were genuine. What wasn't reported at the time was that, during the trial, the public benches broke out in song:

> You take the High Road
> And I'll take the Low Road
> But I'll be in Scotland afore ye . . .

It must have been the first and certainly the last time that the Old Bailey was treated to a rendition of 'The Bonnie, Bonnie Banks of Loch Lomond' but it was all to no avail. Helen Duncan was shipped off to jail, branded a fraudster.

It was only reported after the war that she received a very special visitor while she was inside – no less than Prime Minister Winston Churchill. Churchill must have been a busy man in the last year of the war yet he still took the time to visit Duncan. He had tried to have the charges against her dropped but couldn't. There was another good reason for the visit – Churchill believed in spiritualism. He wasn't alone among world leaders.

Adolf Hitler not only consulted psychics before major offensives, he also had psychic symbols portrayed in certain of his troops' uniforms. Stalin spent more on scientists trying to unlock psychic secrets than he did in the race with USA to develop the atomic bomb. In turn, President Franklin D. Roosevelt, though a psychic sceptic, had a great interest in matters spiritual. There's no doubt that, for better or worse, World War II was influenced by psychics.

Is that why Helen Duncan was charged with witchcraft? Because the world leaders believed her to know too much, not from the enemy but from the other side?

Duncan's was the last trial for witchcraft in Britain. When she was released from prison, she continued attending séances and displaying her powers of materialisation. But she was quieter than before, accepting fewer bookings and not wanting to attract attention to herself. She may have had psychic powers but did she really think the powers of law and order would forgive and forget?

In 1956, while she was conducting a séance, cops burst into the room and arrested Helen Duncan. They weren't too gentle in their approach in spite of her being a frail fifty-eight-year-old woman. After the arrest, strange burns appeared on her stomach – burns that weren't easily explained by the manhandling she had received.

Helen Duncan's health deteriorated rapidly and she died a short time later. Another victim of a witch-hunt? Our last?

THE FIEND

'Most of us ran in teams. You had to, no matter how hard you were. How else did you protect you and yours from other gangs?' recalled one ancient survivor of those post-war years. 'But one guy ran with nobody. We didn't want him and he didn't want us. Hard? Hard enough. But dangerous? Fucking lethal.'

For decades the Protestant Billy Boys and Roman Catholic Norman Conks had battled it out with razors and coshes on Glasgow's streets. So huge was the issue that Glasgow headhunted the man they called The Gangbuster.

Sir Percy Sillitoe, as he came to be titled, will forever be recognised for his role of Chief Constable of Glasgow. Yet, when he was recruited to the job in 1931, he already had a great track record of dealing with gangs in the steel-hard city of Sheffield.

In Glasgow, Sir Percy set about hiring the toughest men he could find as beat bobbies. Scores and scores of big, hardy men were recruited from the Highlands and other rural areas. They were given basic training and a uniform and told to mix it with the gangs every chance they got. Most relished the work.

Yet, by 1938, the Billy Boys and Norman Conks were joined by the San Toi, Tongs, The Fleet, Govan Team, Bingo Boys and scores of other mobs, all of them just as strong as the other two. Some were even getting political.

Billy Fullerton, founder and leader of the Billy Boys, always claimed he only did so after he'd been beaten up by a gang of Roman Catholic youths for performing well in a football match against their team. He saw himself as a responsible man who'd been forced to take action to defend himself and others like him.

The Billy Boys adopted military-style behaviour. They marched on parade, had their own bands and composed their own songs and music. Members were expected to dress to a particular standard and paid a weekly levy to help others when in need – and not just to pay off fines. With the onset of war, Billy Fullerton and the Billy Boys became involved, forming a Glasgow branch of Sir Oswald Mosley's Blackshirts. They'd march on Glasgow Green, on Orange Walks and other significant days, though their major role was as part of Mosley's bodyguard. Who better to guard him than a Glasgow gang?

But there were others – the individual hard men. They had no aims or plan or allegiance – they were simply moved by the love of violence and dishing out pain. These were the men who really worried the citizens of Glasgow – they were also the ones Sir Percy Sillitoe couldn't control. No one could.

Every area of Glasgow had at least a handful of brutal renegades like that but the most notorious of all was the man they called The Fiend of the Gorbals, Patrick Carraher.

Born in 1906 into a decent working-class family, Carraher went off the rails as soon as he could walk. By the time he was fourteen, he was shipped off for his first spell of borstal and he would be in and out of jails for the rest of his life.

Scottish prisons were hard, brutal places then – even more so than today. Knifings, scaldings and lynchings were all part of the risks a prisoner ran. Carraher loved it.

For most other cons, jails are academies of crime that taught their students how to steal better and bigger stashes. But Patrick Carraher wasn't that interested in making money. Fighting was his thing, especially with a blade. Rules of combat? He didn't recognise them. Carraher is what they used to call an 'Indian fighter' – no rules, just winning.

By 1938, aged thirty-two, he had stabbed, slashed and gouged his way through life – more often than not, the victims were hapless, innocent bystanders. Worse, he had developed a serious booze problem that made his temper simmer constantly.

Carraher's reputation was well formed but not everyone was scared of him. They should have been.

A young woman he'd been going out with ended the relationship and he wasn't happy. One night he ordered a pal of hers to pass on a message that he wanted to see her and pronto. Knowing that her friend wouldn't be interested, she thought it best not to tell her anything. It would just have worried her.

Later that same night, Carraher, now very drunk, spotted the woman out walking with her young man, James Durie, a sensible, honest bloke who worked hard as window cleaner. Realising his orders had been ignored, Carraher abused the woman, calling her every name under the sun and threatening worse. Jim Durie, of course, though knowing all about Patrick Carraher's brutal reputation, acted as the gallant gentleman. The young man, however, declined The Fiend's invitation to a fight. It might have been something to do with the big blade Carraher was waving in the air.

Later that night, Durie's older brothers heard of the incident and decided that they had to see to Carraher to protect their brother, Jim. Along with some pals, they caught up with Carraher but he refused to fight saying he was too drunk. Yet he continued bawling and shouting at the Duries as they walked away. At that point, a passing serviceman on leave, James Shaw, advised Carraher to be quiet. In a flash, Shaw was lying on the ground and Carraher walking away.

The young soldier was wounded in the neck and died within the hour at Glasgow Royal Infirmary. Soon, word reached the police that The Fiend of the Gorbals had been at his old tricks – well, he was feared and infamous in the city – and he was arrested. All the Duries stood as witnesses against him as did others to whom Carraher had drunkenly boasted of the killing.

At his trial at Glasgow High Court, it was plain that he had actually knifed Shaw but then his brilliant lawyer got to work. By coordinating the evidence, he proved to the jury that no one actually saw Patrick Carraher knife the man. They found him not guilty of murder but guilty of the lesser culpable homicide and he was jailed for three years. The Glasgow public must have been wondering how lawyers sleep at night. The Fiend had escaped the gallows.

By the time Carraher walked free through the gates of Barlinnie in 1941, World War II was in full swing. He was called up, of course, the army not being able to afford the luxury of refusing people with criminal records in those dark days. Besides, he was one of the most violent men in Glasgow – perfect for a war – except he was declared unfit to serve. Incredibly, the man who terrorised the streets of Glasgow was rejected as unfit to fight for his country due to a dodgy stomach and bad chest.

However, Carraher's health didn't stop him going on just as before. During the blackout years of the war, his violent behaviour became worse. Most of it went unreported due to the information controls of wartime but ordinary people don't need to be told that their streets are lethal.

Usually a loner, Carraher took up with Daniel Bonnar, the brother of his then girlfriend, Sarah. Carraher on his own was bad. The two together were hell on legs.

The number of police was down to a minimum at that time as all able-bodied folks joined the war effort. The cops had other serious problems like security to tackle and had little time to deal with a mental chib merchant. Carraher's evil went unchecked.

Yet, after a day-and-night-long orgy of violence inflicted on innocent Glaswegians, Carraher was once again arrested and sent to jail for three years in 1943. As the war was fought out in Europe, Africa and the Far East, Glasgow became a safer place simply because Patrick Carraher had been flung in jail.

By the time of his release in November 1945, the war was over and the city buzzed with servicemen on leave – men like John Gordon, a career soldier with twenty years' experience with the Seaforth Highlanders who had spent years of the war in a German

PoW camp. Demobbed and having a few celebratory drinks with his brothers, he thought his troubles were over.

Later that night Daniel Bonnar bumped into the Gordon crew all drunk and merry. There was an outstanding issue between Bonnar and one of the Gordons and the latter invited him to a street fight. Bonnar took to his heels. Like his mate, Carraher, a square go wasn't his style.

Learning of this, Patrick Carraher decided to settle the matter and, with Bonnar in tow, went looking for the Gordons. Eventually they found John Gordon along with his brother-in-law Duncan Reevie, one of the thousands of army deserters hiding out in the Scotland at that time.

When the scuffle started, Bonnar once again ran but Carraher simply reached out and punched John Gordon in the neck. Well, that's what it looked like. As people including his own girlfriend would testify, Carraher had slipped a razor-sharp chisel into his pocket as he left home to hunt the Gordons. He hadn't punched John Gordon but thrust the blade deep into his neck. The man died in hospital less than an hour later.

Curiously, Carraher was arrested by a cop called John Johnstone, the same man who had lifted him on his first murder charge. Now Johnstone was going to get another chance to get Carraher off the streets.

The evidence against Carraher was undeniable – especially when his so-called pal Daniel Bonnar turned King's evidence, trading charges of murder against him in the process. Carraher was done for. All the chib merchant's defence could do was claim diminished responsibility, bring in expert doctors to say he was a psychopath, and hope for a lesser sentence. They had a point. It didn't wash. The jury took only twenty minutes to find Patrick Carraher guilty – but would he hang?

Glasgow, like most other cities, had not hanged any civilians during the war – officially. Bad for public morale was the line. But, if Carraher thought that trend would continue, he was sadly mistaken.

Though it was never admitted, through the war years, crime on the street increased massively. But now the war was over and it was time to restore order in our cities.

All the gangsters had noted with horror that hanging was back. A young man called John Lyon had the dubious honour of being Glasgow's first post-war execution when he was hanged in Glasgow for a gang-related killing in February 1946. He wasn't to be the last.

On 6 April 1946, Carraher was in a cell in Barlinnie Prison, where he had spent so many years for violent crimes. Aged forty, he had spent twenty years in one type of jail or another – half his life. But it was the first time he'd been in that cell – the condemned cell.

Many citizens of Glasgow believed that The Fiend of the Gorbals should never have been free. After all, they'd say, he had already cheated the hangman once to go out and murder again.

When the time came for Carraher to walk the long short walk, he didn't dally. He marched in double quick time, leaving the wardens trailing behind. It was as if he was in a hurry to get it all over with.

Did he agree with Glasgow citizens that he'd been alive for too long? Unlikely. That slow walk to the hanging shed must be the most terrifying walk imaginable. Hangmen used to report on those who died well or badly – meaning bravely or in a cowardly way – and they believed the slower the walk the greater the fear.

Was that it? Was Patrick Carraher scared to lose face? Had The Fiend of the Gorbals finally found fear?

A LONELY PLACE

It was a place of refuge – a place to shelter from the raining bombs. Now it was disused and empty . . . well, not quite. Death lurked in the corner.

'PHYLLIS!' The woman's shouts rang out through the Edinburgh streets. Passers by turned to stare and kids playing on the streets followed at a discreet distance mocking the woman's distressed state. 'PHYLLIS!' Each time she called out, her voice became more shrill, the sadness in her heart crying into the east-coast wind. And cry she might – her young daughter was missing.

It was 12 July 1945 in Edinburgh. The war in Europe was over and the country was pulling together, struggling to get back to normal life. Then, as the tales of bloody battles abroad dwindled to a close, an eight-year-old child went missing and brought terror back to the streets.

As in other cities during World War II, many Edinburgh folk were saved and comforted by the air-raid shelters that peppered the city. Yet there were those who believed that enemy bombs were more likely to hit the shelters so, instead, they hid under their kitchen tables – a superstitious minority.

But, now that the air-raid shelters were being decommissioned, the doors lay open and they were slowly being taken over sometimes for unsavoury or sinister uses like casual sex, cheap booze parties thrown by down-and-outs and black-market trading. Such activities made the shelters places to avoid for most decent citizens, especially after dark. But, in the daytime, kids invaded the air-raid shelters and played there. It didn't go unnoticed.

There had already been several reported incidents of kids being sexually abused by strangers in the shelters and most parents would tell their wee ones to stay well clear of the buildings. Young Phyllis Merritt knew about the warning. She wouldn't go there. But where had she gone?

No one missed eight-year-old Phyllis to start with. Her mother thought she was with her gran at 8 St John's Hill and her gran thought she had gone home to her mum's at 6 St James Place. The girl had gone back and forwards between the houses so often before, there was no danger to her – or so they thought.

Gran knew that she had gone to see an aunt that morning and afterwards was playing with some friends in Holyrood Park. She'd had lunch with her seventeen-year-old uncle, Robert Rigg, in a café and then had gone back to her mum's. Well, that's what her gran assumed she'd done.

Phyllis's mum took to the streets, calling for her. Till then Edinburgh had seemed such a small, familiar place to her and full of friendly faces. Now it had transformed into a big city, with dark closes and lonely streets and every face was the face of someone who might harm her girl. For hours, she walked and called out – walked and called out till the light started to fail and she could call no more. She went to the police, knowing that just walking through the door of the station meant that she was conceding grief. Phyllis wasn't just late. She was missing.

That day, the police sent out search parties, helped by family and friends of the missing girl. Among the keenest to help was Phyllis's young uncle, Robert Rigg, who wouldn't rest in his search for her. After all, they were close and he'd taken her for lunch that day. Not unusual but he was the last person to see her before she went off. The poor lad, the police thought, he must be blaming himself.

The day after Phyllis Meritt had gone missing, Robert Rigg walked in to the local police station, weeping and distraught. He'd found her in an air-raid shelter. Dead. The shelter walls were splashed with the wee girl's blood. Pathologists soon ascertained she had been grabbed by the throat and her head bashed against the brick walls and concrete floor time and again before her killer had finally smashed her skull with boulders.

It wasn't the sex killing that everyone dreaded would happen in one of the disused, dark shelters but a mindless, frenzied attack. With war came an easier acceptance of death and violence that was never present during peacetime. There were men now back at home who had seen and done terrible things at the front. Maybe some couldn't stop? The police started looking for sad loners who'd recently been demobbed – last month heroes, the next month suspects.

The death of any child breaks the heart of a community. But Phyllis Merritt was a wee bit special. Good looking, bright and sociable, she was well known and loved by everyone. The heat was on the Edinburgh cops to find the killer promptly. They didn't need to look far.

Phyllis's uncle Robert offered to help the cops in any way he could – whatever it took. Yet there was something about him – his manner, his nervousness – they didn't trust. And he was the last person known to have seen Phyllis alive. They knew that now – aside from the killer, that is.

Before long the cops charged Robert Rigg with Phyllis's murder. To start with, they hadn't a great deal to go on but reckoned that the tongue-tied, awkward teenager would soon break and tell the truth once he had been charged. They were too optimistic. Robert Rigg said nothing incriminating. The case was stuck with the police appealing to Robert over and over again to get it off his chest and just tell them the truth.

'If you get me Merrilees,' Robert finally said, changing his tune, 'I'll give him something.'

Superintendent William Merrilees was the most famous policeman in Britain at that time and with good reason. His true-life story reads like a *Boy's Own* adventure. Merrilees had been rejected by the police because he was way too short and had some fingers missing from one hand. Then, in 1924, he was the hero in a daring rescue of a number of people from a boat fire on the Water of Leith. He saved their lives and changed his own. In the publicity following the rescue, Merrilees revealed he had been rejected by the cops. A stack of dignitaries wrote to the Secretary of State asking that special dispensation be allowed in his case. He agreed and set off one of the most remarkable detective careers ever.

Early on, Merrilees established a reputation for cracking difficult cases and going to extreme lengths to catch the crooks. Like the fictional sleuth Sherlock Holmes, he was especially fond of using disguises to get close to the cons. On one occasion a man had been sexually molesting nannies as they walked babies in prams in an Edinburgh park. Imagine the look of horror on the abuser's face when one day a 'baby' jumped out of a pram and nabbed him. Merrilees' lack of height had served him well that time.

During World War II, he tracked down and arrested the only two German spies to have been caught in Scotland. Nor did he stop there. Merrilees got the female spy to work as a double agent while her male partner was executed.

There's much more about Superintendent William Merrilees but, to people like Robert Rigg, he was the top man, a legend. So, during the investigation, Rigg asked to speak to Merrilees, promising he'd give him significant info about Phyllis's murder. After just one meeting with the accused, Merrilees reported that he'd cracked the case and the young man had confessed. The local cops who had been grilling Robert Rigg for a week with no luck must have marvelled at the diminutive detective's skill.

Rigg went to trial at Edinburgh High Court charged with murder. His defence that he had been insane at the time suggests Rigg and his lawyers thought there was a strong case against him too. This was the most high-profile trial in the immediate post-war period in Edinburgh, possibly in Scotland. The courtroom was packed and people mingled outside. Now that the war had ended, it was business as usual. The cops needed a conviction. They agreed with some politicians in predicting that the country was in danger of becoming more lawless after the extreme conditions of war. A conviction and hanging would send the right message out.

It looked as if the case against Robert Rigg was all but won but then a legal bombshell hit the court. When the Crown tried to call Superintendent William Merrilees, the defence lawyers objected. Although Merrilees had formally cautioned Rigg, he had spoken with him on his own. The defence felt that such evidence should not be allowed – even from a man of his reputation. The judge agreed.

With no confession, the Crown case collapsed and Robert Rigg was found not guilty. From the public benches, young Phyllis's mother howled with grief, begging the judge to let her give more evidence. Of course, her request was refused and the poor woman collapsed in anguish, having to be carried from the court.

The reputation of a lesser cop might have been ruined by that episode but not one of Merrilees' standing. He went on to become Chief Constable of Lothian and Peebles Police and, to this day, remains the only top cop asked to work on for years after he reached retirement age.

No one else was ever charged with Phyllis Merritt's murder. That failure didn't help the parents of Edinburgh sleep at night. Many believed that Robert Rigg was guilty and he'd been freed to walk the streets. Others feared there was another mindless murderer of children at loose. Either way, they feared for their children.

Never again would parents feel at ease when their children played in the streets. The days of innocence had died.

THE TARTAN DAHLIA

A shrill scream rang out, travelling far through the freezing winter night air. Someone was in trouble – or so it seemed. Then a man's voice said, 'Not one light. Are they all dead in Torry?' They were asleep, not dead, but someone else was.

Ten minutes later another scream rang out. A different pitch, a different woman. A policewoman. Another policewoman. Involved in a murder investigation.

It was Aberdeen in December 1945. World War II had just drawn to a close a few short months before yet the local police force was busier than ever. A woman's arm had been found in the docks.

Old Alex King was the unfortunate soul who found it. The seventy-four-year-old had been doing a bit of beachcombing at the docks near the city's Torry area. Aberdeen had been a busy port during the war and much bombed. Added together, it meant that there were rich pickings to be had. Then he saw it.

Many people who discover bodies in water report there was something about it that attracted their attention. Not that they realised right away what it was. Just some bell of recognition ringing loud and clear in the dark recesses of their subconsciousness. So it was with this arm.

Alex had to go right up close to realise it was a full human arm and hand. It might be imagined that, in a city that had just come through a long bloody war as a major target and port, the inhabitants would have become used to corpses. Maybe but not Alex King. He picked up the arm and ran as fast as he could to a police telephone box a few streets way in Torry. The biggest police operation in Aberdeen's history had just begun.

Very quickly the extremely experienced police surgeon, Dr Robert Richards, worked out that the arm belonged to a female of around eighteen years old, who had died in the last few days and whose arm had been cut off with a fine-toothed saw. It wasn't an accident, in other words, but murder.

Swarms of cops were sent down to the beach and docks searching for other clues. Local fishermen took to the sea in boats trawling every inch of the surrounding area. Day after day, they all knew that they were likely to stumble upon some body part of the unfortunate young woman. Then a call went up that they'd found a severed arm – a man's arm as it turned out. Well, the war had just finished and the North Sea carried its fair share of cadavers.

However, the cops didn't have too long to wait for an ID from the female's arm. The simple act of taking fingerprints from the found limb gave a positive match in their files. The dead woman had a minor criminal record. Nothing worth talking about but at least they now knew who they were looking for.

Elizabeth Hadden, known as Betty, lived with her mother at 9 Manor Walk in the Middlesfield area of Aberdeen. Betty was only seventeen and a bit of a free spirit – so free it might well have killed her.

The list of Betty's jobs reads like the vacancy pages of a newspaper. There didn't seem to be anything she hadn't worked at – at least till she got bored. Betty got bored very quickly. She'd long since given up ordinary work for the city's pubs and clubs, intent on a good time and on snaring a man who'd treat her like a princess. Inevitably, Betty had kissed a good many frogs, not one of whom had transformed into Prince Charming.

That Betty was sexually vulnerable there is no doubt. The cops quickly came to a view that she'd fallen into the wrong company – evil company – and he or they had probably raped her and killed her to keep her quiet. Betty might have been a free spirit but she was also strong-willed. The man or men would have known she would have gone straight to the cops. So they didn't let her.

Now armed with a picture of a handsome, serious-eyed Betty, the cops went to town, literally, trying to trace her last steps. The good people of Aberdeen responded well. War had just ended and already they were confronted by a terrible murder of one of their own – probably *by* one of their own. Many sightings of Betty had been made over what turned out to be the last few days of her life. Yet still no definite leads were forthcoming.

They even called in Sydney Smith, the top forensic scientist from Edinburgh, who was able to confirm the local police surgeon's views and, indeed, add to them. He believed Betty had been killed in the early hours of Wednesday, 12 December 1945.

The police by now were convinced that Betty had been killed some place in Torry, dissected and then dumped in the sea. They even experimented with pigs' legs, casting them into the water then watching where they were brought into the shore. Aside from this, they carried out the most thorough door-to-door searches in their history, confident that Betty had been totally dismembered in that area. It all produced nothing. That's where the scream came in.

Locals in Torry had come forward independently to say that they had heard screams in the early hours of 12 December. A woman's terrified screams. So the cops took the unusual step of placing an advert in the local paper asking for anyone who had heard screams or had themselves screamed on that day at that time to come forward. No one did.

Next came the scream test. This was done using different policewomen at different points close to Torry, at points where the screams had been heard and at the same times. They were extraordinary lengths to go to but what the police wanted was to see in which parts of Torry the screams could be heard. That's where their suspect would be.

While good cops the world over have a special capacity to keep an open mind, they also have their theories about suspects.

Aberdeen cops were no different. Most of the senior officers believed they knew who had killed and chopped up young Betty – a Torry man they had been keeping an eye on for a while. On the night of the scream test some were praying that there would be a reaction with lights going on and concerned citizens coming to investigate from this man's neck of the woods. That would give them an excuse to dig deeper – go into his house and check for signs of blood and other forensic evidence.

It was not to be. The freezing policewomen screamed in vain for it elicited not one response.

Eventually, Betty Hadden's case was consigned to the 'Unsolved' pile, the one that collects dust in some untended corner of an office. Police officers involved in the investigation went on to retire and, when asked what the biggest challenge of their career was, they wouldn't, as might have been expected, say policing during the hell of war. They all had a simple answer – 'Not finding Betty Hadden or her killer.'

A young woman who was free as a bird and was killed by a man. Isn't that so often the way?

SEX OR SLAUGHTER?

'You promised,' she said. 'You keep your promises don't you?' Everyday words? Perhaps but not this time. This time it was a matter of murder. Or was it?

Agnes Paton was well known to the Edinburgh cops as trouble. She was a drinker, fighter, prostitute and petty thief and she'd been in jail more than once in her twenty-seven years. She was heading for a bad end for sure and now it had arrived.

The old cops who knew Agnes wouldn't have been surprised to find her battered, bloody and dead up some lane. Yet here they were staring down at her body looking for all the world like she'd gone for a nap. But she was dead all right.

Agnes was found near a boathouse at St Margaret's Loch close to Arthur's Seat. She was lying on her back with her head resting on a red handbag and her arms folded across her stomach. Her clothes were tidy about her body and she looked like she'd lain down for forty winks and died in her sleep. But that wasn't what happened.

'She's hurt,' he said. 'Hurt bad.'

'How bad?'

'I think I done her in.'

It was early on 16 July 1946. A former soldier, thirty-five-year-old John Rutherford, had walked into Central Police Station, in an agitated state, asking that an ambulance be sent immediately to St Margaret's Loch. It was an emergency, he said – they had to hurry.

John Rutherford wasn't wrong. But the cops couldn't work out how Agnes Paton had died. There was no sign of a struggle – she wasn't wounded and even her hair was in place. All a search of the scene produced was half of a man's torn necktie. It might not even have had anything to do with the death. Rutherford put them right when he produced the other half of the tie.

'I killed her with this,' he said, shaking and weeping. 'I didn't want to but I did. Pulled it so hard it ripped.' Then his sobs became uncontrollable, muffling the words in his mouth.

John Rutherford was a very respectable man. He had been a professional soldier since 1931 and had served in several major conflicts during World War II, including Dunkirk. A short while before this incident, he had been demobbed from the army with excellent references. How did a man like that get hooked up with someone like Agnes Paton, never mind murder her?

Rutherford's story shocked the cops. He had 'taken up' with Agnes a short while before – polite language of the time for having a sexual relationship. He was smitten with Agnes and liked to please her. He'd buy her presents and they'd go drinking together, with him paying for everything. But it wasn't enough.

According to Rutherford, what Agnes really wanted was for him to strangle her. When she had first asked, he thought she was joking. She was serious – deadly serious – and she went on and on about it, insisting that, if he loved her, he would strangle her.

Finally, a few weeks before, she had written her request down on a piece of paper and the pair had signed it as a contract. The night before, 15 July, they had gone to an isolated spot by St Margaret's Loch and, sitting on a park bench, she had removed his tie and wrapped it round her neck, demanding that he kept his promise.

'Never meant to kill her,' Rutherford kept blurting out to the police. 'I thought it was just some sort of game.'

Rutherford claimed to have tightened the tie just a little, then a little more as she demanded, expecting her to call out when the pressure was too much. Then he realised she was dead.

The Edinburgh cops had heard it all now. The signed piece of paper might have convinced them Rutherford's tale was true but, in a panic, he had destroyed it the night before – or so he said. The police had no choice but to charge him with murder.

At his trial at the High Court in September 1946, the cynical cops and unbelieving public had their eyes opened. John Rutherford wasn't the only one who knew of Agnes Paton's obsession with being strangled. Other members of the public – all men – reported that she had asked them to strangle her and others that she had sometimes tried to strangle herself. These witnesses were mainly drinking friends of Agnes Paton and may have lacked credibility with the jury but the defence had an ace up their sleeve.

The warders at the local police cells reported that Paton had tried to strangle herself while in custody. One witness thought it was an attempt at suicide while another assumed that Paton was playing a joke on them.

What is now clear is that Agnes Paton is likely to have had a sexual fascination with being strangled. We understand that now in the twenty-first century. We also know that such behaviour can go so fatally wrong, as happened with rock singer Michael Hutchence.

In 1946 some Freudian psychiatrists understood this deviant sexual behaviour but it would be decades before it would reach the public domain, let alone be allowed as evidence in court. However, the jury were persuaded that Paton had been obsessed with being strangled and that John Rutherford had not intended to kill her.

Accepting the victim's role in her own death was a giant step forward for criminal justice in Scotland. They found Rutherford not guilty of murder but guilty of culpable homicide and he was sentenced to seven years in prison.

Some would argue that Rutherford was unlucky to have been jailed at all yet the man came so close to being hanged. What is certain is that he was unlucky to have met and fallen for Agnes Paton.

Rutherford was lonely and in love. All he wanted to do was make Agnes happy even if that meant strangling her. But did she die happy? Of course, we'll never know.

OLD ALLIES, NEW FOES

Unusual. The cottage was locked and shuttered. Just someone being cautious? Or was the war visiting rural Scotland?

It was 1947 and World War II had been over for two years. Besides, this was rural Scotland where folks had escaped most of the horrors.

The war was the last thing on Archie McIntyre's mind when he reached his parents' isolated cottage and found it locked. But it wouldn't stay that way for long.

The house was Tower Cottage, on the expansive Tombuie Estate in the wild lands round Aberfeldy. With its many acres of rolling hills, heather, bushes and wild grass, the estate was ideal for rearing sheep, shooting and fishing.

Tower Cottage was at the top of a steep hill, all on its own over a country mile from its nearest neighbour – the big house where the laird lived. It was so isolated that the family rarely locked the doors and Archie didn't even have a key.

Archie knew his father would have left early in the morning to go to a market in Perth but where was his mother? Then he remembered his mother was out working that day. The laird and his family were coming home after a long break and she was to spend the day cleaning and airing the house for them. Mystery solved. Archie sat down outside the cottage and waited for her.

Then the local gamekeeper turned up worried about Archie's mother, Catherine McIntyre. He'd called at the big house and found it still locked and no work done. It wasn't like Catherine. Was she ill?

Dread and worry rushed through Archie McIntyre. He would have known if his mother was ill and she was a hard-working woman who always did her work. So where was she?

With a ladder from the barn, Archie climbed up and forced his way in through a bedroom window. He ran frantically from room to room, calling out her name, but there was no sign or response. The usually tidy house was in a mess with cupboards lying open, drawers having been emptied on the floor and furniture higgledy-piggledy. Something was wrong.

Archie found his own bedroom locked – something that never happened. With no key, he hacked the door down with an axe, worry screaming in his brain. And there was his mother, lying on his bed, hands and ankles taped together, a gag in her mouth, eyes staring and covered in blood. Dead.

In one of the most rural, crime-free areas in Scotland, Catherine McIntyre had been battered to death.

With the local bobbies soon at the scene and Archie's father home to the tragic news, they ascertained that Catherine had been brutally battered to death and over £80 stolen, a fair sum in 1947. But worth killing for? It might be for someone who didn't have much. Someone desperate.

Unlike their city counterparts, the Perthshire cops weren't accustomed to dealing with murder cases. But they knew their countryside intimately and searched it thoroughly. They were looking for someone in bloodstained clothing – and it had to be a stranger. Who in that tight-knit community would kill a neighbour?

One of their immediate fears was that it was a tramp passing through. There were very many more gentlemen of the road in those days. Lost souls wandering the lanes and back roads of the countryside trying to escape from God only knows what torment. Except some of them weren't gentlemen. It was an awful thing to contemplate – a tramp, down on his luck, going to doors asking for charity only to turn violent as soon as your back was turned. Such a man would be almost impossible to catch and could turn up any time on any doorstep with evil intent – a nightmare for the police and the rural public.

Then the cops made a breakthrough. A few hundred yards from Tower Cottage a space had been flattened in high bushes. There they found a man's razor, handkerchief, boiler suit and a sawn-off shotgun. Almost everything was covered in blood. The shotgun was broken in two and the butt was smeared in dried blood. They had found the murder weapon.

This was more worrying than the existence of a psycho tramp – the scene told the cops that the murderer had lain in wait till Catherine McIntyre was on her own and then struck. He'd planned the robbery and went equipped with the shooter. This was a callous, calculated killer.

They had one sure thing to go on – the shotgun. They could tell the barrel had only recently been sawn down, maybe somebody could recognise it. In circulating the description of the gun, they took the very unusual step of doing the same on BBC radio – everyone listened to it in those pre-TV days. They weren't overreacting. The murder of a defenceless woman in what most thought of as a rural idyll had terrified much of Scotland's population – particularly those who lived in the countryside.

Farther to the north near Oldmeldrum, Aberdeenshire, a farmer had reported a shotgun of the same description having been stolen. He had loaned the shotgun to a farm labourer. Then the gun disappeared when that same labourer suddenly left the area. The farmer gave a detailed description of the man and said his name was Stanislaw Myszka, a deserter from the Polish Army in exile in Scotland.

The cops knew they had to circulate this man's name and description before he killed again. They did so promptly but worried about the public reaction. There were many thousands of ex-Allied soldiers and former prisoners of war still based in Scotland. Many of them couldn't go home because their countries, like Poland, had been occupied by the USSR. Others were being kept here to help the country recover by working on farms. There were thousands of them. What if the public started fearing every one was a killer?

The next breakthrough was a contact from a Polish couple who had settled in Upper Kinknockie Farm, north of Aberdeen. They were friends of twenty-three-year-old Stanislaw Myszka and had seen him recently when he visited and asked them if he could stay for a while. His friends were sure that the description fitted Stanislaw and thought that the events at Tombuie might explain why he had left their house suddenly without warning.

The police net was closing in as they swept over the territory from the north of Aberdeen to the North Sea coast. After a tip-off that a strange man had been sighted, they quietly drove out to a disused airport near Peterhead. There they found and arrested Myszka.

From that day on, whenever the cops took Myszka for a court appearance or to the cop shop for more interviews, huge crowds gathered, howling for his blood. A great deal of anti-foreigner sentiment filled the air. The general view was that Scotland had given this man asylum and he had repaid that by murdering an innocent woman.

At his trial at the High Court in Perth, Myszka's lawyer submitted a plea of insanity. Three independent psychiatrists, including a Polish doctor, found this not to be the case so his plea was changed to not guilty to the murder charge but guilty to the robbery one.

Myszka's lawyer battled well in the face of the strong evidence against his client but the forensic bods were to have the ace card up their sleeve. Professor Glaister of the Department of Forensic Science at Glasgow University had been called in to the case. During the trial, he asked for a sample of Myszka's hair. The defence and Myszka, of course, had no objections. What good would hair do the doctor?

Citing a complex forensic analysis of the structure and the protein of the hair, Professor Glaister then demonstrated how that hair came from the same body as hair found on the razor discovered in the clearing near Tower Cottage. The blood-splattered gun, boiler suit and handkerchief were strong evidence but it was a few strands of hair that tied Myszka to the murder.

The jury found Myszka guilty of murder in less than twenty minutes.

On 6 February 1948, the famous hangman Albert Pierrepoint made his farthest trip north, to Perth Prison. There he executed Stanislaw Myszka, the last person to be hanged in Perth and the only foreign national to be hanged in Scotland in the twentieth century.

1950 TO 1959

HEROES AND HORRORS

World war may have been over but war kicked off in Korea (1950–53), the Suez Crisis erupted (1956), the Soviets crushed an uprising in Hungary (1956), the Mau Mau rebelled in bloody civil war in Kenya (1952) and, after a revolution, Fidel Castro took over Cuba (1959).

At Queen Elizabeth's coronation, the world wondered at someone so young taking on such a role (1953). Everest was climbed for the first time (1953) and the Russians launched Sputnik 1, the first-ever orbiting artificial satellite (1957).

The rock'n'roll era began, the top twenty was introduced (1952) and the first stereo recordings went on sale (1958).

The first photograph of the dark side of the moon was taken (1959) and the first hydrogen bomb was detonated (1952) with the British version coming a short time later (1956). At home, parking meters were introduced (1958) and the first motorway opened (1959).

British scientists, Watson and Crick, quietly made a discovery that would change the face of crime detection when they discovered DNA (1953). The House of Commons voted to retain the death penalty (1954).

Tom Goodall, a young Glasgow detective was allocated the task of working on eight murders. He would crack the case and go on to be the most famous cop of his era – the man he was chasing? Read on.

HEAVY RAIN IN HELL

'Your mum will back soon,' said the kindly woman to the fretting child she was looking after. 'You know she loves you, don't you?' He nodded his head, tears drying on his cheeks. Young as he was, he loved and missed his mother – a good mother. 'Well, she wouldn't leave you, would she? Not if she could help it.' But could she?

Fat, warm, soaking Glasgow rain fell steadily making the streets shimmer in the night. But there was no mistaking the crumpled bundle lying at the side of the street. It was a body.

It was on Prospecthill Road in Glasgow's southside. It's a busy road now but, in 1950, there weren't many cars about. Besides, folk then, as now, didn't like getting involved.

Two members of the public alerted the cops anonymously by phone. They probably thought that it was a drunk crashed out or maybe some guy who had been giving a kicking – both sights were as common on Glasgow streets in 1950 as they are now. More so even.

PC William Kevan was sent to check up. Little did he know that he was about to help make Scottish legal history – a historical first that he and his colleagues would take pride in and feel shame over both at the same time.

Instantly PC Kevan realised it wasn't a drunk or even a beaten man. It was a woman and he could see she was badly injured. Maybe even dead.

The ambulance arrived at speed and the paramedics confirmed PC Kevan's fears. The woman was dead – knocked over by a car most likely but the beat bobby wasn't so sure. In a simple hit-and-run, there would have been just the one set of tyre marks at either side of the body. Here, there were several. Another thing worried PC Kevan and his superiors – the woman had no identification on her at all. Nothing. In those post-war years, people were still in the habit of carrying some form of ID, their ration card usually. This was most unusual.

Glasgow Police had no option but to release information to the local newspapers appealing for anyone who might recognise the woman to come forward. It didn't take long for a Mrs Johnston to get in touch with them.

On 28 July 1950, Mrs Johnston's friend, Catherine McCluskey, asked her to look after her toddler for the night. Catherine was forty years old, a single parent of an infant and two older children, all by different fathers. At that time people tended to look down on women on their own, especially if they were sexually active – and proof positive of this was provided by the kids. They were seen as fallen women, little better than prostitutes, and for them life was difficult.

Mrs Johnston had agreed to babysit the wee one but now she was worried, very worried. Catherine McCluskey hadn't turned up and wasn't at her home in 239 Nicholson Street in Glasgow's southside.

Catherine McCluskey wasn't coming home ever again. She died on 28 July lying on Prospecthill Road in the rain.

'Oh the poor woman,' Mrs Johnston sighed tearfully, 'what a tragic accident.' The cops nodded in agreement and made her more tea. As she went to leave the police station she stopped and turned. 'She was making a new life for herself, you know,' she said. 'Was going to settle down with a new man. The baby's daddy. A decent man with a good job. In fact he's one of you lot.'

What the cops already knew but had decided not to tell Mrs Johnston or any member of the public yet was that Catherine McCluskey's death was no accident. A post-mortem had found that her legs weren't broken, most unusual when a pedestrian is knocked down by the force of a car. There was only one explanation – she was already on the ground when the car ran over her.

Worse than that, her internal injuries supported the early views of sharp-eyed PC Kevan. There were no skid marks, as might be expected in an accident, yet a car had run over her torso several times. Her head and facial injuries were also more consistent with a beating than a car accident.

It was murder all right.

The first person they had to track down, if only to rule him out, was her lover. Mrs Johnston had never met the man and only knew his surname – Robertson.

There were a good few Robertsons in the City of Glasgow Police and the investigation team were facing a long slow job till they got a phone call from an alert desk sergeant at Orkney Street Police Station, Govan. He had picked up on the unofficial grapevine – men and cops are some of the biggest gossips – that the team were looking for a policeman by the name of Robertson. He suggested they start with a copper he knew, PC James Robertson, who was having marital problems and had been seeing someone else.

PC James Robertson denied knowing Catherine McCluskey but the interviewing cops were going to be thorough. They chase husbands, wives and lovers in murder inquiries for one very good reason – too often they are the killers. The thought that one of their own could be a murderer was too much to contemplate. So they'd be thorough, be beyond public criticism and make sure they got the right man.

They learned that Robertson was out on the beat at the time of the killing. When they interviewed Robertson's regular partner and partner that night, PC Dugald Moffat, the man's face went puce.

Moffat had been covering for Robertson for some time. He had a 'bit on the side' – a 'fancy woman'. Robertson's wife watched every move he made and it was difficult for him to see his lover. So, while they were on quiet shifts, Moffat would cover for him while Robertson slipped off to spend a couple of hours with her. That's exactly what had happened on the night of 28 July 1950. Robertson had gone off to see his woman around 11 p.m. and turned up again at about 1 a.m. – the period covering the death of Catherine McCluskey.

The cops had a suspect in a brutal murder. Normally that would be very satisfying but this time they had problems – it was another cop.

Robertson's beat on the night of 28 July was quite a distance from the scene of crime. No bus driver or the like had reported a cop travelling that route at that time and it was too far to walk, commit murder and get back on shift in two hours. Maybe he had driven. Robertson had an old Austin saloon car. The cops pulled that in for checks and it didn't take them long to find what they were looking for. A simple torch shone on the undercarriage revealed blood and fragments of flesh and clothes. The cops had their man.

Charged with murder, James Robertson still denied all the charges. He did then admit to knowing Catherine McCluskey but not to having an affair with her or killing her. He claimed he had sneaked off shift to see her that night and had hidden his car up a street near his beat just for that purpose. When they met they had argued fiercely, he claimed, and he had stormed off, jumping in the car and driving away at speed.

Feeling bad about the row he had changed his mind, braked hard and reversed back to where Catherine was. Then he heard a dull thump and felt a bump. Getting out of the car, he saw that he had driven over Catherine. Driving off in a panic, he had hidden his car in a side street and rejoined his partner as if nothing had happened.

An accidental death – that was PC James Robertson's defence when he turned up for trial at the High Court, Glasgow, on 6 November 1950.

Scotland was appalled. The charges amounted to a terrible and brutal murder of a woman and the cops were accusing a cop. But would there be justice?

Hangman John Ellis was official executioner for twenty-three years. In total, he hanged 203 souls, including six in one day. After he retired, he committed suicide in front of his family by cutting his throat. ('The Disappearing Act' and 'Blood Red Rotten Row')

This is the famous hangman Albert Pierrepoint who was part of a dynasty of executioners that included his brother Thomas and father Henry. Albert made legal history when he hanged the only policeman to be found guilty of committing murder whilst on duty – a Scot, of course. ('Heavy Rain in Hell' and others)

Tower Cottage on the Tombuie Estate was where Catherine McIntyre met a bloody end at the hands of the transient Pole, Stanislaw Myszka.
('Old Allies, New Foes')

Despite looking every bit the happy family man in this photo, PC James Robertson killed his lover, Catherine McCluskey, in 1950.

This is the stolen car PC Robertson used to kill Catherine by driving over her several times, hoping to make it look like a hit-and-run accident.

Catherine's body lies in the road and several sets of tyre marks are clearly visible. During her ordeal, the poor woman lost her shoes – one can be seen by the kerb and the other is in the road. ('Heavy Rain in Hell')

Donald Merrett led a privileged life but, when money became tight, he stole thousands of pounds from his mother, before allegedly murdering her. In 1945, he found himself strapped for cash and, once again, resorted to murder. ('The Rotter')

Lady Menzies attending a society wedding. Her son-in-law Donald Merrett murdered his wife Vera in order to get his hands on her money. On his way out of the house after the killing, he encountered Lady Menzies and murdered her too.

Fights in Glasgow's many dance halls were commonplace in the 1950s. Normally, when a scuffle started, a space on the dance floor would appear and, after some punches had been traded, things would settle down again. Sadly for some, like James Smith, it didn't end there. ('Just Another Night Out')

A smiling assassin? This is Peter Manuel, the first man ever to have the term 'serial killer' applied to him.

The Smarts, along with their son Michael, were amongst Manuel's victims. They were shot dead in their beds in Uddingston in 1958.

In 1956, Manuel had also shot and killed Margaret Brown (right).

Anne Kneilands (left) and Isabelle Cooke also died at the hands of Manuel. Although he was found not guilty of murdering Anne, he later confessed that he did.

Marion Watts and her daughter Vivienne (right) were both shot at close range. Margaret Brown (opposite), Marion's sister, was staying with the family when Manuel broke in.

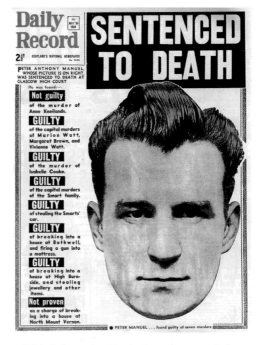

This is how the *Daily Record* reported the outcome of Manuel's trial on 30 May 1958. ('Man of the Night')

The Aberdeen dock where, in the mid 1950s, James Boyle confessed he had disposed of the body of his baby. Because the infant was an inconvenience to his plans to move south, callous Boyle murdered baby Andrew, put him in a shopping bag weighted with bricks and tossed him into the dock. ('Babyface Baby?')

The house at 5 Marshall's Court in Edinburgh where, in 1953, the murdered bodies of two little girls were found dumped in the outside toilet.

Before confessing to the double murder of the two little girls, John Lynch was, ironically, given his name, heard shouting about how he would lynch the murderer if he could get his hands on him. ('The Ghost Who Confessed')

Teenager Linda Peacock wasn't interested in anything rebellious so, when she didn't come home one summer's night in 1967 after meeting some friends, her parents were understandably alarmed.

Gordon Hay was staying at an approved school not far from the place where Linda Peacock's body was discovered. He seemed to have an alibi but, for the first time, dental forensic detection was to catch a killer. ('Too Good a Girl')

The Torry Battery in Aberdeen which overlooks the foreshore where the arm of local girl, Betty Hadden, washed up. Despite the police's best efforts, the rest of Betty's body was never found. ('The Tartan Dahlia')

Margaret Guyan's marriage had always been a bit rocky but, when she moved out of the family home in Aberdeen to live with Henry Burnett, she could never have dreamt what the consequences would be. ('Lethal Lust in a Cold Climate')

The Williamswood bank in the Glasgow suburb of Clarkston where Howard Wilson and his two sidekicks stole almost £21,000 in 1969.

Inspector Andrew Hyslop had a sixth sense where crime was concerned and never more so than when an ex-cop might be involved. Suspecting Howard Wilson was up to no good, he asked to look in some cases Wilson was unloading. Wilson obliged and then opened fire on Hyslop.

Howard Wilson is led away by police after being found guilty of bank robbery and the cold-blooded murders of Constables McKenzie and Barnett who'd arrived as backup for Inspector Hyslop. ('A Deadly Conceit')

Robertson's lawyer did a heroic job of defending him against a weight of forensic and circumstantial evidence. But at the end of the day the only two people present at that time were Robertson and Catherine McCluskey. She couldn't speak for herself. He said it had been an accident. Would they believe him?

Not after the police gave evidence on his car. And it wasn't just the blood and flesh on the car's underside – it was a stolen vehicle, with false number plates and registration papers. The accused claimed he had found the car on waste ground in the Gorbals and was given the false documents by a police informant – as if that was any better than stealing them. No one in the court believed him.

James Robertson was proven to be a thief and, more importantly, a liar. It took the jury an hour to find PC James Robertson guilty of beating Catherine unconscious then deliberately running over her again and again in his car – guilty of murder.

On 16 December 1950, at Barlinnie Prison, Albert Pierrepoint made Scottish legal history when he hanged James Robertson. Since records began, PC James Robertson is the only serving policeman to be executed for a crime committed while on duty.

The cops had caught and punished one of their own. Justice was done that day, so they thought. But were they proud? Ashamed more like.

THE ROTTER

'CHAAAARGE!' the young officer roared. He had a Bren gun in his arms and he was running very quickly up the beach. Who was he roaring to? Himself, of course – his comrades were dead, wounded or taking shelter. But charge he did, scattering the enemy troops as he ran, spraying a wide curve of deadly bullets. And on he ran as if he didn't care if he died. The very picture of the hero. He was more than that. Much worse than that.

That was in World War II, in 1943 – a time when ordinary men became heroes and extraordinary men whimpered. An unusual time, a surprising and deadly time. To understand our man we have to go back a bit in time.

Born in 1908, Donald Merrett's New Zealander daddy abandoned his mammy and him when he was still an infant and they were living in Russia. Back in England, his mother Bertha pretended she was a war widow and brought up her young son on her own. Life's much easier when you have money and Bertha Merrett was loaded. Her boy, Donald, was born with a silver spoon in his mouth but he was trouble from the start.

Though getting as much pocket money as a labourer earned in a week, the teenage Donald had taken to stealing from his mother's purse. He had discovered sex and couldn't be bothered with the courting game. High-class, top-dollar call girls would do him – subsidised from his mother's purse.

Bertha thought Donald was just high-spirited like a lot of upper-class kids so she enrolled him at the expensive Malvern

152

College for the best education she could buy. But he preferred his lady friends and driving a motorbike he'd bought with cash stolen from his mother. She should've spotted the signs back then. Shame on her – for her – she didn't.

Desperate, Bertha moved them to Edinburgh – the very posh 31 Buckingham Terrace. Edinburgh University was one of the best in the country and she could pay for his entrance. Donald could go there while living at home with her, she thought. Donald had other ideas.

Soon his socialising and expensive call girls in Edinburgh's clubs and hotels demanded more than stealing a few pounds from his mother's purse. Forging her signature on her chequebook would cover it, though.

In a few weeks in 1926 Donald Merrett emptied his mother's bank account of £300 – easily worth five figures now. The inevitable happened. The account was overdrawn and the bank notified his mother. Time was running out for Merrett. Or was it?

One morning in March 1926, their maid left mother and son both reading quietly in the dining room, as was their routine.

'BOOM!' It was a shattering noise that shocked the maid so badly that she dropped a dish and clutched her ears. Donald ran through saying his mother had shot herself. Sure enough, the poor woman was lying on the ground, bleeding from the head, and nearby lay a pistol.

Bertha Merrett wasn't the type to try suicide – everyone who knew her knew that – yet the cops accepted she had. She wasn't the type to have guns lying around – unlike her son who had secretly bought pistols since his teens. But she wasn't the type to die easily either. She survived.

With his mother lying ill in hospital Donald had a ball with wine, women and song, moved into a plush hotel and bought himself a new motorbike – all with Mum's forged cheques of course.

Yet with Bertha conscious she was also talking. She had been sitting at the table in her dining room, felt Donald come up behind her and told him to go away – she was busy. Next thing a big bang went off in her head. Bertha made this damning statement to a relative but it was mixed up with some confused gibberish. Bertha had been shot in the head, after all, and she was struggling.

Then events took a turn for the worse. A few weeks later Bertha died from complications. Now all her money would be Donald Merrett's. Or would it? Bertha wasn't so soft. She had left him all her money and investments but she'd put the matter into the hands of a public trustee – a careful, conscientious one who called for an investigation.

The cops were finally interested when the public trustee informed them that somehow the mortally ill, bed-bound Bertha Merrett had been out on a spending spree in her last weeks of life. Donald Merrett was arrested and charged not only with forgery but also with murdering his mother.

As his trial started at the High Court, Edinburgh, in February 1927, the media was full of the case. An upper-class man of great privilege being accused of murdering his mother – this was a major scandal. Donald Merrett on the other hand was relaxed, carefree, glib. That was his style.

There was no forensic evidence, there were no witnesses and the maid was a little shaky on recalling events – well, her job saved her from poverty. So, in spite of the deathbed statements from Bertha, the lawyers simply debated whether anyone really believed a young man from such a well-to-do family would stoop to killing his own mother over something as common as money.

It was a sign of those class-ridden times when the jury found the murder case against Merrett not proven. However, he was found guilty of forgery and jailed for twelve months. In those days, ordinary people were being sent to penal colonies for taking a few pounds. Merrett had stolen thousands and got a mere twelve months' jail.

A sensible man would've sighed with relief at escaping the hangman and lived like a saint. Not Donald Merrett. As soon as he was free he visited an old pal of his mother, a Lady Menzies, and promptly eloped with her comely teenage daughter, Vera.

Though Donald had to change his surname to Chesney to conceal the infamy caused by the publicity of his trial, life looked up for him once again. On his twenty-first birthday he inherited £50,000, a vast fortune, left to him by his maternal grandfather – the father of the woman he undoubtedly killed.

He and Vera, by then his wife, took off for the Mediterranean and lived a life of yachts, flash cars and parties. On the side, just for kicks, he ran a smuggling racket between North Africa and Spain. Sex and adventure, those were his highs.

But Merrett had yet another weakness – gambling – and he was bad at it. So his fortune was dwindling and, in a rare moment of apparent selflessness, he laid down an £8,500 endowment in Vera's name. It was something they'd both regret.

When World War II broke out, he was given a commission in the navy and immediately made a name for himself. Reckless wasn't the word. He crashed at least four boats, often into enemy positions. His bravery was noted at the battle for Tobruk when he took off alone up a beach into a line of German soldiers, blasting them with a Bren gun. The day he bellowed, 'CHAAAARGE!' to himself.

His mates thought he was Errol Flynn in the flesh. Little did they suspect that he'd murdered his own mother for money. Right there on the beach, they probably didn't care.

Somehow surviving the war, he was based in Germany before being demobbed. There, he amused himself in the black market, running anything he could steal from the Allied troops to sell to the ration-starved population of neighbouring countries and even trading weapons to the new enemy – the Russians.

After the war, he once again floated about Europe, changing countries as often as he changed his women. He and Vera had split up as the war started and she was living in Edinburgh. Poor Vera couldn't keep up with Merrett's pace of life and, by the 1950s, had turned to booze big time.

He, on the other hand, had found the love of his life – again. The beautiful Germanic blonde Sonia was as energetic as him and craved his life of adventure but problems were coming their way. Cop forces all over Europe had sussed out his smuggling rackets. You couldn't sell army lorries, guns, explosives and food to the Russians and expect to go unnoticed. Then there was that old problem – he was broke again. But Merrett knew where he could get some cash.

In January 1954, he took a trip to Edinburgh to see Vera, still his legal wife, and, one night, he took her to every busy pub and hotel he could find – and Edinburgh had many. Other customers noticed the couple. Vera, still handsome, was drinking big time. Merrett was tall, tanned and heavily built. And, with his beard, his thick long hair and the large gold earring he wore, he would have cut an imposing figure at any time but he must have been most unusual in 1954.

Merrett left the next day, telling Vera it had been a farewell visit before he moved to New Zealand. Instead, he returned to Sonia but, two weeks later, he was on his way back to Edinburgh. This time, he had short hair, no beard and no earring. He wore plain glass specs, walked with a limp and used a forged passport. Nobody would have thought he was the same man as the swashbuckling boozer who had trawled the Edinburgh pubs two weeks before. Out the back of Vera's house – 22 Montpelier Road, Bruntsfield – he waited till only her bedroom light shone.

Climbing over the rear garden wall, he let himself in through some French windows which he knew had a faulty catch. He had anticipated correctly that Vera would be too disorganised to get round to having them fixed. Calmly, he walked through the house up to Vera's bedroom where he found her too drunk to be shocked by his unexpected appearance.

Merrett sat in the bedroom talking and drinking with his wife till she passed out. He coolly ran a bath, carried her to the bathroom and lowered her into the water. Vera was so drunk she didn't struggle – she just drowned.

Retracing his steps through the house, Donald Merrett must have thought he had pulled off the perfect murder and he must also have thought about how he would be rich soon thanks to that £8,500 endowment in Vera's name that would come to him as her husband. Then, in the dark, he bumped into his mother-in-law, Lady Menzies. He had been careful but not careful enough and hadn't known she was visiting her daughter.

She may have been a lady but she was game. Demanding to know what he was doing there, Lady Menzies grabbed Merrett's lapels. The much bigger, stronger man pushed to get free but couldn't. In a panic, he reached out in the dark. In his desperation, his fingers wrapped round a hefty coffee pot. He raised it above his head and brought it crashing down on her skull. Lady Menzies let go. She was dead.

All the way back to the home he shared with Sonia in Cologne, Donald Merrett must have realised he had blown it. Forensics had moved on so much since he had killed his mother. Now his fingerprints and other clues would be all over the scene of Lady Menzies' murder. Now they'd get him. His situation couldn't be worse. Or could it?

In Cologne, the man who usually did the leaving discovered that Sonia had left him. The love of his life had flown. A short while later he called a taxi and gave the driver directions.

Two weeks later, a man walking his dog deep in the woods discovered Donald Merrett all alone there, in the middle of a vast German forest. Foxes and rats had been at him, gnawing away at his flesh, but it was plain enough to see what had happened. Donald Merrett had pulled out a revolver, stuck it in his mouth and blown his brains out.

He'd had a privileged life but he had soiled it. After all, what does a rotter do but lead a rotten life?

BABYFACE BABY . . .?

He had the sweetest face. Everyone who knew him knew that. The sweetest baby face that made men trust him and women want to take him home. Everyone knew that – apart from him. All he knew was that anger and hate burned so fiercely they could kill.

Urban myths exist everywhere. In Scotland there's one about the first murder conviction where no body has been found. Most folk believe the first was The Spanish Assassin, Ricardo Blanco, and his associates. They were found guilty of murdering drug dealer Paul Thorne on Fenwick Moor in 1988. Thorne was buried in an as-yet-undiscovered unmarked grave out on that moor. Others are even sloppier and think it was Elgin's Nat Fraser. His estranged wife Arlene disappeared on 28 April 1998 and has never been found yet he was jailed for her murder.

But they'd be wrong. It was earlier than both of those – much earlier.

Crime records become sparser the further we go back. Yet we know that, in 1749, Anne Phillip was found guilty of killing her baby by throwing him into the sea at Stonehaven. Phillip was found guilty of murder in spite of no one seeing a killing. All they saw was her walking to some cliffs with the child and returning with only his clothes – damning for sure. In spite of the baby's body never being found, Phillip was due to be hanged. At the last minute, she was reprieved and given a royal pardon. Even back then, they recognised the poor woman was dreadfully ill.

In modern times, the records are good and they provide precise details on such a conviction decades before Blanco and Fraser. It happened in Aberdeen in 1955 and a gruesome tale it is.

Convicted-murderer-turned-sculptor Jimmy 'Babyface' Boyle had a history of causing the prison authorities headaches. Because of his dirty protests and his involvement in riots and assaults, they created the so–called animal pits at Inverness's Porterfield Prison to try to control him and the Special Unit at BarL was also home to Boyle for a time. However, he wasn't the first 'Babyface' Boyle to be in trouble. His namesake, James Boyle from Paisley, was given that nickname as a teenager back in the 1940s. But these Boyles had something else in common – neither was as sweet as they looked.

Boyle was a chauffeur by profession though he'd drive any vehicle to make a living. He was the driver for one of the bosses at a large engineering firm in Glasgow when he met teenager Barbra Irving, who worked at the same company as a clerical worker – a toff's job in those times. Within days of meeting, the pair were an item and, within months, naive Barbra was pregnant. When they met, Boyle had described himself as young, free and single – two out of three wasn't bad. Under pressure to marry Barbra and make a 'respectable' woman of her, he had to confess he was already married, with a wife and three kids living in Paisley.

But Boyle had plans. The couple would tell no one about the pregnancy but would just move on. Aberdeen seemed far enough away. Calling themselves Mr and Mrs Boyle, they took digs in the city for a month and he got a job as a bus driver. All was fine and dandy till the baby was born. It was a wee boy. He was fit, healthy and strong and they called him Andrew. The baby was no trouble but problems were brewing close by.

A few weeks after Andrew was born, James Boyle started work as a bus driver in Newcastle. For unknown reasons, he had been planning to move to that city for some time. When signing on with the bus company, he had to give his details. Big mistake – within a few days, he was arrested by the cops, charged with serious neglect of his kids back in Paisley and taken back to the west of Scotland to go on trial.

Barbra then returned to live with her parents in Glasgow's Govan area. She sat in the court with her father the day Boyle was sentenced to a month in jail. That night, her old man noticed she was looking worried and ill – that she'd looked that way since she moved back in with them. Was it just James' predicament or was there something else?

There was something else. Something that wasn't there. Something old Mr Irving knew nothing about. Something Barbra had told no one about. Something she'd been forced to keep quiet because her man, James, told her to. It was the baby. Eventually, Barbra blurted out that she and James had had a baby boy. The baby had been adopted and she felt guilty about it – wretched and guilt-ridden.

Sad as he was about his grandson being adopted, Mr Irving was relieved it wasn't something even more serious. He wasn't to feel relieved for long.

Two days later, Barbra had another story to tell – a story that would disgust any decent person. A few days after baby Andrew was allowed home, she and Boyle had been sitting in their rented room in Aberdeen when he said they should move to Newcastle. That was too far for such a young baby to travel, she had said. Couldn't they wait a while? No – Babyface Boyle was an impatient man and saw himself as the boss of their family. They'd move to Newcastle but without the baby. She'd have to have him adopted.

Looking at her babe fast asleep, Barbra said there was no way she could do that. The couple were so short of cash that wee Andrew didn't even have a cot but slept in an old case with a pillow for a mattress.

'Isn't there another way we could get rid of it?' Boyle said. It was more of a suggestion than a question.

Soon after, he went to work, leaving Barbra crying.

When he returned from work, he started again, right from where he had left off. 'Can't you strangle it?' he'd asked.

Of course she couldn't.

'Well, he's not mine – I'm not the father – so I could.'

Of course the baby was his. She'd been a virgin when she took up with him.

Barbra thought he was just angry – the way he could get angry even over trivial things – and, as usual, it would all blow over. Later she went to the bathroom to wash her tear-stained face. When she came out, both Boyle and Andrew were gone. Then she heard Andrew's cry – a muffled cry from the bedroom. Barbra rattled the door handle but it was locked. She cried out to Boyle to let her in but he didn't reply. The only noise she heard was wee Andrew's sobs – muffled sobs as if he was very far away.

Sometime later she went back to the bathroom. There she collapsed on the floor and sat weeping her eyes out. About twenty minutes later, she emerged, nervously picking her way through the small flat, and found both Boyle and Andrew gone.

An hour later, a very upset James Boyle returned home. He wouldn't say to Barbra what he had done or where the baby was.

Some will judge Barbra Irving badly for not going straight to the cops or for even leaving Andrew alone with Boyle at all. But she was a young, immature teenager and he was a very manipulative man.

God knows what Barbra Irving's dad made of this horror story. First he heard he had a grandson and then he was also told the baby had been murdered by the wee one's own father. What we do know is that the old man went straight to the cops.

Within days, James Boyle was interviewed by the police in Barlinnie Prison where he was serving his month's sentence for child neglect. Boyle admitted disposing of baby Andrew by putting him in Barbra's wine–coloured shopping bag, weighing it down with bricks and throwing him into Aberdeen's deep Victoria Docks. But he denied murder, claiming that the mother, Barbra Irving, had murdered the child.

The day before Boyle's trial for murder started at the High Court in Aberdeen, Barbra Irving and her father travelled up there and registered the birth of baby Andrew. Registering a baby's birth when they knew he was dead – it must have been the saddest journey imaginable.

A terrible winter hit the north-east of Scotland on the day James Boyle's trial started on 31 January 1956. There were those at the time who said the weather was hell because Boyle, the baby killer, was in town.

The cops had tried their hardest to find baby Andrew. Again and again, divers had gone down into the dark waters of Victoria Dock but with no success.

Without a victim's corpse, any independent witnesses or forensic evidence, it was a straightforward matter. James Boyle said Barbra killed the baby and Barbra said that Boyle murdered him – choose.

Maybe it would have made no difference to the verdict but the Crown was taking no chances. They had made sure that the balance of the jury was eight women to seven men, betting that women would feel more sympathy with the mother – a majority of female jurors was still something of an oddity then. The jury believed the mother and James Boyle was found guilty. He was sentenced to death and removed immediately to the condemned cell at Craiginches Prison, Aberdeen.

Ahead of the verdict, the cops had planned their tactics well. An angry mob was hanging around and they would have gladly ripped Boyle limb from limb. Many would have done the same to Barbra too as they held her responsible as well. Couldn't she – shouldn't she – have stopped him?

Shortly after the trial, the mob spotted the prison wagon and took after it howling. A few minutes later, a police van quietly pulled out of the court and turned in the opposite direction. In the back sat the condemned man, Babyface Boyle. Just as the police had hoped, the bloodthirsty throng had chased a decoy.

Boyle's lawyers submitted an appeal, as was fast becoming the norm in murder convictions. It was heard on 22 February 1956 and it failed but all hope wasn't lost.

On the very same day that Boyle was sentenced to death, Labour MP Sydney Silverman had submitted a private members' bill to suspend the death sentence.

On 5 March 1956 the Lord Provost of Aberdeen, George Stephen, got togged up in all his ceremonial finery. He had important business to carry out but it was the least public of all his duties as an elected official.

There in the condemned cell at Craiginches Prison, with James Boyle suffering from flu and lying in bed, Lord Provost Stephen read out a formal letter from the Secretary of State for Scotland.

Boyle was to be reprieved and would spend life in prison instead.

'Thank you,' is all Babyface Boyle said at being told he could live. It doesn't sound much but most people in Aberdeen at the time didn't think his life was worth much.

Baby Andrew was nine days old when he was murdered. His body has never been found. His father, his killer lived longer. Was he troubled much by the ghost of his dead boy? Troubled? Not him. He was a charmer. After all they named him well – Babyface Baby Killer.

JUST ANOTHER NIGHT OUT

Accordions were wheezing, the drums rat-tat-tatting and the fiddle singing the devil's tune – not exactly modern music but it would do. Funny though – it didn't sound like a last anthem.

'You dancin'?'

'You askin'?'

It's not exactly the best chat-up line ever and, these days, it's more than likely to result in a knock-back. Yes, it's bad, but murder?

It's not known if those exact words were used at the Ancient Order of Hibernians' Hall, Royston, Glasgow, on 16 November 1951. What is known is that a young woman had just agreed to dance with a young man called James Smith when he added, rather ungallantly, 'Jist a wee minute, hen.'

Smith crossed the dance floor, put his left hand on the shoulder of a local bloke called William Loudon and then struck him with his right hand. Was this just another minor incident in the booze-fuelled world of violent street life? Maybe, but it was the end of the dance and the start of hell.

The Hibernian Hall was slap bang in the middle of what we now call Royston. The area used to be called The Garngad and, along with the notorious scheme of Blackhill to the north, it has a long-established reputation for uncompromising street violence. In years to come, it would be the base of Arthur 'The Godfather' Thompson and the infamous Welsh crew and it was the happy hunting ground of Paul Ferris. All that was the future but The Garngad was never peaceful.

It's a predominantly Catholic area and, until recently, cars entering it from the M8 would be greeted with the gable end warning of:

YOU ARE NOW ENTERING FREE GARNGAD.

Newspapers supporting the IRA were sold in its pubs. Money was collected for Republican causes, pro-Republican petitions were signed and marches organised. Once a year, a Hibernian Walk would take off from The Garngad and the marchers would go through the streets of adjoining Protestant areas before ending up circling a block of flats back in their own patch. There, it was rumoured, the local housing department had placed many Protestants. Every year there'd be a pitched battle.

Armed with blades and hammers, the kids from the local secondary school, St Roch's, would engage in street battles against kids from the neighbouring Protestant schools and much damage was done. Some of these so-called schoolkids' spats even ended in death – the deaths of children. Why? The answer is that old beast that has haunted Glasgow and haunts it still – sectarianism.

There were those from The Garngad who would happily fight and die for the Republican cause. If that wasn't on, in the meantime, they'd fight each other.

A long, trailing, built-up area crammed with tenements, everyone in The Garngad knew each other. It was that type of area. But that didn't mean it was all sweetness and light – not among the young men and especially not at weekends and social occasions when strong drink had been taken.

Mary Malone was standing in the Hibernian Hall chatting to a friend and her own husband, Martin Malone. Trouble had been brewing all night between groups of young men – nothing unusual in that. Just as happened at Scottish weddings, it was almost traditional that someone scrapped at these dances.

Across the hall there was scuffle. Martin could see that his best friend, William Loudon, was in a fight with some young guys and he immediately rushed across the hall to the rescue. Within seconds, Martin Malone was stabbed. Dead.

The whole community went into mourning. It was bad enough when their young men met with grief outside the area but to start killing each other? This was bad.

Everyone in that hall knew each other, so it was no surprise that, by the following day, twenty-one-year-old James Smith had been identified, arrested and charged with Malone's murder. Smith admitted to assaulting Malone but pled not guilty to murder, claiming self-defence. A standard ploy? Maybe but, in this case, there was some considerable doubt.

Jamie Smith – a popular young man in the area – went to trial for murder at the High Court, Glasgow on 26 February 1952. Outside the old High Court, spilling over on to Glasgow Green, hundreds of protestors had travelled down from The Garngad. They knew Jamie Smith and knew he was no killer.

Witness after witness said it had been a night of sporadic violence all through The Garngad. An earlier fight had resulted in four young men being thrown out of the Hibernian Hall. But, in the packed space with all that action, people weren't clear about who exactly had been involved.

Smith himself claimed the trouble had started earlier when Loudon and Malone had severely assaulted one of his friends. He admitted that there was an issue to be sorted, revenge to be dished out, but there was other business on hand – women.

'You dancin'?' he'd asked a young woman.

'You askin'?' she'd replied, showing her consent with a smile and moving out on to the small, packed dance floor.

'Jist a wee minute, hen,' Smith had said to her before he walked quickly across the floor. All she could see was that he thumped William Loudon and then all hell broke loose.

Under oath, Smith admitted that he had gone across to thump William Loudon for the beating he and Malone had dished out on his pal earlier but, according to Smith, Loudon had pulled a blade on him.

Smith claimed he wasn't carrying a knife – that it wasn't his style, especially at the dancing – so he had backed off quickly. Except he wasn't quick enough. Martin Malone had rushed across at Smith with a blade already drawn. There were punches, wrestling, kicks, grappling. These fights are much, much messier than Hollywood portrays. Within a few seconds, Martin Malone had hit the floor bleeding and dying.

In the panic of violence in such a confined space, people remember sparse detail, being too concerned for their own safety. Smith insisted at his trial that Malone had been wielding a knife. But he was in trouble – no knife was found in Malone's possession.

After such fights, it is the standard procedure for friends of the combatants to pick up their weapons and make them disappear. It's a pals' thing, Glasgow style. Fingerprints, blood and weapons are damning evidence to be used by the cops – the common enemy.

Not one witness could support Smith's version of events. But a knife had been found – a secret knife.

On the second day of the trial, the prosecution were eventually and reluctantly forced to admit that a second knife had indeed been found in the hall – a knife that could have been Malone's, as Smith had alleged. The trouble was that the police and prosecution had failed to order forensic tests or fingerprints on that weapon, missing the opportunity to identify the owner. These days, science has progressed enough for that weapon still to be useful evidence but, back in 1952, months after the event, it was too late.

Smith was found guilty. Outside the High Court, people howled in angry protest and pushed against a line of uniformed cops. They knew Jamie Smith. They knew he wasn't a killer.

Smith immediately appealed. Over four days of detailed debate – one of the longest criminal appeals at that time – the three appeal court judges declared that the knife wasn't central to the conviction since there was no evidence, even circumstantial, that it was Malone's knife.

In the mêlée of bodies in that cramped hall with scared people screaming and scrambling to avoid the violence, if just one person had sworn they had seen a knife in Malone's fist, there might have been a different result. As it was, the appeal was dismissed.

The Garngad was alight with protest. They knew Jamie Smith. They knew he was no killer. But it was all too late.

On Saturday 12 April 1952, James Smith went to the dancing again – this time at Barlinnie Prison at the end of the hangman's noose. He was only twenty-one years old and, even as he took that long short walk, he swore he was innocent. Now we'll never know the truth.

THE GHOST WHO
CONFESSED

'Who'd be a bobby?' laughed the policeman aloud, addressing no one but himself as he stamped his feet on the ground to keep the cold out. Just as well he had a sense of humour. Well, he had to laugh. Guarding an outside toilet in the dark? Wasn't that a joke? No joke but murder. And soon the killer was going to come looking for him.

It had started earlier on 11 December 1953 in Edinburgh's Greenside Row, just an ordinary day for all concerned – especially for two wee lassies, Lesley Nisbet and Margaret Curran. The girls were close neighbours, close friends and, at four and three years old, close in age.

That day, like every day, they played together round their homes at 5 Marshall's Court, Greenside Row. It was a tight-knit community where everyone knew everyone – they were safe as safe as could be. Then they went missing.

Lesley's mum, Janet, first spotted something was wrong. The lassies were always in and out of her house with some story or looking for a piece and jam. When they hadn't been in for a while she went looking for them – looking and calling and going farther from the close than the wee ones were allowed to go. They were well-behaved girls but even good girls get into trouble some time.

They weren't to be seen anywhere. Janet Nisbet panicked and called on all the neighbours. Everybody dropped what they were doing and started searching the streets. Nothing.

A couple of hours later, around 5.30 p.m., a frantic Janet went to fetch her common-law husband, John Sinclair. She knew that, as usual, he'd have stopped off in his local pub for one pint of beer.

When Janet arrived at the pub everyone turned and stared. Women weren't in the habit of walking into pubs on their own – that was a male preserve in 1953 – but there was worse. Even the old drunks slumped in the corner could see she was beside herself with worry.

Immediately a group of men had gathered round Janet as she wept and told her man how Lesley and Margaret had gone missing, how long for and how the neighbours and she had searched the whole area.

Janet Nisbet knew most of the men in the pub. One in particular, John Lynch, was a close neighbour and he'd been having a drink with her man. Lynch was a bit the worse for wear and offered to buy Janet a port and lemon to help her calm down.

The good woman refused the drink, saying she didn't want to waste time with her lassie out there, lost. That didn't stop Lynch having another drink himself but he promised to join the search party soon.

All the other men left the pub to look for the girls. The pub owner even let one of his staff go and help and said not to worry about his wages. Like all the poorest of communities, this one was rich in humanity.

After the police had been involved for six long, fruitless hours and hundreds of volunteers had scoured the streets, the back closes, the nooks and crannies, there was still no sign of the youngsters. It was now late at night and folk were exhausted and they'd run out of places to look. Gradually, reluctantly, the neighbours and friends gave up the search for the night, promising to be back first thing in the morning. They wouldn't have to wait that long.

Young Elizabeth McKail, a close neighbour of the missing wee girls, had a problem. She hated sharing toilets with other people. It was bad enough that the only facility her tenement had was an outside cludgie and she had to share with all the other families, spiders and occasional rat but now not even that was possible. All afternoon the door of the outside toilet had been stuck shut. Elizabeth had gut ache and needed to go fast. Now she was contemplating having to use the toilet next door.

She shared her predicament with her mother who knew how much Elizabeth hated using strangers' toilets. Her mother gave her a big kitchen knife and suggested she could try to prise the door open.

Desperate, Elizabeth was willing to try anything. Out in the pitch dark of the back close, she wedged the blade into the slight crack in the door opening and pushed down with all her weight. Nothing. She pushed down again. When it cracked then creaked free she must have smiled with relief – till she opened the door.

There crumpled on the cold concrete floor of the toilet were the bodies of Lesley and Margaret, their dead eyes staring up through the dark, twinkling in the yellow light of the moon. Elizabeth McKail must have jumped with the shock and horror. It's not recorded but it's a good bet that she either emptied her aching bowels right then or instantly forgot she needed to go.

With the cops and the girls' parents soon on the scene, it was confirmed that the bodies were those of Lesley and Margaret and both were dead – and had been for some time or so it looked.

As the bodies were carried away for post-mortems, the cops regrouped and decided on tactics. Hundreds of people had been searching the area for hours yet the girls were found in the back close next door to where they lived.

All afternoon and all night, searchers must have tried that cludgie door, only to find it jammed tight, and moved on. The girls might have lain in there unconscious but alive for a while with life slowly ebbing out of them. Could they maybe have been saved?

The police decided they would start interviewing every single local person early in the morning. Meantime, they had to guard the scene of crime so the forensic team could search it properly in daylight and that's where DC Thomas Gow came in. Gow was an experienced cop who had dealt with all sorts of atrocities that humans inflict on humans and he'd picked up the pieces of more than one corpse. But guarding that outside toilet throughout the night was his worst shift ever.

Early on, there was some weak, yellow light glowing from the back windows of the nearby flats and a sickly moon. One by one, the families went to bed, switching off the lights as they did so, and, as clouds gathered and swamped the moon, he was left in darkness. On his own, feet away from that toilet, he couldn't stop thinking of those wee lassies being murdered and dumped just there, just feet from where he stood. It was the graveyard shift all right.

Then he had company. The man was staggering. He was very drunk and very loud, his voice booming out through the still air. It was John Lynch who lived in that close and who'd offered Lesley's mum the drink in the pub. He had kept his word and joined the search party but, unlike the sad and serious others, he always had something to say. This time was going to be no different.

'I'd fucking kill who did this,' Lynch bawled, his breath stinking of stale beer and cheap whisky. 'Ah WOULD!'

DC Gow told the man to keep his voice down, that it was the early hours of the morning and people were sleeping.

John Lynch heeded the cop's advice but that didn't stop him going on and on about what he would do to the killer. 'You wouldnae need Pierrepoint – Ah'd hang them masel'.'

When John Lynch eventually staggered off to bed, DC Gow just dismissed him as a concerned but drunk neighbour. Understandably, emotions were running high in the area and they would get higher still before all this was over.

DC Gow hadn't been the only one to work through the night. Trying to help the investigation, a Dr Fiddes had been examining both girls' bodies so that he could brief the cops fully in the morning. And he would. He concluded that both lassies had been strangled yet there was no obvious sign of sexual assault, the most common motive in such slayings. But there was more helpful and more obvious evidence than that.

Wee Margaret had a woman's stocking tied tightly around her neck and under it was caught a small piece of floral material. Lesley had a safety pin missing from her clothes. In those hard-up days kids' clothes were often bought too large so they'd last for years. No need to sew the hems up when you could pin them.

It was exactly the type of evidence the cops needed and armed with this they set off on their door-to-door interviews.

Starting at the girls' home and working out, it wasn't long before they knocked on the door of John Lynch. The cops had hardly crossed the threshold when Lynch called out, 'Take me. It was me. Me. Ah did it.'

The guy had been behaving weirdly since the girls went missing. The cops thought this might just be another hysterical reaction from him. They quickly changed their minds when Lynch's partner, Annie Hall, revealed that one of her stockings was missing from the washing, an apron she owned had a tear in it and the material matched that found on Margaret's neck.

Annie had done the washing the morning before, hung up her apron and then gone out. Many witnesses would swear she was with them when the girls went missing – when the girls were murdered. John Lynch had acted alone.

The cops' case became even stronger when they found a safety pin in the ashes of his coal fire. Though it was badly charred, they could prove it was the same type Lesley's mother used.

A huge crowd turned up outside the High Court on 23 March 1954, when John Lynch went on trial for double murder. They weren't the moneyed businessmen from the New Town or the toffs from Morningside but the working class of Greenside Row and every other down-at-heel area in Edinburgh.

The murder of the two girls had outraged them all and it was worse that it had been one of their own who'd done it. They were there for John Lynch's blood and to send a message to every potential child killer – we'll get you.

Inside court Lynch retracted his confession. He claimed that he had called out that the police were fitting him up. It was a claim that washed with no one, not even Annie Hall, his lover, who walked away a sad and broken woman.

The jury decided that Lynch had, for reasons unknown, strangled both girls, dumped their bodies in the toilet and then jammed the door shut. He then calmly went to the local pub where he sat drinking with the father of one of his victims. He'd offered to buy the missing girl's mother a drink and he swore to anyone who'd listen that he'd kill the killer. He was cruel all right and callous with it.

When, early on 23 April 1954, Saughton Prison announced that John Lynch had been hanged, the huge mob outside cheered and celebrated big time. As far as they were concerned, a double child killer had been given his due.

Over in Greenside Row the parents of Lesley and Margaret sat and wept. They had a lifetime of grieving to look forward to. What was there to celebrate? They suffered the anxiety of parents whose innocent children had been snatched from them, snatched from life for no given reason.

They wouldn't be the last. Maybe they knew that.

MAN OF THE NIGHT

'Is he mad?' asked one journalist turning to an older colleague as a buzz ran through the packed court.

'Mad? Oh, he's mad all right,' replied the older man. 'The question is can he pull this off?'

'It's some gamble,' continued the younger man, scribbling shorthand on his pad, 'big stakes.' The older man smiled and scratched the stubble on his chin from yet another hurried morning, when he'd had to rise early to queue among the other hacks to make sure he got a seat.

'Gambling with his life?'

'Aye, that's . . .'

'Or his final show?'

'A show?'

'He likes a show does our boy. Maybe this is all he wants.'

It's what the crowd wanted, that was for sure. But this was an unexpected twist. An accused person had simply used his right to sack his lawyers and represent himself. It's a move that judges always consider ill advised but was it pure madness in this case?

From day one on 12 May 1958, hundreds of people had queued overnight, desperate for a seat in the public benches in the famous North Court in Glasgow. Newspapers had run front-page headlines for months. It was the biggest murder trial on record in Scotland and his name was on everyone's lips – Peter Manuel.

Accused of eight horrific murders, he would hang even if he was found guilty of just one. The evidence against him together with his own confession meant the case against was strong – very strong. Yet here he was pleading not guilty and sacking some of the best lawyers in the land. Who exactly was this Peter Manuel?

Manuel was American – by birth, at least. His parents had moved to New York searching for a better life for their family and he'd been born there. After a few years spent in New York and Detroit, the family returned to their home turf, Birkenshaw near Uddingston in Lanarkshire and, almost immediately, their middle child, Peter, was in trouble.

Kids can be cruel. Maybe it was five-year-old Peter's broad Yankee accent, his lack of height or his Walter Mitty fantasies – whatever it was, they gave him hell and a loner was born.

Manuel was well known to the Lanarkshire cops as a petty thief from the age of ten. By eleven, he was on probation for breaking into a shop. But housebreaking was his real buzz, especially when the occupants were in. Although he was often caught, he still went back to it, getting a high from tiptoeing around someone's home while they slept feet away in their own bed. For the young Manuel, it was an addiction.

Soon the burglaries landed him in reform schools, which were truly hellish institutions. That worried the cops and his parents but it's what they didn't know that should have terrified them.

Manuel loved the night. After dark, the loner would wander the fields near Uddingston at night and any unsuspecting sheep, horse or cow got the sharp end of his blade. Yet this same man loved his own family dog, an Alsatian called Rusty. When the poor mutt died of natural causes, Manuel wept and wept and was inconsolable for months. Still he went out at night.

With the hormone rush of puberty came new tastes – women. Manuel would tail girls down the lonely country lanes he knew so well he could find his way round them in the dark. When he reckoned he'd be safe from passers-by, he'd grab some lassie, pull her into the bushes and pull down her underwear. That was all. No touching, feeling or rape – just pull down her pants. It was minor stuff, the cops thought, and mostly didn't even charge him.

By the age of fifteen years Manuel had turned nasty. At one reform school he assaulted a female member of staff and yanked off her underwear, leaving her bleeding, bruised and humiliated. And he'd done this in a corridor of his own school where he was bound to get caught. Then, one night, he broke into a young woman's house, woke her up, pulled her pants down and battered her about the head with a hammer. Did he wake her up so she'd be conscious while he looked at her body and beat her?

While on the run, he attacked other females, including a pregnant woman, in a similar way. Never raping them, he confined the attacks to beating them and exposing them.

Eventually, all the charges went to court and landed Manuel nine years in Peterhead Prison, then the toughest nick in Scotland. His offences were almost all sexual assaults on women with added violence. These days, he would be put into a separate unit for sex offenders but not in the 1950s. Back then, he was thrown in among the most serious gangsters in Scotland – well, the ones who had got caught. Manuel loved his new company.

He tried so hard to impress the old cons. When his fantasy tales of big bank robberies didn't wash, he fought the screws and spent years in solitary confinement. The cons still weren't impressed but Manuel wasn't giving in that easily.

When he was released from Peterhead, he now had contacts in the world of organised crime. The 1950s were producing a new breed of Glasgow gangster – Dandy McKay, Arthur Thompson, Walter Norval – men who were more Capone than Al. Manuel wanted to be one of them and to be respected by them. He would hang around their pubs and clubs, telling tales of his derring-do – more often than not, they'd be made up. To the real players, Peter Manuel was either a bit of a joke or a nuisance and that's why he decided to do something that would grab and hold their attention. Someone else was going to pay the price.

The beginning of the end for Manuel started at High Burnside in the Watt household in September 1956. A home help called that morning to assist Mrs Watt who was disabled. It was to be a day the home help wished she hadn't gone to work. Upstairs, in separate rooms, lying in bed were Marion Watt, her sixteen-year-old daughter, Vivienne, and Marion's sister, Margaret Brown. All had been shot in the head at close range. Marion and Margaret were already dead and Vivienne died before an ambulance could reach her.

Some minor items had been stolen and the killer had calmly eaten some food. Vivienne's nightdress had been pulled up to expose her naked body but she hadn't been raped. No big theft or rape – what could the motive have been?

The streets of Glasgow shook with fear. Who could breeze into a house in the middle of the night and shoot three women as they slept? Unless it was personal . . .

The tranquil setting of Loch Fyne was a striking contrast to the bloody scene in Glasgow. That's where Marion's husband, William, was – he'd gone on a fishing trip to Lochgilphead, Argyll.

When cops broke the news to the man, he was distraught and broke down. They were suspicious. The police reckoned Watt could've driven down from Argyll in the middle of the night, killed the women, driven back and been in his bed at his hotel the next morning where staff swore he had been. After the case had been carried on the front pages for days, a worker on the Renfrew Ferry swore that Watt had crossed over on the night of the killings. That was enough for the police and William Watt was charged with murder. He was thrown into the remand wing at Barlinnie Prison – a hellhole of a jail that was hated by even hardened cons, never mind men in prison for the first time. Worse, every other con knew what Watt had been jailed for and they didn't take kindly to the shooting of women. Life for William Watt was very difficult but Glasgow citizens sighed with relief that there wasn't a psycho killer on the loose. They were right about that but for the wrong reasons.

Watt's lawyer, the famous Lawrence Dowdall, started getting letters from a Barlinnie prisoner. Shortly after the Watt killings, Peter Manuel had been sentenced for robbing a colliery and he wasn't a happy man. In detailed, well-written letters, Manuel outlined that Watt was innocent because another prisoner had confessed to him that he was the murderer. Wary that this might be just another loony trying to get some buzz out of association with a horror crime, Dowdall encouraged the correspondence and, page by page, Manuel revealed more and more specific information. Why? All his life Manuel the loner craved attention – whatever it took.

When Manuel revealed that one of the women had been shot twice – something never revealed to the public – the cops released William Watt. Now they were hunting Peter Manuel. Interviews with Manuel in Barlinnie and searches of his parents' home revealed nothing. The prisoner with the busy pen just insisted that another man had confessed to him. Not believing that line for a second, the cops would have to play a waiting game.

Manuel was released from prison in November 1957 and terror stalked the streets again.

A young woman, Isabelle Cooke, disappeared one dark night on her way home to Carrick Drive, Mount Vernon. On 6 January 1958, in bed at their family home in Sheepburn Road, Uddingston, Peter Smart, his wife Doris and their eleven-year-old son Michael were found shot dead. Mrs Smart's clothes had been pulled up to expose her body but she hadn't been sexually interfered with. Downstairs in the kitchen, the killer had eaten well and even fed the family cat. A pattern was emerging and the cops had only one name in mind – Peter Manuel.

The west of Scotland fell into panic. The killer of the Watts and the Smarts was on the loose. Who'd be next?

Then the cops got help from an unexpected source. Gangsters didn't like Peter Manuel and were sickened by these killings. They told the cops that the usually skint Manuel had been flashing money around in east-end pubs.

Pub landlords cooperated too and it was soon identified that all Manuel's money came from a batch of brand-new notes – exactly those issued to Peter Smart who'd withdrawn money on the day of his death for a holiday. Now the cops could move in.

During the police raid on Manuel's parents' house in Birkenshaw, specific items stolen from the Smarts as well as things from other burglaries were discovered. Finally, Manuel was arrested.

Manuel denied everything, claiming a well-known Glasgow gangster – Samuel 'Dandy' McKay – was the killer. When the furious McKay heard this, he and his mates provided the cops with a stack more evidence against Manuel.

Then William Watt had got another clue. Against all advice, he had met Manuel to discuss the latter's letters from jail. Watt was convinced that Manuel was the killer but wanted to be sure. While they were talking, a smiling, smug Manuel slowly tore up a picture. Horrified, Watt recognised it was of a young woman called Anne Kneilands whose half-naked body had been found on an East Kilbride golf course ten months before the slaughter at his home.

In custody, Manuel denied everything. Then the cops took a gamble and arranged for him to meet with his very law-abiding parents.

'Tell us everything, Peter,' pled his tiny, ladylike mother. 'Tell the truth.'

With tears steaming down his face, Peter Manuel, the killer of mothers who loved his own mother over everything, did just that and confessed to killing Anne Kneilands, the Watts, Margaret Brown and the Smart family.

Manuel was now the centre of attention at last and he loved it. He even added extras.

He'd killed Isabelle Cooke and took the cops to where he had buried her. She was found half naked but, once again, no rape or sexual interference had taken place.

A few days after being let out of jail in November 1957, he'd taken a train to Newcastle, caught a taxi at the station and, on a country road, shot the driver in the back of the head and slit his throat. Sure enough Newcastle cops confirmed that unsolved murder.

Manuel even told them exactly where in the River Clyde he'd dumped his guns – a Webley revolver and a Beretta automatic. For the first time in the UK, the cops used divers to recover evidence. It wouldn't be the last time since, after a few days, both guns were recovered.

Forensics, murder guns, linked goods, a signed confession to multiple murders with details only the killer and the cops could have – it was all stacking up against Manuel. Though signed confessions alone aren't enough to convict in Scotland, it was as strong a case as the police could hope for. Yet there was Peter Manuel in the High Court in May 1958 sacking his lawyers and conducting his own defence.

Was he mad? No – he was the centre of attention.

For twelve long days, he showed great skill in the art of court debate. He'd done this before when he was charged with sexual assault years earlier and, that time, he'd won a not proven verdict. But here he was facing eight murder raps – this was a different matter entirely.

In his summing-up to the jury before they went to make their decisions, the judge, Lord Cameron, ruled that there should be a not guilty verdict on the murder of Anne Kneilands for lack of corroboration. He went on to commend Manuel's defence as being conducted with 'a skill that is quite remarkable'.

Remarkable for sure – but had it been good enough to save his life? Less than three hours later, the jury returned with guilty verdicts on all seven murder charges. Manuel would hang.

Even as the verdicts rang out criminologists were studying Peter Manuel closely. Here they had an acutely intelligent man, a loner who craved attention, who loved his pet but was cruel to animals, who killed women but doted on his own mother, who saw himself as a lady's man but was impotent, only reaching orgasm while inflicting agony and death.

How to describe such a man? They invented the phrase 'serial killer' and, to Scotland's everlasting shame, Manuel was first in the world to be labelled as such.

In the condemned cell at Barlinnie Prison, Manuel confessed to another nine murders – Anne Steele and Ellen 'English Nellie' Petrie, who'd both been battered and stabbed to death in Glasgow, a London prostitute, a teenage girl in Coventry and other innocents. He'd been practising killing for a long time.

If Manuel's confessions are to be believed, he might well have murdered eighteen innocent souls. Perhaps the weight of that struck home when, in Barlinnie, he drank disinfectant in a failed suicide effort.

Peter Manuel was the most feared and hated man of the 1950s – not just in Scotland but in the whole of Britain. Most folk wanted him dead and quickly. Yet there others who wanted to see who this man was, to get a sense of what made him tick. But Manuel was seeing no outsider – unless it was one of the faces he admired so much who was asking to see him.

Sammy Docherty was a well-known bookie with connections throughout Glasgow's underworld. He was friendly with a young newspaper photographer, Harry Benson. One word from Docherty and Benson was given the ticket of the decade, a visiting pass to see Peter Manuel. For weeks, Benson was a regular visitor, sitting with this polite, articulate man whose manner belied his murderous record. The pair also corresponded. But, when letters arrived at Benson's home, his mother, with whom he lived, picked up the mail and, seeing who the sender was, promptly destroyed the letters. That's the effect Peter Manuel had on good citizens – terror even from his written word.

Harry Benson, of course, went on to be one of the most famous photographers in the world. He captured iconic images of The Beatles in their early years and was there when his close friend Senator Robert Kennedy was assassinated. For Manuel, there was no such rosy future to look forward to.

For his last fortnight in his condemned cell, Peter Manuel said nothing, not a word, and just sat staring at the wall, listening to the radio. The night before his date with death, he broke his silence, looking up at one warden and promising, 'If you turn up the wireless, I'll go quietly.'

On 11 July 1958, Peter Manuel did indeed go peacefully, the tunes of the day still playing in his head. As he dropped to his death, he gave birth – the first serial killer to have been tagged as such was born.

WASTED

'NANCY BOY!' The rough male voice from across the street made heads turn. 'Aye, fucking you Ah'm speaking to.' The shouter stood and pointed at the slightly built middle-aged man in the hand-stitched suit and expensive-looking glasses. 'FUCKING SHIRT-TAIL LIFTER, so ye are. You and your wee boyfriend.'

'Come on, Robert,' said the man in the good suit, 'just ignore him.' He put his hand on the young man's shoulder to lead him away but he hadn't noticed his companion's blushes or the angry tears in his eyes.

'Leave me be,' replied the young man, violently shrugging the hand off his shoulder and walking off quickly. The older man trailed behind him. He wasn't going to let him go that easily – not a good-looking, vigorous boy like that.

Love story or exploitation? Who knows? But it was lust for sure and love in part. The part of the older man and that was the problem.

It was 1954 when seventeen-year-old Robert Scott met the older man, William Vincent – Bill to his friends. Robert had popped into a coffee bar in the east end of the city not far from his home in Forge Street in the Parkhead area of Glasgow. It was and is the area of Celtic FC's ground but football wasn't the sport Bill Vincent was after that day. Vincent was a homosexual with a taste for young lads. He didn't distinguish between whether they were adults or children. Why should he? All homosexuality was illegal then. As long as they were handsome and strongly built – just like Robert Scott was – they would do him nicely.

Vincent was skilled in the art of picking up. An affluent car merchant with a showroom in Park Terrace Lane – one of the wealthier parts of the city – he had the money to treat young men well. That usually did the trick.

The war was fading in folk's memories, especially the young folk. The austerity years were coming to an end and new styles, new music and new ambitions were flooding in from America. The trouble was that most working-class Scots didn't have the money to pay for these lifestyles – unless, that is, they met a wealthy friend. Bill Vincent was every ambitious young man's benefactor.

Robert Scott was good looking and ambitious. He wanted to be rich, famous, stylish and trendy. Not for him the drudgery of work in the heavy industries that Glasgow still depended on. Within days of returning from London after a failed trip to seek his fortune, Robert just happened to be in St Vincent Place in the city centre where he accidentally bumped into Bill Vincent – or so he'd later claim. Then, as now, St Vincent Place was renowned as a pick-up place for gay men looking for quick thrills.

Within a week, Bill Vincent was taking Robert out to swanky pubs and clubs – his treat, of course. Soon, Robert was staying over nights at Bill's house and in Bill's bed. Robert Scott denied he was gay, of course – most gay men did in the 1950s. He was Bill Vincent's regular companion and bedfellow but, in public, he would display no sign of affection or closeness. One night, in trendy Park Circus, at The Crocodile Club, a well-known haunt of homosexual men, Scott and Vincent were with male friends who, quite openly, started passing round pornographic pictures of men. Even though homosexuality was illegal, for many years certain pubs and clubs had catered for them. It was illegal but tolerated – most of the time.

Robert lost the plot big time about the porn pictures, tore some up, shouted, 'Disgusting fuckers!' and stormed out. It wasn't the pictures that upset Robert but the pictures being shown publicly. Someone might spot him and suss his sexual preference. He shouldn't be judged badly on this. The 1950s were an extremely difficult time for gay men – especially young gay men. Like many others, Robert Scott decided he couldn't take the public pressure and threat of discovery. It was just too much and he'd rather walk away. His chance was to come soon.

Robert was called up to do his National Service. In the post-war years, with peace still fitting uneasily on the world and smaller conflicts raging across the globe, all young men had to serve their two years if they were fit. Scott hadn't been looking forward to serving but now he embraced it with open arms.

Based at Longtown, Cumberland, in the north of England, Robert and Bill exchanged frequent, affectionate letters to start with but, gradually, Robert stopped replying, taking his big chance to break off the relationship with Bill Vincent. The older lover wasn't to be shaken off that easily and took to phoning Scott's commanding officer frequently and even visiting the camp. All to no avail.

Bill Vincent might well have been in what he took for love with young Robert Scott but he wasn't a celibate monk. All the while he was trying to woo Robert back, he was seducing young men. Once it had a disastrous outcome for him when one young lover beat him up and stole a load of valuables from his home. It was part of the risk of being a gay man in the 1950s. Yet Bill Vincent was no mere victim – far from it.

Like many others in the car trade, Vincent was a police informer. At times, he had even informed on so-called friends having gay orgies, just to settle some minor slight. On more than one occasion, he appeased the parents of underage boys he had seduced by giving them a load of money. Sleazy? Certainly but he was also used to having his own way – just as he planned to have his way again with Robert Scott.

After Scott was discharged from National Service at the beginning of 1958, he returned to Glasgow and that's when Vincent threatened to tell his parents about their sexual relationship unless he jumped back into his bed. This blackmail was too much. By April 1958, Robert Scott had had enough and decided to settle it once and for all.

The cop car headlights caught the young man standing beside the yellow car. Not just any car but a brand new Sunbeam Talbot Alpine in canary yellow – the absolute business in 1958. No matter how fancy the car was, it was still stuck in deep mud in a country road near Longtown in Cumberland.

'I have done a murder,' he had said down the phone to the police in sleepy Gretna. They must have thought it was a prank but, no, Robert Scott was deadly serious. When he opened the boot of the Sunbeam, there was a body in the foetal position, eyes staring blankly. Bill Vincent was dead.

Robert Scott confessed to the murder. In court, he would tell his tale though never saying that he was homosexual and always implying that he had never had an intimate relationship with his victim. A murder charge was one thing but to lose face was to lose everything.

According to Scott, on that night of 12 April 1958, he had gone round to Vincent's mews flat to settle matters once and for all. As soon as Vincent had let him in, he jumped at the young bloke, trying to kiss him. Scott told the court that he was repulsed and, just to show him he wasn't like that, he'd grabbed the older man by the throat. He was telling him this and shouting at him that their friendship was over when he'd looked at his face and realised Bill Vincent was dead.

Scott admitted to panicking and deciding to get rid of the body in some remote country area. He'd put Vincent's body in the boot of his own car and drive down south near his old service camp, a place he knew well, and dump it. His plan might have worked as well had the car not stuck in mud. It might still have worked had the guards at the camp gates been able to give him help. It might even have worked had the same guards not put him through on the phone to the police at Gretna. Even then, it might have worked if he hadn't found himself confessing to them down the line.

The jury at the High Court, Glasgow took less than an hour to find Scott guilty of murder. The judge blasted him as an immoral soul, clearly refusing to buy his tale of Vincent's unrequited lust, but then showed some mercy. Scott wouldn't hang – he would, however, be imprisoned for life.

Up in Perth Prison, Scott seemed to adjust well. He was even allowed to work with the plumber, a cushy and interesting job in prisoners' estimation. Then one day in November 1959 while the plumber had gone for a break, Robert Scott threw a rope round a rafter and hanged himself.

Why? He never said. A victim of his time, perhaps? A time of new hopes but old morals. A time of wider horizons though few freedoms. Was it simply because he was gay in the wrong era? What a waste.

1960 TO 1969

SWINGING

John F. Kennedy was elected president of the USA (1961), only to be assassinated (1963). The Civil Rights movement in America seemed to be winning at last then Martin Luther King fell to a bullet (1968).

The Russians put the first man in space (1961) and then the first woman in space (1963) – while, not to be outdone, the Americans put a man on the moon (1969).

The world hovered on the brink of crisis. The Berlin Wall was built (1961), the USA and USSR squared up over the Cuban Missile Crisis (1962), India and Pakistan went to war (1965) and the Troubles started in Ireland (1969).

The Beatles arrived big time (1963), *Coronation Street* hit the TV (1960), *Carry On* films were a hit at the movies and so were *Psycho*, *Spartacus* and *The Magnificent Seven*. Hippies celebrated peace and love at the Woodstock Festival (1969).

The first heart transplant operation was carried out in South Africa (1967) while in Britain NHS prescription charges were introduced.

The first police personal radios were introduced to Scotland in Pollok, Glasgow (1965) and Scottish cops start using Panda cars (1967). The first Regional Crime Squad was formed, drawing detectives from most forces to combat serious organised crime on a national basis.

BLOOD ON THE GRASS

'COME!' The man's voice rang assertive but warm through the night air. 'Come on, you stupid dog. I can't see you there in the dark.' But he could hear his best friend barking a short distance away – barking excitedly – and he knew that the Alsatian must have found something. 'You'd better not be hunting rabbits,' the man growled with no one to hear but himself. 'You know what happened the last time,' he said, remembering the blood on the dog's face and how pathetic he looked as he sat in the bath to get washed. 'No, you didn't like that one bit, did you, eh?' He walked cautiously through the park in the dark night, following the noise of the dog barking. 'There's nothing worse than a bath, eh?'

The kindly dog owner was right and wrong. His dog had found something and there are many things worse than baths – much worse – and he was about to stumble on one.

They call Glasgow the Dear Green Place and with some justification. But the history of some of the city's public parks is bloodier than can be imagined. Queen's Park in south Glasgow is just one example. In 1920, two men, James Fraser and James Rollins, were hanged for the savage murder of a man in the park. For years afterwards people avoided the place but, by 1960, the memories had faded and people returned to Queen's Park but with that came fatal consequences.

In the spring of 1960, the muggings started slowly but with a familiar pattern. Two young men would approach a man on his own, ask him for the time, a light for their cigarette or directions to some street and, as he offered help, they would jump him. At first, the physical damage to the victims was minimal though all were shocked and robbed. Many of the attacks were not formally reported to the police as grown men were often too embarrassed at having been overcome by fresh-faced boys. Also, Queen's Park was renowned as a place men could go in search of casual sex with men or women but mainly men.

Young male prostitutes loitered on the edge of the park looking for johns. Even if the victims of these muggings had genuinely been wanting to help out strangers, they were two young men, one clearly still a teenage child. What would people think? They kept quiet rather than run that risk.

Gradually, inevitably, knives, bottles and heavy sticks started being used by the muggers. The weapons were more frightening and so produced quicker results and more loot as terrified men emptied their pockets. But a weapon carried is a weapon used. A disaster was waiting to happen and that's where the dog came in.

Very late on the night of 6 April 1960, Thomas Brown took his Alsatian into Queen's Park for a last walk of the day, feeling safe in the company of such a large dog. And he was. Through the pitch dark he heard his pet bark excitedly, insistently. A rabbit or maybe a fox on the prowl? But the dog had found larger prey.

Brown could see his dog standing over a dark shape in the grass. A bag of rubbish? Not interesting enough for his dog. Maybe a litter of unwanted kittens or puppies? That would excite the dog and infuriate Thomas Brown. He couldn't stand how people were cruel to poor animals. Then he looked down at the bundle and gagged on acid bile.

The man lay face down on the grass, his skull smashed and very dead. The police were swiftly on the scene and in no doubt that forty-nine-year-old John Cremin had been murdered, battered to death, but there were no clues as to the identity of the culprits. Queen's Park is a vast place where it is possible to murder someone in broad daylight with no witnesses. So it appeared this was a hopeless case destined to gather dust on the 'Unsolved

Murder' pile – except that the robberies in the park did not stop. In the following four months, violent attacks continued unabated with knives and weapons always being used now.

Eventually the police received information that sixteen-year-old Crawford Mure might be involved in the robberies. They knew that lad. When they arrested and interrogated Mure, he denied any involvement but instead revealed that an associate of his, sixteen-year-old Douglas Denovan, had boasted to him that he knew the murderer of John Cremin. 'Just showing off' was how Mure described Denovan's revelation but the cops weren't going to take any chances. The man he named was almost a boy himself – nineteen-year-old Anthony Miller.

But Denovan wasn't in the clear. The few mugging victims who had come forward had all mentioned there being two attackers and their descriptions matched Miller and Denovan. They were both arrested and charged with Cremin's murder.

At their trial at Glasgow High Court on 14 November 1960, the older accused, Miller, gave no evidence but young Denovan sang like a bird, providing plenty of detailed information on a host of attacks the pair had carried out and describing how they escalated over time to more audacious, more violent escapades. All Tony Miller's idea, of course, or so Denovan claimed.

According to Denovan, their attack on Cremin followed a typical routine. He had approached Cremin, who they reckoned was a gay man cruising the park looking for a pick-up, while Miller stood a little distance off pretending to be drunk and feeling sick and sorry for himself. As Cremin chatted to the fresh-faced boy, Miller suddenly picked up a hefty plank of wood, ran at him and smashed him on the back of the skull. While John Cremin lay groaning and bleeding to death on the ground, the pair emptied his pockets.

Denovan's ploy of giving full evidence had worked. The jury found him guilty of culpable homicide and he was imprisoned. If he had been less informative at the trial he might well have been found guilty of murder and gone into the history books as the youngest man to be hanged in Scotland last century. As it was he was released just nine years later on 1 May 1969.

The silent Miller was not so fortunate and was found guilty of murder. In spite of an appeal, Anthony Miller was executed on 22 December 1960. He was one of the youngest people to have been executed in Scotland in the twentieth century. As it was, he was the last man ever to be hanged in Barlinnie Prison, Glasgow.

The question is, should he have swung alone?

TOO GOOD A GIRL

'LINDA!' The shouts rang out through the small village.

'LINDA!' Almost everyone in the place had volunteered to search.

'LINDA!' In the night, one call went from one end of the village to another. Surely she'd hear them?

'LINDA!' There was no answer. Where could she be?

Closer than they thought.

The sleepy, gentle village of Biggar was ideal for raising children. Linda Peacock was fifteen years old and still charmed by what the area had to offer – especially horses – unlike some other teenagers who'd turned rebellious and promiscuous in those heady 1967 days. Not her.

But, on the evening of 6 August, she had gone out to meet some girlfriends as she often did, just to walk around, chat and laugh – all innocent teenage behaviour. That's all that Linda did. Yet she hadn't returned. That wasn't Linda. She never did things like that. She was a good girl.

Her parents were frantic with worry and went to the police. With some of the other local lassies known to be a bit wild, the cops would have gone straight to the local spots where lovers met in secret. But not Linda. They knew too she was a good girl.

Parents, police and neighbours searched all night. Early on 7 August, in the graveyard of St Mary's Church, a lonely bobby hunting his beat found her under a large, thick bush, her body drizzled with dew. Dead.

Like any small community, Biggar had had its scandals, its characters, its people falling from grace. But the murder of an innocent fifteen-year-old lassie? Not on their territory would the killer walk free.

Immediately, it seemed as if every soul in the wider area had volunteered to help search for the killer. The cop in charge was Detective Chief Superintendent William Muncie, top brass of Lanarkshire CID. The killer wasn't going to walk free on Muncie's shift either.

The forensic bods soon made their awful report. Linda had been bashed on the head with some heavy implement and then strangled from behind – the burn marks of some rope were black on her white neck. Her clothes were undone and unzipped and her body exposed but she hadn't had sex – willingly or unwillingly – ever.

Below her body, the earth was disturbed and her fingernails were broken and bloody. Wee Linda had struggled and fought every inch of the way. A good girl.

DCS Muncie was on the case and that meant he'd call in whoever could help. The Regional Crime Squad from Glasgow, more accustomed to murder hunts, was called in and every force in the Central Belt willingly gave troops.

The horror of Linda Peacock's murder had grabbed the sympathy of the cops as much as it had the public. It was just, well – she was a good girl.

As the hunt went on for the killer, Linda Peacock was buried in the same graveyard where she'd been murdered. One of the coffin carriers that day was DCS Muncie. This was now personal.

The forensic team had spotted something they reckoned would be top evidence – a deep bite mark on her right breast. They called in Dr Warren Harvey, an expert in forensic odontology from Glasgow University. His view was that the bite was unique, particularly because both canine teeth had holes or pits in them. They started examining the teeth of men all over the area.

The *Daily Record* was on the case and sent someone up in a plane to take detailed aerial photographs. The photos were then

passed to the cops. Everyone wanted to help. From one of these pictures, a detective noticed that the Loaningdale Approved School was within very easy walking distance of the crime scene. Not by road but as the crow flies. The school was a residential unit for male teenagers, still legally children, who were sent there by the authorities for offending. Many residents had a background of violence but it was mainly in gang fights, not targeting women or teenage girls – if that had been the case, they would have been dispatched elsewhere and not to Loaningdale.

Yet, as the most experienced cops knew, a previous pattern of similar violence was often not present in such murders. Sex killers have to start somewhere. What they were more hopeful of was an ID – using that bite mark. The teeth of all the Loaningdale boys were checked. Everyone aside from three of them were quickly eliminated. Then it was down to one – seventeen-year-old Gordon Hay.

Hay, from Aberdeen, was a thief with no record of violence or having any problem with females. There was no pattern in his previous behaviour suggesting he was an extreme risk to anyone. But the forensic bods were certain that bite mark was unique and it belonged to Gordon Hay.

Hay denied murder and had a very strong alibi. On that night, he was in bed in his dorm at school. While Loaningdale wasn't a locked secure unit, it was staffed at all times. As far as the school's records were concerned that was exactly where Gordon Hay was that night – in his bed. The cops realised this was a good alibi but all hope wasn't lost. They were going to get help from an unexpected quarter.

Loaningdale School was full of career criminals of the future – young men who had already taken the stance that they didn't cooperate with the cops – but, like their senior counterparts in the criminal world, they didn't like sex killers. So they talked. Many boys slipped out of the school at night, they said, to meet local girls who would often wait in the wooded grounds giving owl hoots as signals to draw their attention. Gordon Hay was one of

those boys. Moreover, according to three other Loaningdale boys, he had slipped out of school the night Linda was killed.

That was enough for the DCS Muncie. Gordon Hay was charged with Linda Peacock's murder.

At his trial on 26 February 1968 at the High Court, Edinburgh, this evidence was spelled out in full. Some local people had also spotted the couple near to the murder spot and one person had heard a girl's scream but had done nothing, thinking it was kids in high spirits.

The Crown painted a picture of Hay having slipped out of the school, meeting Linda and trying to have sex with her. When the young girl refused, he lost his temper, battered her head in with a boat hook he'd stolen from another boy and strangled her with a cord. The cops had part of the cord and they'd found blood on Hay's clothes but they needed more. It all came down to that bite mark.

The defence lawyers knew this and tried to have the presiding judge, Lord Grant, disallow the evidence, claiming not that it was unscientific or wrong but that the warrant used to force Hay to cooperate in having impressions made of his teeth wasn't legal. If they'd won the debate, a killer could have walked free. They lost and the evidence was heard.

In the time-honoured way of courts, expert witnesses argued for both sides. Dr Keith Simpson, pathologist for the Home Office – the top man, in other words – was called as an outside expert. Simpson agreed that the bite was unique. So did the jury. Gordon Hay was found guilty of murder and sent to jail at Her Majesty's pleasure – the first person in the UK to be found guilty of murder on the basis of forensic dentistry.

That wasn't the end of the issue. The trial had revealed to the public that troubled teenagers could walk out of an institution that was meant to have them under control at will. If it could happen with Loaningdale in Biggar, it could happen with any of the dozen similar schools throughout Scotland.

Demands were voiced to make all such schools more secure and to keep the young offenders – even if they were legally children – under lock and key.

The management of Loaningdale explained that Gordon Hay had no previous record of violence, never mind extreme violence to women. No one could have predicted that Hay would turn killer. That didn't reassure local Biggar people even after the national outcry had calmed down.

It wasn't good enough that the innocents of their community should be put at any risk. That dangerous young men should be allowed to wander almost freely among them. That one night another girl could be brutally killed. A girl like Linda Peacock. A good girl.

Max and Sheila Garvie are seen here enjoying the high life in their plane but Max needed something more exciting than flying in his life.

At first, attractive Sheila wanted nothing to do with the sessions of wife-swapping and group sex that Max set up but soon she was a willing participant.

The Garvies' home which locals dubbed 'Kinky Cottage'. Max had a triangle of thick bushes planted to screen the alfresco orgies that went on there from prying eyes.

Here, Max Garvie is on an evening out with his lover, cop's wife Trudi Birse. Sheila also took a lover and what started out as some playful sexual experimentation ended in murder. ('Swinging and Killing')

James Griffiths had a morbid fear of going to jail so, when, in 1969, the cops went to question him about the murder of an elderly woman in Ayr, it was a dead cert he wasn't going to surrender without a struggle.

Daily Record

A policeman: A boy: 2 women: 9 men

13 SHOT IN CITY STREETS

105 minutes of terror, then the wanted man is carried away dead

FULL STORY—BACK PAGE • MORE PICTURES—PAGES 13, 14, 15

Griffiths, armed with two guns, vainly tried to shoot his way out of trouble. Here, he can be seen at the window of a house in Kay Street, in Springburn, where he had holed up.

Police shot Griffiths through the letterbox of the Kay Street flat and he died before the ambulance arrived. He was given a pauper's burial in Glasgow's Linn Cemetery.

Police believed Griffiths's accomplice in the Ayr murder was this man – Paddy Meehan. With Griffiths dead, Meehan had no alibi and he spent seven years in jail, trying to prove his innocence.
('A Murderous Misunderstanding')

This aerial view shows the woods not far from the Keenans' home where, in 1969, William Townsley, a member of a travelling family who were passing through the area, found a woman's torso. ('The Gypsies' Gift')

Lanark couple James and Elizabeth Keenan. James reported his wife missing around the same time as the police found severed body parts at several different locations in Scotland. Coincidence or something more sinister?

In the late 1960s, the murders of three women who had all been out for an evening's dancing had the folk of Glasgow terrified. The major suspect was a man named John who quoted from the Bible. This is an artist's impression of 'Bible John' – the man who had Glasgow's citizens scared to leave their homes at night.

Detective Superintendent Joe Beattie was in charge of the massive hunt for Bible John. He has never been found and theories about whether or not the three women died at the hands of just one man still abound today – as do the speculations about Bible John's whereabouts. ('Streets of Fear')

In 1966, the actions of Aberdeen man Adam Sherriffs left the police and everyone who knew him absolutely stumped. Seemingly happily married and with a little daughter he adored, he inexplicably murdered his family before killing himself.
('No Rhyme, No Reason')

Matthew Lygate saw himself as a Scottish Che Guevara. In the early 1970s, he and some colleagues from the Workers' Party of Scotland took to armed robbery – 'liberating the spoils of capitalism', they called it – to fund their revolution . . . and some extravagant living.
('Marx, Mao and Mugs')

In 1974, James Crosbie, pictured here on the right during a jaunt to Las Vegas, became Scotland's most wanted man. A successful businessman who enjoyed the good life, Crosbie seems to have taken to armed bank robbery in order to inject some excitement and danger into his world.
('The Recidivist')

Eighteen-year-old Helga Konrad left her home in Germany and eloped with Dutchman Ernest Dumoulin. They married in Edinburgh in October 1972 and, a few hours later, he pushed her off Salisbury Crags to her death. The very next day, he tried to cash in the massive life insurance policy he'd recently taken out on her. Hard to say which of the two was the more naive.
('No Luck, No Love')

One person who certainly wasn't naive is this man – Walter Norval. He ran his operations just as a military general would. Money from bank robberies, payroll heists and other scams poured in but it was just a matter of time before the cops caught up with him. ('Walter's Army')

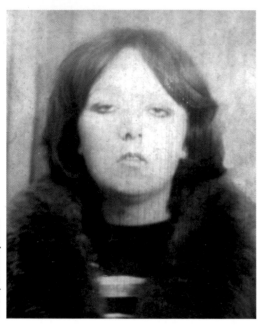

Christine Eadie (left) and Helen Scott were last seen alive in the company of two men they'd just met in Edinburgh's World's End pub in 1977. Their badly beaten bodies were found a few miles apart in East Lothian the following day.

Billboards asking for people to come forward with any information they might have about the two young women are put up on the corner of capital's High Street, opposite The World's End.

Police inquiries into what became known as 'The World's End Murders' were coordinated from this incident room but the case wasn't solved at the time. Would advances in forensic detection ever bring justice for Christine and Helen? ('No Hiding Place?')

Dr Brenda Page, a lecturer at the University of Aberdeen in the mid 1970s, seemed to have a great life. Why, then, was she found murdered in her city-centre flat? Might it have something to do with the escort work she did in her spare time? ('Doctor Sweet, Doctor Secret')

When Thomas McCulloch shot a chef in the face because his bread roll didn't have enough butter on it, there was only one place he could be sent – the State Hospital, Carstairs.

In Carstairs, McCulloch met Robert Mone who was serving time for the brutal murder of a schoolteacher. The result was a pairing straight from hell. For months, they planned their escape and, when the appointed day came, it brought bloody mayhem.

This is Christopher 'Sony' Mone, Robert Mone's father. A detested character, he would boast about his son's evildoings. He then committed a horrendous crime of his own – one that even outdid Robert's in terms of its barbarity. ('The Stuff of Nightmares')

Carol X was gang raped and slashed about the face and legs. The Crown decided Carol X's life as a prostitute made her an unreliable witness and refused to take her case to trial so she brought a private prosecution against the three vile men who'd raped and disfigured her. ('Ill Repute?')

To most folk, David and Veronica Little seemed a normal happy couple but, at their home in Dumfries, he had subjected her to terrible physical and sexual abuse, even flaunting his affair with Elaine Haggarty, the couple's teenage babysitter, under her nose.

Veronica Little is supported by police after being found guilty of procuring the murder of her husband. In 1982, she enlisted the help of Elaine Haggarty and Elaine's friend, William McKenzie, to kill the man who'd tormented her for years.

William McKenzie fired five bullets into David Little before burying him in a shallow grave in a field outside Dumfries. Veronica paid him just £120 to murder her husband. ('Behind Closed Doors')

LETHAL LUST IN A COLD CLIMATE

The stench hung heavy in the cold air. Women in long, thick aprons, their hair tied back to stay out of the mess, their breath gentle puffs of cloud in the freezing air, bent over large trestles of fish, slicing and gutting, slicing and gutting. It was a strange place for love and lust to flourish.

It was Christmas time 1962 and Margaret Guyan had just started working in John R. Stephen Fish Curers in Aberdeen. It was hard, smelly work but that didn't stop that something special in Margaret shining through. One young man noticed.

In many ways the city of Aberdeen is a small village. It didn't take long for twenty-year-old Henry Burnett to find out that Margaret Guyan was married with two children. In the early 1960s, before the notion of free love and sex caught on, other young men have may run a mile but not the beguiled Burnett. He was hooked on that handsome smile of hers – dangerously hooked.

Besides, the gossip mill had also whispered that the woman had a troubled marriage. Five years earlier, in 1957, Margaret had married Thomas Guyan and settled into their home in Jackson Terrace in the city. Their first child, Charles, was born in September 1958 and, to the outside world, all was well with the couple when their second child, Keith, was born early in 1961. But children don't always equate with happiness.

The couple were far from happy and had some miserable secrets. Keith was not Thomas Guyan's son but the result of a fling

Margaret had had. In spite of this, Thomas wanted their relationship to continue, promising to bring up the boy as his own – a
good man with a kind heart.

Although she continued to live with her husband, Margaret
wasn't so sure that the relationship was for her and, by the
autumn of 1962, she had consulted a solicitor about divorce – still
a radical step for a working-class woman in the early 1960s. That
was when she started work in the fish curers where she met young
Henry Burnett. Love blossomed at the back of the curing sheds –
well, lust at least. But both Henry and Margaret wanted more – or
so they thought.

By May 1963, Margaret and her son Keith had moved in with
Burnett at Skene Terrace. Almost immediately things started to go
sour. Besotted Burnett's immaturity and inexperience began to
show big time. He was madly jealous – so jealous, he was
convinced that Margaret would leave him any minute and took to
locking her in their home while he was out. For a free-spirited
woman like Margaret Guyan life must have been hell.

Only a few weeks after leaving her husband Thomas, she met
him by chance on the street. They stopped and talked and her man
made it clear that he wanted her back. No recriminations, no rows
– all he wanted was her. Margaret Guyan agreed on the spot to
return to the marital home. There was just one problem, her
two-year-old son, Keith, was back at Skene Terrace with Henry
Burnett who was bound to create a scene, maybe worse. Margaret
didn't want to face the young man alone and trouble between the
men had to be avoided so her grandmother, Georgina Cattanagh,
accompanied her. Margaret hoped that the elderly lady would be
a calming influence – some hope.

Arriving at Skene Terrace, the women stood at the threshold as
Margaret Guyan explained the situation. Burnett wasn't having
any of it. He pleaded and roared, ordering Margaret Guyan to stay
with him, but it was all to no avail. So he grabbed Margaret, drew
a knife, held the blade at her throat and pulled her into the house,
slamming the door shut.

Georgina Cattanagh banged on the locked front door with all the strength she could muster, calling out for Burnett to be reasonable. For some unspoken reason, perhaps fear, Burnett soon released Margaret, unbolted the door, threw her on to the pavement and took to his heels off down the street.

The terrified women grabbed young Keith from the house and headed for home fast. Safely there, they told Thomas Guyan the full story. Horrific as the experience had been, they all agreed that that was now the end of it. Young Henry Burnett might be madly possessive but he didn't have the bottle to tackle a man, Thomas Guyan.

Later that evening on 31 May, a knock sounded at the front door. Without a second thought, grandmother Georgina Cattanagh went to see who was there. Back in the kitchen, Margaret and Thomas Guyan heard the old woman scream, 'NAW, NAW! Ye cannae come in here!'

Rushing to her aid, Thomas Guyan halted abruptly at the kitchen door as he found himself staring down the barrel of a shotgun. With no warning, no threat, Henry Burnett shot Guyan at point-blank range in the face, sending shards of his skull, grey matter from his brain and blood across the room. Thomas Guyan fell dying.

Shouting and screaming at Margaret, Burnett didn't hesitate as he yanked her by one arm, pulling her towards the street, the shotgun still in his other mitt. Crazily waving the gun at anyone who appeared, Burnett dragged Margaret into nearby Seaforth Road. There he stole a car and sped off along the coast road towards Peterhead.

Though it was far from crime-free, gun incidents were rare in 1960s' Aberdeen and the police had little experience of dealing with such incidents. But what could have turned into a bloody shoot-out ended with a whimper. Within half an hour, police caught up with Burnett, who immediately and peacefully surrendered.

At the High Court in Aberdeen on 23 July 1963, it emerged that, after the knife incident with Margaret, Burnett had hurried to his brother's house at nearby Bridge of Don and taken his shotgun. Guns were easily available in such predominantly rural areas at that time, with licences being freely granted on application for such things as the control of vermin. But too often the rats weren't on the sharp end of the guns.

It's certain that Burnett would have pled a defence of crime of passion if it had been allowed under Scots Law. Instead he claimed a double-headed defence of being totally insane at the time or at least of diminished responsibility. The jury believed none of it and, after twenty-five minutes, they found him guilty of murder. Lord Justice Wheatley donned the black cap and sentenced Henry Burnett to be hanged.

It was a verdict that shocked none of the public. What was shocking was that there were those who begged for the life of the young killer. The families of both the accused and the victim campaigned for clemency. It was one of those rare events that made even good, caring people feel humbled by the forgiveness shown. Thomas Guyan was a good loving man, after all, who'd been killed for loving a woman. A wish for revenge by his family would have been understandable. Instead they pled for clemency but failed.

Less than a year after he had met Margaret Guyan, on 15 August 1963, twenty-one-year-old Henry Burnett was hanged. He was the only man to be hanged in Aberdeen in the twentieth century and the last man ever to be hanged in Scotland.

While even his victim's family wept on the day of the hanging, in a short time one man was to be grateful of Burnett's distinction as the last person to be hanged in Scotland – very grateful indeed.

A DEADLY CONCEIT

It was decent pub with plush red carpets and thick wallpaper that felt like velvet – and there were no drunks or rowdy singers. You could even get ice with your drink – unusual in 1960s' Glasgow. The group of men in their suits sitting quietly fitted in well. They seemed like the kind of respectable customers the manager wanted to encourage – if he had only known what they were plotting.

'Let's rob a bank.'

At first, his mates had all laughed, assuming he was joking – except they were wrong, as wrong as could be. He was serious – deadly serious. The ideas man was Howard Wilson. Tall, smartly dressed, his hair neatly cut, bright and articulate, he was the dominant character in a small group of business pals. He was also an ex-cop – some said a bitter ex-cop who was angry at the world.

Wilson had expected to be promoted rapidly through the ranks. When that didn't happen, he resigned even though he was doing well. He just wanted more and he wanted it faster. Till then, the worst his associates would say about him was that he was arrogant or conceited and a few of them didn't trust him one bit. They were spot on.

Wilson wasn't finished though. He had faith in his own abilities, this time as a businessman – a bit too much faith as it turned out for his two greengrocer shops in Glasgow were losing money fast.

Now, in 1969, Wilson was broke and desperate – desperate enough to rob a bank. He was in good company. His pals – Ian

Donaldson and John Sim – were an ex-cop and ex-prison warder and both of them were also struggling in civilian life.

In that posh pub in Shawlands in Glasgow, when Wilson was proposing a bank job, they had sat open-mouthed.

'You joking, Howard? Fuck, you're no', are you?' said one.

'Would I joke about something like that?' Wilson replied po-faced, taking himself, as usual, very seriously indeed. 'Well, would I?'

They wouldn't admit it but the other two were, if not frightened, certainly intimidated by Wilson. But he was bright, they knew that.

'We've all met robbers and hard men, eh?' He was referring to their previous careers and, of course, he was right. 'Are we not smarter than they are?'

The two men thought for a second till one asked, 'Aye, of course, but how would we go about it?'

'Would this do for a start?' Wilson slyly shifted his coat which was lying on a chair beside him so that his friends and only his friends could see it – a pistol. The bank job was on. All were members of Bearsden Shooting Club and he had quite legally bought a Russian Vostok .22 pistol from the club president – the very type of move that was to be banned after the massacre of Dunblane. After recruiting a young man, Archibald McGeachie, as the getaway driver, they were all set.

One day in July 1969, three smart businessmen walked into the British Linen Bank in Williamwood. No one suspected a thing till they pulled a gun and squirted ammonia in the staff's eyes. Three minutes later, Wilson and his crew were driving away fast, £20,876 richer – a fair sum in those days.

The men weren't stupid. They had a quiet celebratory drink, split the proceeds and got on with life as usual – there would be no new cars, fancy holidays or splashing the cash in pubs. Ex-cop Wilson knew that was a certain way to get nabbed. It was all very sensible and trouble-free but there was one problem – all three had businesses running in the red and, by Christmas, they were broke again. They had crossed the line once so why not cross it again and rob another bank? All agreed apart, that is, from young McGeachie who declined the job. Exactly why we don't know and we'll never know because, on 23 December 1969, he disappeared from his home and was never seen again. Was he seen as a weak link by the gang? One who had to be shut up?

At the time, the huge Kingston Bridge spanning the River Clyde was being built. Word on the street then and now was that young McGeachie was dumped in one of the massive concrete stanchions that support the bridge. Only one of the team was capable of that – Howard Wilson.

On 30 December 1969, Wilson's team hit the Clydesdale Bank, Renfrew. This time they got off with £14,212 and a large metal box full of coins. For the time, it was a fair haul and it was enough to sort out their small failing shops.

Back at a flat Wilson had at 51 Allison Street, Govanhill, they unloaded the car. The cash was in suitcases and the metal box was in a cardboard box so passers-by wouldn't suspect anything. However, unbeknown to them, they were being watched by no ordinary citizen. Across the way in a shop, Inspector Andrew Hyslop had spotted Wilson. Hyslop knew Wilson from his time in the cops – knew him and never trusted him. Hyslop hadn't yet heard about the robbery – after all, it had only happened twenty minutes before and police communications back then weren't as slick then as they are now. So Inspector Hyslop was working entirely on his cop's sixth sense. His curiosity about what the men were unloading had been aroused and he decided to look closer.

First Hyslop radioed his colleagues to ask them to meet him at the flat and then he went up the close. At the flat door, Howard Wilson greeted him in a friendly way, inviting him in and offering him a drink. It was close to Hogmanay after all.

Wilson gave Hyslop permission to look in one of the cases. As the cop opened it and discovered it packed with bank notes, Wilson pulled a gun, stuck it in the cop's face and pulled the trigger – it jammed. He fired again and sent a bullet crashing into Hyslop's skull, dumping him on the floor alive but paralysed.

Almost instantly, Constables Sellars, McKenzie and Barnett arrived at the scene and, hearing the shot, ran into the room. A trained police marksman, Wilson swiftly shot McKenzie and Barnett in the head. Sellars narrowly escaped and took refuge in the bathroom.

McKenzie was still alive. Coldly, Wilson stooped over him, placed the gun against his forehead and fired – a fatal shot.

With one bullet left, Wilson turned and, noticing that Hyslop was still alive, bent over and placed the barrel of his gun on the paralysed cop's head. Just then a DC Campbell barged into the room, sussed the score immediately and dived on Wilson. The gun went off but the last bullet crashed into the ceiling. Battle over.

McKenzie was dead. Young Barnett died soon after from the bullet lodged in his brain. Hyslop survived but only through good luck and would spend the rest of his days in pain with bullet fragments remaining in his skull ruining his health till the day he died.

At his trial in 1970, Wilson's accomplices in the bank robberies, Sim and Donaldson, who had tried to stop the shooting, were found guilty only of the robberies and sentenced to twelve years each. With his two team members and cops Hyslop and Campbell giving evidence against him, Wilson had no choice but to accept full responsibility for the murders and he became Scotland's only cop-turned-cop-killer in written history.

Sentenced to twenty-five years inside, Wilson was in trouble. Cons hate cops – even cop-killing ex-cops. These days, Wilson would have been housed in a protective unit along with the child abusers and the informants but, back in the 1960s, there were no such units. He was simply thrown into the lions' den.

Once again Howard Wilson's arrogance got him through. If the other inmates were going to gang up on him and shove a jail-made blade through his ribs because they suspected he was still one of the uniformed enemy, there was only one thing for him to do – prove he hated the system even more than they did. And he did – hate it and proved it. No pretence was required. Howard Wilson truly despised anyone telling him what to do. It was the likely reason he suddenly started blasting away that fateful day – no cop was going to take him in, even if they did catch him with the loot. Now no prison screw was going to control him – not one.

From the off, he fought the system in riots and attacks, spending weeks in solitary only to come out batting again. He was so difficult to manage, he ended up at Porterfield Prison, Inverness, in the cages that were designed to hold a handful of men that mainstream prison simply couldn't cope with. One of Wilson's fellow lags at Porterfield was convicted murderer and Glasgow gangster, Jimmy Boyle. Ironically, former cop Wilson had once staked out Boyle.

After some years, Wilson settled down in jail and, like many of his rebellious contemporaries, took to creative work – in his case, writing. His novel, *Angels of Death,* was a best-seller and won the Koestler Award for creative writing in prisons. At last he'd found the praise that he'd craved all his life – found it behind bars.

After thirty-three years in jail, Howard Wilson was released and slipped quietly into obscurity. Alone with his thoughts now, does he recall the time after he was sentenced? When thousands of women and kids – policemen's families from all over Scotland – demonstrated in George Square, Glasgow calling for the return of the death penalty for killing cops, which had been abolished only two weeks before the murders.

'Wilson must hang,' the women and kids called out. So horrified were the politicians by his crimes that they considered giving in to the demands. But it was not to be. If the government wouldn't hang Howard Wilson, who would they hang? No one. With Wilson's conviction, capital punishment truly ended.

But the killing? That went on.

SWINGING AND KILLING

'Do you, Maxwell Garvie, take this woman to be your lawful wedded wife?' There was never any doubt in the answer, no suspicion of last-minute changes of mind. She was young, beautiful and bright and he was going to have her as his wife. But would it all end it tears?

Sheila Watson was beautiful and bright, for sure. When handsome, debonair and wealthy Max Garvie courted her, no one in the small north-east Scotland community was surprised. Married in 1955, they seemed destined to prosper and last. But would they?

Max and Sheila Garvie settled into his family's luxury farm at Fordoun, Kincardineshire, and had two daughters and a son in the first few years of their marriage. Still only in their late twenties, they seemed to have everything – money, healthy children, a loving relationship – then it all went sour.

It was the 1960s and times were changing. Sex, drugs and rock'n'roll were all the rage for those who could afford them – and the Garvies could.

Max had been getting bored for some time. Described as a farmer, he was more of a manager with other people doing the work and him reaping substantial profits. First fast cars filled his time and then he got a private aeroplane. But he was still bored. Danger was in the air but no one smelled it. Max took to drinking heavily and downing handfuls of tranquillisers, often while flying his private plane in hand-free daredevil stunts over the North

Sea. For a while, such risks gave him the buzz he craved but that too wore off soon. It was his other, more intimate, tastes that started the rot – sex.

Max organised for a triangle of trees and thick bushes to be planted near their home. No one thought anything of it. Farmers did that type of thing to provide shelter against the north-east's strong elements. His shelter wasn't for crops, though – it was for naked people.

A nudist colony is what Max built. At first, only friends were invited and just in the summer months – the only time of year anyone would dare strip off in that cold corner of Scotland. It was just some well-to-do folks having a laugh. These were not times for the shy or self-conscious.

Sex orgies followed soon after. To start with, they involved close friends in small groups and, at first, Sheila refused point blank to participate. It led to rows between her and Max who called her a fuddy-duddy and square and old-fashioned. What had she to lose? She might like it. Max was persuasive. Soon Sheila was into the sex orgies and as enthusiastic as her husband.

The Garvies were flamboyant – Max had his plane and his cars and Sheila dressed in the best of fashion, her short skirts and tight tops from Carnaby Street showing her fine figure to advantage. Even in that area of large estates and farms, the neighbours were beginning to notice what the Garvies and their pals were up to. The sober-minded, conservative and often Presbyterian Doric-speaking villagers dubbed the Garvies' home 'Kinky Cottage'. If only they'd known the half of it.

Max Garvie was slowly losing the plot. The sex orgies had broken one taboo but now he had to move on to new challenges. What about men?

Garvie was an office-bearer in the SNP. At SNP meetings, he met a handsome young man, twenty-year-old Brian Tevendale. Max had sex with Tevendale but wanted more than that – much more.

Tevendale was frequently invited to the Garvies' home. Max would leave the young man alone with Sheila and later demand to know from his wife if the two had had sex. Sheila was upset at the very thought. The orgies with friends were something she and Max did together. For her to have sex with another man on her own was too much like an infidelity. Sheila wasn't that type – not then.

Then, one night in 1967, Tevendale was staying over at the Garvies' yet again and, in the early hours, his bedroom door was suddenly opened and a naked, shivering Sheila was shoved into the room by her husband. At last, he had broken his wife's will. She didn't leave till the morning.

Now the games took a new turn with Max and Brian tossing a coin some nights to see who would sleep with Sheila. But Max Garvie didn't play fair – ever. When he lost the toss, he insisted the three go to bed together.

Then Max started an affair with Tevendale's sister, Trudi Birse. A policeman's wife, Trudi joined in four-in-a-bed romps with the Garvies and her own brother. Trudi's husband even joined in though Max thoughtfully arranged another female partner for him. Never mind swinging London – Kinky Cottage was where it was all happening.

Max had a low boredom threshold and soon tired of Trudi Birse even though she was a good-looking woman and a willing participant in his games. He decided that he and Sheila should dump their sexual playmates and find new ones. Trudi was up for it but Sheila refused – for good reasons.

To his horror, Max realised that Sheila and young Brian Tevendale had fallen for each other. Sheila might have gone along with his ideas of the Swinging Sixties but she wasn't really cut out for it. At heart, Sheila was an old-fashioned dame who fell in love. Used to always getting his own way, Max tried to come between them. The man who had forced them together now tried to prise them apart – a big mistake.

On the morning of 15 May 1968, Sheila Garvie wakened in bed to find her husband gone – or so she said. Reporting the matter to the police, Sheila said that nothing unusual had happened the night before. Max Garvie was posted as a missing person but it was a puzzle to the local cops. None of Max's cars was missing and nor was his private plane. Even his wardrobe was still full of his clothes. A man like Max Garvie wouldn't just walk out of his life. He'd travel in style and comfort.

In August, for reasons best known to her, Sheila shared some suspicions with her mother, Edith Watson, that her lover, Tevendale, had killed her husband. Law-abiding Mrs Watson went straight to the cops.

While Sheila was busy denying to the cops that there was any significance in her comments, bad news came in. They'd found a body.

On 17 August 1968, Max Garvie's putrefied corpse was found in the drains of Laurieston Castle, St Cyrus – Tevendale's home village. Immediately, Sheila Garvie, Brian Tevendale and one of his friends, twenty-year-old Alan Peters, were charged with Max's murder.

Sordid – that was how judges, lawyers and the media described the events leading to the trial at Aberdeen High Court on 19 November 1968. As the sexual shenanigans unfolded, Sheila Garvie and Brian Tevendale blamed each other. Sheila claimed she woke in the middle of the night to discover Tevendale and Peters had murdered Max. Tevendale said that the killing was Sheila's idea and he had gone along with it out of infatuation. The prosecution claimed that Sheila and Brian had coldly plotted the murder.

According to the Crown, Sheila persuaded Tevendale to murder Max so they could be free to pursue their relationship. On the night in question, Sheila went to bed with Max and had sex with him. In the early hours, she slipped out of bed, let Tevendale and Alan Peters into the house, handing them a .22 rifle belonging to Max.

With Sheila watching from the bedroom doorway, Tevendale smashed Max's skull with the rifle butt as he slept. Then, placing a pillow over the man's face, he shot him once in the head.

The three then went downstairs and, their nerves shattered, quickly drank a whole bottle of whisky. The two men wrapped Max's corpse in a blanket, dumped him in the boot of Peters' car and took him to what they thought would be his last resting place in the deep drains of Laurieston Castle.

It was a complex and distasteful case. The media had a field day feeding the public's desire for more and more titillating details. Church groups spoke out about sinning leading to destruction. Preachers hit the streets ranting about the devil's music being the root of all this evil.

Back in the High Court, Aberdeen, the jury found the case against Alan Peters not proven and acquitted him. Brian Tevendale was unanimously found guilty of murder. Sheila Garvie was also found guilty of murder but only by a narrow majority verdict. She almost slipped away from court an innocent woman but, under Scots Law, a simple majority of one will do.

A short time before, the pair would undoubtedly have been hanged for their crime. But capital punishment had been abolished and they were sentenced to life.

A few months after the end of the trial, from Gateside Prison in Greenock, Sheila wrote to Tevendale in Perth Prison, saying, 'I have decided to have nothing more to do with you ever again.' The great passion that had led them to cold murder had died. Sheila and Tevendale were never to meet again.

Both were both released in 1978. Tevendale married and became the landlord of a pub in Perthshire till he died suddenly in 2003.

An insurance company confirmed that, on Max's death, Sheila had stood to gain £55,000 on one policy alone. There were other policies too, as well as the farm, investments and capital. Sheila Garvie went on to marry again twice – she divorced the first time and then was widowed. Always refusing to talk of the murder, she has led a steady, respectable existence, running a B&B in the small coastal village of Stonehaven.

Her days are certainly quieter than her swinging years as mistress of Kinky Cottage. We have to wonder if she misses them.

A MURDEROUS
MISUNDERSTANDING

'This is going to be a bad one,' said one policeman to the other as they drove towards their job.

'Why? We're only needing some information. What is it to him?'

'Have you never dealt with him before, then?'

'Nuh.'

'Well, take it from me – he's a strange one.'

'So . . .'

'Dangerous. Bloody lethal.'

He wasn't wrong.

In the 1960s, Glasgow's streets had never been more violent. Razor gangs ruled with teams like the Blackhill Toi, Drummy, Cumbie and Tongs all comprised of hundreds of members – and they were all tooled-up and ready for warfare for any trivial reason.

The city's notoriety was worldwide. So much so that one of the world's top entertainers of the time, Frankie Vaughan, tried to help. Top marks for caring yet it did no good.

Loan sharks, like Jimmy Boyle, had graduated from the gangs and ruled their patches with terror. Boyle was charged with murder on two occasions but witnesses were slashed and bombs were thrown at the cops and the courts – he walked free both times. However, on a third murder charge, Boyle had run out of luck. As he went to jail for life, his lawyer was found guilty of intimidating witnesses and was sent to the pokey for eight years. Hard times.

For all that blood and gore, early on the morning of 15 July 1969, the city was about to explode in the most shocking episode yet. Tragically, it started with a mistake – a misunderstanding.

James Griffiths was an accident waiting to happen. Brought up in Rochdale, he was into crime from an early age, graduating to armed robbery and safe blowing by the age of thirteen.

Women loved dark-haired, sallow-skinned Griffiths but he never earned the respect of his fellow cons. He'd boast to them of his antics and they'd turn away. He'd swear to them that, one day, he'd use a gun on the cops and they sneered. If only they'd known.

In the high security of Parkhurst Prison on the Isle of Wight, Griffiths shared a cell with two Scots. One was Archibald Hall, The Demon Butler, who'd go on to be a serial killer in England. And then there was Paddy Meehan, a top safecracker and pal of Arthur 'The Godfather' Thompson.

Meehan was a bit dour and didn't make friends easily. Yet he must've been impressed when Griffiths escaped from Parkhurst and actually got off the island. Damn few folk had managed that and, even more impressively, Griffiths had had the audacity to spend the ferry crossing chatting to a prison warder and his wife.

Griffiths was recaptured but his escape had made such an impact on Meehan that he invited him to come to Glasgow when was freed. Meehan wasn't to know that Griffiths was a powder keg who'd meant what he said when he'd sworn the police would never take him alive and he'd turn a gun on the cops if that's what it took.

On 6 July 1969, two men broke into the Ayr home of elderly Abraham and Rachel Ross. They assaulted and tortured the pair, forcing them to say where their valuables were. Two days after her ordeal, Rachel Ross died.

It was a terrible murder and the cops knew that Paddy Meehan had been in Ayrshire that night. They always kept an eye on Meehan. When he was arrested and a very frail, grief-stricken Abraham Ross ID-ed him, Meehan was in big trouble.

Meehan had been in Ayrshire all right – passing through with Griffiths to case an office in Stranraer. Griffiths was his alibi, simple

214

as that. Dour as he might have been, Meehan was old-fashioned. That meant his street code wouldn't allow him to finger Griffiths and Griffiths wasn't for handing himself in – to do so would mean certain jail for planning the heist. And Griffiths hated jail – it terrified him.

Eventually, knowing he was facing a murder rap and looking at life in prison, Meehan told the cops Griffiths was living under the name of Douglas at 29 Holyrood Crescent in Glasgow's west end. Two detectives were sent there on 15 July 1969 to question Griffiths and see if he would support Meehan's alibi. As one cop predicted trouble and the other pooh-poohed him, they didn't realise they were being watched. Griffiths saw them coming.

The cops knocked on the door – no answer. Knocked again – still no answer though they knew Griffiths was at home. So they broke the door down and BOOOM! They ran right into James Griffiths screaming, swearing and firing a shotgun at them. The cops headed back down the stairs double quick but not quick enough. One was shot square in the back and sent tumbling.

Now barricaded in his flat, Griffiths threw open a window and started blasting at anyone who moved. A short while later, he took off out of the flat down on to the street, still shooting. Quickly he made his way to his car and, from the boot, he lifted a sniper's hunting rifle and belts of bullets before scampering back to the flat. Griffiths might be strange but he had prepared for just such a shoot-out very thoroughly indeed.

Cops arrived at Holyrood Crescent team-handed as bullets and pellets whizzed into the street. Suddenly there was silence. Had Griffiths seen sense? The police waited and considered calling out to the flat to negotiate with the gunman. Then they realised they were looking at an empty flat – Griffiths was on the move. Clambering out of an attic window, he had scampered over roofs and down into a back close.

Out on Henderson Street, near The Grapes bar, salesman James Kerr was sitting in his Ford Anglia minding his own business when a shadow fell over him. Glaring through the car window was a dark-haired desperado with bandoliers of bullets criss-crossing his chest and a gun in each hand. Kerr's ears burned and then went deaf as Griffiths blasted a shot, threw open the car door and yanked the poor man out. He was lucky.

Now the mad gunman was on the loose, driving the Anglia through the west end and firing shots at pedestrians – just random folks minding their own business. This wasn't about getting away from the cops any more – this was murder stalking the street.

In Carnbrae Street, Possil, Griffiths crashed the motor. Unhurt, he clambered out and made a dash to the nearest pub, The Round Toll. Pubs in Possil are used to trouble but this was a first. Waving his rifle at the scattering customers, he blasted two shots into the ceiling, yelling, in his thick Rochdale accent, 'Don't mess. I've shot two coppers already.'

Grabbing a bottle of brandy from the gantry, he stood there gulping it from the neck as terrified punters looked on. One old guy, William Hughes, twitched and Griffiths spun round, shooting the man twice. He'd die days later of his wounds.

The bar manager, James Connelly screamed, 'You dirty, fucking bastard. What did you do that for? He was just an old man.' Amazingly, the barman grabbed Griffiths by the scruff of the neck and threw him out of the pub, dumping him on to the pavement. No one messes with Possil barmen . . . or bar women, come to think of it.

No doubt the crazed gunman wanted to go straight back and shoot Connelly for his impertinence but reports of the Possil shootings had reached the cops and their cars were catching up fast, sirens blaring. Griffiths heard them and knew he had to get out of there quick.

Oblivious to what was going on, lorry driver John Craig had innocently pulled up at the kerb outside The Round Toll when he heard an explosion. Some car backfiring, maybe? Or some kids with fireworks out of season? The last thing he thought of was that a gunman was on the loose in the middle of Glasgow in broad daylight. Then bullets started whizzing over his cab and he saw the demented Griffiths running at him.

Craig didn't need two tellings – he was out of his cab and off. But Griffiths stopped and tried to shoot him as poor Craig tried to shelter behind a lamp post.

Behind the wheel of the lorry and firing sporadically out of the window, Griffiths was off again. This time he ended up in Springburn, an area of the city he wasn't familiar with. It was to be his downfall. The howl of sirens seemed to be coming from both sides as well as from behind him. Griffiths was a very good driver – he had been since he was a kid stealing cars. As long as he could hear the cop cars, he could avoid them is what he would've thought. All he had to do was keep moving forward and adjusting his direction – and that's exactly what the cops were banking on.

The lorry screeched to a halt in Kay Street – a dead end. The cops had known what they were doing. By coming at him from different angles, they pushed him in a certain direction – a direction that would lead to him driving into that dead end.

At 26 Kay Street, a tenement, he broke into a flat and started blasting through a window. As people dashed for cover, scores of cops swarmed around the street and a phone call was made to the army asking for help. They agreed and began mustering troops pronto. James Griffiths was going nowhere. He was staying put and creating mayhem.

A baby in a pram lay stranded on Kay Street as bullets battered into the ground. A brave cop crawled out, grabbed the baby and passed it into the safety of a ground-floor flat window. In a nearby children's playground, an eight-year-old girl was shot as her pals howled in terror and parents rushed to corral them to safety. A newly married eighteen-year-old woman was hit and her husband had to be jumped on and restrained as he ran in fury towards Griffiths and certain death. One poor guy had just come out of the hospital where he had been recovering from a knife attack by some heavies. Griffiths shot him in the neck.

The cops had to do something.

With guns in their mitts, two detectives made it unnoticed to the close mouth and slowly, carefully, quietly climbed the stairs. At the door to the flat where Griffiths was holed up, one cop eased open the letterbox and peeked in. The metal screeched, Griffiths turned and, with his rifle raised to fire, he came howling towards the door.

The cop stuck the barrel of his gun through the letterbox and fired blind once. The bullet struck Griffiths on the shoulder and he hit the deck.

Instantly, the cops were on him. They disarmed him and were carrying him downstairs towards their colleagues and a police van but, before they reached the street, James Griffiths was dead – the first wanted man on record to be shot dead by Scottish cops.

The cops only wanted to find out if Griffiths was with Paddy Meehan on the night Rachel Ross was murdered. Now Meehan's alibi was dead. He would be convicted of Mrs Ross's murder and rot in jail till a campaign, led by lawyer Joe Beltrami, secured him a royal pardon in May 1976 – seven needless years in jail.

James Griffiths, the man who could have cleared him but, instead, went on a murderous rampage, was disowned by family and friends. Given a pauper's funeral, he lies in Linn Cemetery, Glasgow.

A loner in life, a loner in death. His grave remains unmarked to this day. And all because of a misunderstanding.

THE GYPSIES' GIFT

Old prams, litters of dead puppies, mattresses, rusty bikes and every other conceivable thing imaginable – that's what they were used to finding on that job. Sometimes they even got a laugh – like the time they found a new pair of ladies' shoes sitting there in the middle of the railway track as if someone had just taken them off. Well, it broke the monotony. But sometimes that can go too far.

Peewee men walk the railway line, day after day, checking the track. A boring job? Not the day when one discovered a severed leg.

It was 24 March 1969 on the Edinburgh–Fife line. The bloke was well used to all sorts of rubbish being dumped near the tracks but that brown paper parcel was neatly wrapped. He'd have a look inside. Horror time.

It didn't take a forensic expert to see it was a woman's leg. Smooth and shapely, the leg still wore a silky stocking. That increased the horror somehow. Like the leg had been attached to a good-looking woman. Like he could imagine her. See her in his nightmares.

Nine hours later, the Edinburgh cops were under pressure. Another female leg had been found on their patch, wrapped in brown paper and dumped in the shallows of the Water of Leith. Was there a madman on the loose in the city?

The legs were very neatly severed and indicated the woman had been just over five foot tall and aged between twenty and forty. It wasn't much to go on but it was something. What they really needed was the torso. Almost instantly, 'The Missing Torso Case' was coined by the media.

Both legs had been found near bridges and major motor routes so the killer could have easily travelled a distance to dump the legs. He wouldn't want them to be found in his own backyard, would he?

All the surrounding cop forces were called in to the murder inquiry. In spite of Scotland's high murder rate, chopped up cadavers were distinctly uncommon and they scared the public witless for obvious reasons. The cops had to crack this case early on.

A murder squad of around thirty detectives were given an open overtime agreement and as much in the way of other resources as they asked for. They looked through missing persons files and, by doing so, actually traced 462 folk, some of whom weren't best pleased. They made TV appeals and had all sorts of other crimes reported. They hoovered crime scenes for linked clues and spoke to every prostitute in the Central Belt to see if any of their pals hadn't been around for a while. Then they systematically worked through every report of a missing woman in Edinburgh, Lanarkshire, Fife and Stirling. That was some list.

It all seemed hopeless. The other body parts could be anywhere. The killer could have moved on, far away. He and the victim might not even be from Scotland. But they were about to make a breakthrough.

The Lanark police had received yet another phone call complaining about travelling folk. The woods and lanes around the town were a traditional stopping-off point for travellers. The trouble was that they often parked their caravans on other people's land without permission. Prejudices against travellers still ran high in some quarters and, in the 1960s, they were still referred to as gypsies or, more commonly in Scotland, tinks.

The cops had the dirty of job of making the travellers move on. It was a job some cops hated – they couldn't see what the harm was. But that's what the Lanark cops did on 1 May 1969 when they'd received a phone call complaining that a family called

Townsley had parked up their lorries and caravans on a lay-by off the A73 Biggar to Lanark road. The family weren't causing any trouble so the cops gave them till 10 a.m. the next morning to move on.

The next morning the Townsleys were taking their time. William Townsley decided he'd go for a walk in the forest next to the lay-by. That's when he found it wrapped in an old blanket and tied up with twine – a human torso with the arms attached but no legs.

The cops, forensic bods and scene-of-crime photographers were swarming over that forest within the hour. Pathologists would get many more clues and they soon confirmed that, despite the headless trunk and the legs having been found some considerable distance apart, they did belong together. There would be more clues too from the blanket and twine. That was all well and good but there was nothing to point them in the direction of a suspect.

Travelling south on the A74 to Carlisle, the killer could easily have turned off to dump the torso where Townsley had found it. UK-wide appeals for help went out and all sorts of English police forces responded. Meantime, the Scottish cops thought they'd look closer to home.

A mile away from where the torso was found was the village of Thankerton and a little farther away the town of Lanark. There was someone there who the Lanarkshire cops wanted to see.

James Keenan was, at first glance, a most unlikely suspect. All his neighbours thought he was a most helpful man and some even called him Mr Kindness. With his younger wife, Elizabeth, and fifteen-month-old baby, Veronica, at their home in 40 Wellwood Avenue, they were seen as an ideal, happy family. That was until Elizabeth left her man. With no warning, no row and no fall-out, she had simply disappeared – or so James Keenan had told the cops. Husbands and wives split up all the time – the police knew that. It was the timing of Elizabeth's disappearance that intrigued them – it had been reported two days after the legs were found.

A cop crew took footprints from the severed legs and tried to raise some prints in Keenan's house, looking for a match – no joy.

So they'd taken away some of Elizabeth's shoes. Now that the torso had been found with arms and hands attached, they took fingerprints and went back to his house to check for a match yet again.

Keenan had shown all the outward signs of being a heartbroken man worried sick about his missing wife. He'd gone to the cops repeatedly, he'd taken part in public appeals for her to contact him and he'd been interviewed by the newspapers, when he'd often burst into tears. Ordinary citizens may have felt bad about him being investigated in the missing torso case but the cops weren't paid to worry about upsetting feelings.

The police informed Keenan that they could now tell more about the woman whose severed body parts had been found. She was brunette, aged between mid twenties and mid thirties, in good physical shape and she'd had a baby – a bit like his missing wife, as it happened.

James Keenan broke down and confessed. It was his wife, Elizabeth. Did they want to know where her head was?

Over the next few hours, Keenan explained to the cops what had happened. They had been sitting talking in their home one night. Elizabeth had been feeding the baby and she dropped the spoon. She had picked it up off the floor and just continued using it without cleaning or washing it. Keenan just snapped and thumped her with an axe. He had then sawn her limb from limb with a hacksaw, wrapped the body parts up and driven round in his Vauxhall dumping them in different isolated places.

Sure enough, Keenan led the cops to a group of young trees near Carnwath and walked right up to a package. It was Elizabeth's skull.

Later, at his trial, James Keenan would claim he had blacked out and, when he came to, he found he had murdered his wife. But when pressed by the prosecution as to what really happened that night he admitted, 'All I can think of is that spoon. Something happened when Elizabeth fed the baby with it. It was that dirty spoon.'

James Keenan was found to be sane and guilty of murder in The Missing Torso Case. It would be thirty years before such a gruesome find occurred in a Scottish murder again. Almost the same length of time James Keenan would spend in prison. He was jailed for life.

STREETS OF FEAR

'My name is John.' He said it in a quaint, old-fashioned way for those hip days of the late 1960s and a macabre legend was born.

As rock'n'roll stars raved on about the Swinging Sixties, free love and peace, Glasgow people were terrified to walk the streets. The decade had started badly back in the old haunted, hunting ground of Queen's Park where two boys had murdered a man for money and one of the boys was hanged for the offence. Fear had kept people off the streets for a while but, by the late 1960s, they were back in Queen's Park looking for pick-ups. But now there were other places they could do this – especially at the dancing.

Trendy young adults would head into the city centre where new clubs were springing up all the time. One place was always popular – the Barrowland Ballroom, especially on Thursday nights when it catered for the over twenty-five-year-olds. It was a good night for a married woman to find a man. It was a great night for a man to find a needy woman.

On 23 February 1968, Patricia Docker was found dead in a doorway. She'd been strangled with her own stockings, bashed in the face after she had died and her handbag was missing. The last time she'd been seen was as she was leaving the Barrowland Ballroom with a tall, slim, red-haired man in a smart suit with a collar and tie. It might have been the last time Patricia was seen but it certainly wasn't the last time people would hear that description.

On 15 August 1969, Jemima McDonald was found dead, her stocking wrapped round her neck, her face bashed after death – just the same as had happened to Pat Docker. Now the cops were worried and the public was terrified – but not terrified enough.

On 30 October 1969 – the night before Halloween – Helen Puttock was found dead in a backcourt in Earl Street, Scotstoun. She'd been strangled with her stockings and her handbag was missing. However, there was one difference this time – the killer had left clues.

Helen had been with her sister, Jean, at the Barrowland Ballroom in the company of the tall man, dressed in a neat suit, with well-groomed red hair.

'My name is John,' he'd said in that old-fashioned way, as he introduced himself to the two sisters. But there was another John in their company – John from Castlemilk – and he knew the other John. All four agreed to travel home together in a taxi – an excuse for some winching more likely – but, when they got outside John from Castlemilk suddenly refused point blank to go. It was as if he'd chickened out . . . but chickened out of what? He was only going to be seeing a woman home, wasn't he?

In the taxi, the other John spoke politely about his religious upbringing, quoting at ease, mainly about Moses. 'I don't drink at Hogmanay,' he said, 'I pray.' And, with that, Bible John, serial killer, was born.

Outside her home in Knightswood, Jean waved her smiling sister off in the back of the taxi with John. When Helen was found, like the others, she'd been strangled with her own stockings and her handbag had been stolen but there were differences – there was a bite mark on her flesh and he'd masturbated on her after she was dead and left semen splattered on her clothes. The semen was useless as a clue in 1969 but the forensic bods knew that would change and kept samples of it which they still hold.

There was another similarity that rocked the public – all the women had been menstruating. Did the killer know that? And, if so, how had he known?

Hysteria screamed in every public corner. People were so scared that dance halls almost closed down due to the fall in numbers.

When the police issued what was to become an iconic photofit of Bible John, men of a similar appearance were attacked in public. The cops were forced to issue them with official cards declaring, 'I am not Bible John.'

A hundred cops worked the case round the clock, taking well over 50,000 statements. BBC television screened a re-enactment, one of the first in the UK. Young cops – both male and brave females – went to the Barrowland Ballroom under cover. It was the biggest police operation Glasgow had ever seen. Yet they arrested no one.

The killings suddenly stopped – in Glasgow at least. Theories abounded about Bible John dying, emigrating, moving south, being in the army but it was all just speculation. However, some experienced cops think Bible John did move abroad, returning to Glasgow every now and then to resume his killing career.

Thirty-seven years on and the hunt for Bible John continues. But there's another hunt that was never finished. What of Castlemilk John? He's never been found. Is that where the truth lies? Is he out there somewhere?

NO RHYME, NO REASON

The farmer was a country man – had been all his life. He knew the area around his farm better than some people know their own homes. But, one day when he took a walk in the woods, he was going to stumble upon something even he didn't know about. Wouldn't have dreamed of – even in his worst nightmares. That walk in those familiar woods would spawn tragedy and one of Scotland's deepest mysteries.

It was love. Isabella McCabe – everyone knew her as Bella – was handsome, hard-working, in her thirties and had been married before. In the late 1950s, that wasn't a recipe for popularity with men, especially when you'd got two kids in tow. But she did meet a good man. Adam Sherriffs was younger than she was by four years. He worked as a steel erector – a good earner. He was strongly built but a gentle man and he fell for her big time, children and all.

In Adam Sherriffs, Bella had met a gem – everyone agreed about that, especially her children – and they were married in 1960 in the Registrar's Office in Aberdeen. A love story.

By 1966, the family were settled in their home in a tenement flat at 27 Logie Avenue in the city. Money was tight but the family were well used to that. Adam was always in regular work, often in new housing developments, and Bella took jobs as a waitress in cafés.

John McCabe, Bella's oldest child from her first marriage, was twenty-one and worked on a trawler in the dangerous, fish-rich North Sea. Young John had got married the year before but he and his wife, Eileen, struggled to find a home in a city strapped for affordable houses so Bella and Adam had welcomed the young couple to their home for periods, as did Eileen's mum. They were young, in love and loved. Life was good.

Bella's second child, thirteen-year-old Murray McCabe, was loved by his stepfather, Adam, and was happy and well balanced. Three years before this, Bella and Adam had had a baby, Jacqueline, and her daddy doted on her. Not that he left Murray out or made him feel bad – Adam Sherriffs had love enough for them all. Then Bella and Murray left him.

That's what Adam told Bella's mother, Georgina Gray, one day in July 1966. She couldn't believe it. There hadn't been any trouble between the couple – they were such a well-suited pair, such a close family.

Adam had called on her to break the bad news. It was just like him to treat her with such consideration. He had turned up at her house with young Jacqueline and, when the girl was happily playing out of earshot, Adam had quietly and calmly told Georgina about Bella walking out on him. Taking care of everybody – that was Adam Sherriffs' way, everyone said so.

Bella had taken her son Murray and, Adam thought, might have gone to stay with relatives outside Aberdeen. He looked worried, upset. Poor man – Georgina felt so sorry for him.

A few days later, John McCabe returned from a stint at sea and called on his grandmother who told him what had happened. He couldn't believe it either. No one could.

In spite of the split, John and his wife Eileen moved into the Sherriffs' flat at Logie Avenue where they would stay for a while as had been agreed a long time before. The flat was empty but given all the upset they weren't surprised and assumed that Adam had taken Jacqueline to stay with other relatives outside Aberdeen. It was so typical of Adam to give the wee girl a holiday and take her mind off the family troubles.

Then, on 27 July 1966, retired farmer Hector Strachan went for a walk in the woods – it was a small but dense wood in the sprawling grounds of Balgownie Old People's Home, just outside the city. A tough old farmer like him felt at home outside in the fresh air. The walk in the woods would be good for him. Then he found the man hanging from a tree.

It must have been terrifying for Hector Strachan to be alone in the woods and suddenly find himself confronted with a hanged man. But Hector kept his wits and soon the cops were on the scene. It wasn't long before they found identification. It was Adam Sherriffs. There was more – a suicide note in Adam's pocket. And it wasn't just a suicide note – it was a confession.

Sherriffs had murdered Bella and young Murray in their home at Logie Avenue. He didn't say why – just that he had strangled them and had hidden their bodies under the floorboards. He had then travelled to Balgownie with young Jacqueline, the three-year-old he doted on and who loved him so much. In a field of corn he had strangled her. God knows what must have been going through that man's mind. God knows what torment he felt.

Having killed his daughter, Adam Sherriffs went for a short stroll to that wood near the River Don and there he hanged himself.

Adam Sherriffs was a triple murderer who'd taken his own life – that much he'd made sure the world knew. What he didn't explain was why.

Sherriffs' family, his workmates and the neighbours at Logie Avenue were lost for reasons. They had no clue that anything was wrong. To them, the Sherriffs were the most loving, stable family in the street. The Sherriffs were just an ordinary family – loving, caring and hard-working. They were luckier than most but still just an ordinary family and Adam was an ordinary man who'd turned to murder.

Why? We'll never know. The reason died the day Adam Sherriffs took a walk in the woods.

1970 TO 1979

DISCOS, DRUGS AND DEATH

As the Vietnam War worked its way to an end (1975), the Watergate scandal brought down President Richard Nixon (1974). Saddam Hussein became president of Iraq (1979) and Margaret Thatcher was the first female prime minister of Britain (1979).

Floppy discs and domestic video recorders were introduced (1975). Walkman portable cassette players hit the streets (1979) and Concorde broke the sound barrier crossing the Atlantic (1976). The first test-tube babies were born (1974) and Louise Brown became the first surviving test-tube baby (1978).

The Beatles split up (1970) and generations went into mourning when Elvis died (1977).

The film *M*A*S*H* (1970) set the anti-war mood of the times while John Travolta showed men how to dance in *Saturday Night Fever* (1970). The Sex Pistols formed as a reaction to disco and punk was born (1976).

In Scotland, the Upper Clyde shipbuilders went on the first work-in taking over the yards (1970). Gordon Brown was the student rector at Edinburgh University (1974). Sixty-six fans died on stairway 13 at Ibrox Stadium during a Rangers versus Celtic game (1971).

David McNee was appointed Chief of Police in Glasgow (1971), resigned to become Commissioner of the Metropolitan Police (1975) and was knighted (1978). Renee Macrae and her three-year-old son, Andrew, went missing, sparking the biggest and longest hunt in Scottish history (1976). A spate of sex killings of young women in Glasgow and Edinburgh baffled the cops (1973–79).

MARX, MAO AND MUGS

'There's only one thing for it, comrades,' said the small, serious-eyed man with the goatee beard. 'We'll have to liberate the spoils of capitalism.'

'The what?'

'Rob a bank. After all, they have stolen the money from the workers. It's not theirs to keep. What's wrong with that? It's revolutionary.'

The 1960s didn't just spawn free love, women's lib and drugs. Radical politics was in and groups sprang up everywhere. In Germany, Italy, France and the USA, it got serious with armed revolutionaries in shoot-outs with the cops, bank raids and bombs. Scotland wasn't immune.

Matthew Lygate was deadly serious – too serious some might say – but that was the way of radical revolutionaries in the 1970s. Lygate liked to talk about Marxism and how things should be but, for him – unlike so many of his peers – talk wasn't enough. He was going to make it happen.

The Workers' Party of Scotland (WPS) was just one of hundreds of extreme left-wing groups formed in the late 1960s. Tiny, with a membership of around sixty, including a section at St Andrews University for some reason, it seemed no different from so many other parties. But the WPS was weird even for those times.

The WPS believed in a mixture of Marxism, Leninism and Scottish Nationalism. It was a close supporter of the strict regimes of Maoist China and Albania where they banned facial hair and skirts above the knee. It formed close associations with Algerian terrorists and even gave the thumbs-up to an eccentric former British army major, Freddy Boothby, who was hell-bent on setting up a provisional government in Scotland.

Few people took the group seriously. Big mistake.

It had been created by former tailor Matthew Lygate. When he stood in a by-election in the Gorbals, he polled a total of seven votes. That might explain why few folk took them seriously but the party members took themselves seriously – deadly seriously.

The WPS was short of funds. How can you run a revolution with no money? Matthew Lygate had the answer – rob banks.

Lygate went about recruiting his team. He thought of them as revolutionary freedom fighters but, in truth, they were a mixture of greedy armed robbers and naive idealists – a very motley crew indeed. They included: William MacPherson, thirty-one, a professional gambler who joined the WPS after visiting their bookshop in the southside of Glasgow; Colin Lawson, twenty-four, who had trained to be a monk before leaving to be a psychiatric nurse; and Ian Doran, twenty-three, from a well-established Glasgow crime family, a professional hit man who was wanted by Scotland Yard for a murder in Soho. The armed gang was completed by the public face of WPS – Lygate himself. He liked to model himself on the great John MacLean, the Scottish revolutionary. Lygate was more accustomed to long political discussions than armed robbery but he was the leader and brains behind the mob.

It could all have been stopped before anything happened but for one thing – the cops didn't listen.

Early in 1970, before the gang had sprung into action, a member of the WPS, Steven Niven, somehow found out about the plans to rob and secretly went to the head of the CID in Edinburgh. Chief Superintendent Ronald Clancy listened to the young man's talk of armed revolutionaries politely enough yet the cop dismissed Niven's claims as 'fanciful'. Niven then went to two newspapers and repeated his story. A full dossier on the WPS, including a list of party members, was handed to the Special Branch in Glasgow. Still no action was taken.

Maybe the cops couldn't believe that there was an armed Marxist gang in Scotland. Maybe they'd failed to learn their history of how Winston Churchill, fearing that John MacLean would spark an armed revolution, filled George Square with soldiers, machine guns and tanks ready for the battle.

With the cops ignoring the warnings, the WPS went to work. Armed with guns and clubs, they robbed two Glasgow banks in quick succession. With the party funds now swollen, they rested. But that wasn't good enough for William MacPherson and Ian Doran. They had expensive personal tastes and habits to support so they went on a freelance armed robbery of their own, not even bothering to wear masks.

Slowly, the police were becoming interested – especially now they had actual crimes to investigate. In particular, they paid a number of visits to MacPherson's mother's house in Mansewood in the suburbs of Glasgow but, finding nothing, still no one was interviewed let alone arrested.

Two more banks and a business were robbed in quick succession. Now the police were worried that a new team, using the same approach every time, was robbing premises at will. Though no one had been hurt so far, during those last two robberies, a shotgun was fired. Was this a sign of nervousness or callousness? Either way, the team was becoming dangerous to people as well as to dosh.

To the cops, this wasn't political – just criminal. Maybe that's why they had so little luck in nabbing the team.

The police were convinced that many robberies throughout Scotland and England showed similar patterns and were being carried out by the same gang. That's how robberies worked in Scotland.

They sifted through all the usual suspects on their books. Names like Arthur Thompson, Walter Norval, cockney Al Brown and gunman William MacPherson came up time after time. But it was the gang they needed. Who was working with who? None of their usual informants knew anything about any new gang. More robberies took place. Yet all the while the cops were sitting on as much information on WPS as they needed to catch the crooks – information they had filed under 'Time Wasters'.

Late in 1971, an anonymous phone call finally made the police treat the WPS seriously. In a raid on the party's Glasgow bookshop, weapons and £10,000 cash were discovered – enough incriminating evidence to arrest Lygate, MacPherson, Doran and Lawson.

Though the police suspected the WPS of many raids throughout Britain, they could only form cases on five robberies in Glasgow. All in all, the proceeds of these heists amounted to a mere £27,000. While the police estimated the real overall haul as being much larger – maybe closer to £250,000, a fortune at that time – they also reckoned that very little went on funding the WPS's revolution. Instead, it was spent on supporting McPherson and Doran's lifestyles. Indeed, when William McPherson was arrested, he was in the process of buying a £159 watch, a very hefty price for a timepiece back in 1971.

At their trial in Glasgow High Court in 1972, all the men pled not guilty. Lygate made a speech about the violence of capitalism against the working class. The robbers were 'liberating' the funds like true revolutionaries so what could they be guilty of? It was the state that was guilty of oppression.

Unfortunately, Lygate was not as articulate as his hero John MacLean whose court speeches at trials in the early twentieth century are still quoted as texts in left-wing thinking. The former tailor was also far too long-winded in the opinion of the judge, Lord Dunpark, who kept interrupting him.

All four were found guilty of participating in some or all of the armed robberies. Lawson, represented by a young Lord James Douglas-Hamilton who'd go on to be a senior Tory politician, got off lightest with a mere six years. But he was definitely the lucky one.

William MacPherson was jailed for twenty-six years, the longest specified jail sentence ever to have been given out in Scotland at that time. MacPherson was a known career criminal and reckoned to be very dangerous. Had there been any problems during the robberies, he would have used his shotgun for sure.

Lygate got twenty-four and Doran twenty-five years – huge sentences for what they were actually found guilty of, given the amount of money recovered and the fact that no one had been hurt. Maybe the gang was being punished for the crimes police believed they had committed rather than those they were charged with. Or maybe the court didn't just take too kindly to Marxist revolutionaries robbing banks in Scotland.

After his sentence in 1972, Matthew Lygate told his solicitor, 'I will be released very soon – when the revolution comes.'

Lygate was released in 1985. He tried to revive the defunct Workers' Party of Scotland but failed. He's still waiting for his revolution.

BABY BABYSITTER
FROM HELL

It had been a great night out – just what the two single mothers needed – but it was time to get home and check on the kids. Home to tragedy.

Mary McGowan and Sheila Laird were good friends whose lives were very similar. Divorced, in their thirties, with kids, no jobs and money tight – an occasional night out was called for. Why not?

That night in September 1972, it was just a drink or two at one of their local pubs – The Blair on Dundee's Princes Street. There they'd met a couple of men. Finding them good company, they'd agreed to go on to a party with them. It was the 1970s, a time of freedom and pleasure-seeking and, after all, they were grown women.

Besides their kids were being cared for all right. Mary McGowan's seven kids were older and her thirteen-year-old, Annette, was babysitting Sheila Laird's younger three – Elizabeth (seven), Susan (five) and wee Helen (three). She'd babysat before with no problem so what did the mothers have to worry about?

Around 1.30 a.m., the women got back to Sheila Laird's flat at Blacklock Crescent. Annette was fast asleep on the couch and, as usual, Sheila went straight through to the bedrooms to check on the wee ones. The older two were fast asleep and fine. There was just one problem – she couldn't find Helen.

Where could she be in the middle of the night? Had she somehow got out of the house while Annette was sleeping?

In a blind panic Sheila shook Annette awake and demanded to know where Helen was. Still half asleep, Annette went to Helen's bed and, pointing to the foot of it said, 'She's there.'

Pulling back the covers, Sheila Laird found her youngest daughter, curled up into herself – not asleep but dead. And not from natural causes but murdered.

For a small city, Dundee punches above its weight. In terms of its industries, imports and exports and even its football teams, it always has done and this is also true for crime. But even the experienced cops and doctors called to the scene were shocked. Who wouldn't be at the brutal murder of a beautiful three-year-old lassie? And it wasn't just that Helen had been murdered – it was also how she had been killed.

Her body was covered in deep bite marks and she had been strangled – a terrible, slow, painful way to die. What terrors she must have gone through in her last moments.

The pathologist was in no doubt – the bite marks matched thirteen-year-old Annette McGowan's teeth. Scotland had yet another child-killing child.

A couple of years later, an Ayrshire boy, Willie Bell would brutally murder his three-year-old sister, Angela, when he was on the run from approved school. The public outrage and anger echoed on for years.

Then in 1991, in woods near Glasgow's Drumchapel scheme, eleven-year-old Joseph Keith would batter three-year old James Campbell to death. Drumchapel people would have gladly saved the need for a trial.

Who can forget James Bulger's killers Jon Venables and Robert Thompson being chased by a howling lynch mob? Some would hunt them still.

These are just a handful of examples of children who kill children. Somehow it has always affronted many people, driving them to fury and threats of violence

But this was not to be the case with Annette McGowan. Annette got sympathy in spite of the brutal killing of Helen. Annette had learning difficulties, a mental disorder and uncontrolled epilepsy. Added to that was the fact that she suffered from a genetic complaint causing her problems with one eye and other physical difficulties. The girl should have been being cared for herself – not caring for younger children.

In Scotland, there is no legal age limit for caring for children. A parent has to leave their child with someone responsible and capable whether forty or fourteen. Due to her disabilities, Annette McGowan was neither.

There was never any dispute that Annette had killed wee Helen and nor was any reason ever given. The doctors were clear – Annette McGowan had acted with diminished responsibility. She probably didn't even understand the enormity of what she had done. But she was frightened – a tiny little figure in the dock, hanging on to the policewoman's hand as if her life depended on it.

It took the jury – many of whom were visibly distressed – less than twenty minutes to find Annette guilty of culpable homicide. Then came the difficult part – what should be done with her?

In Scotland, a child found guilty of murder would usually be sent to one of the high-security, locked units for kids. But this wasn't usual and nor was it simply a matter of protecting other children from Annette – the girl desperately needed the right care and treatment herself. The only appropriate place in the whole of Scotland was the State Hospital, Carstairs. But there she'd be among adult killers and offenders and that wasn't acceptable to the judge, Lord Keith.

The sad fact was that no resources existed. Perhaps, if they had, Annette McGowan would have been helped years before and Helen Laird might still have been alive to this day.

A special arrangement was eventually made to care for Annette at Balgay Approved School in Dundee and the judge finally sentenced her to ten years. But ten years of treatment and help, not jail.

She was only a child after all – and a child who needed help, not hell.

THE RECIDIVIST

He was wealthy by anyone's standards yet he couldn't stop robbing. Where would it all end?

It all began in a single end in Springburn in the 1930s, where three kids and two adults were packed into a tiny space. It was a time of poverty and hardship when people either failed or fought. James Crosbie fought.

No one got by in pre-war Springburn without being handy with their fists and feet and Crosbie was. But, from an early age, he took to robbing factories, shops, warehouses and discovered something – he loved the money and he loved the robbing.

By his twenties, he'd started tackling post offices. Those were the days when most people didn't have chequebooks and postal orders were the way to pay – the days when post offices were loaded with cash.

The cops didn't take kindly to post-office raids and James Crosbie was already well known to them as a likely suspect. He'd been in and out of borstals and jails all his young life but now, having done one job too many, life in Glasgow had got too hot, even for him. It was time to move south to new adventures.

Bobbing and weaving at different money-making enterprises, from smuggling cigarettes to robbing shops, Crosbie soon became known among the London faces. But, if the players knew him, so too did the cops.

Nabbed for handling a couple of thousand stolen cigarettes, Crosbie was sentenced to a whacking three years in jail. In Dorset's Verne Prison, he was allocated work in the printing shop – it was a boring job but one with unexpected extras.

'Would you like to do a job for The Twins?' another con whispered to him one day. Crosbie didn't know who the guy was talking about. It was Reg and Ron Kray.

They wanted someone to copy driving licences. At that time licences were much simpler affairs and they were issued by different local authorities. It would be no problem to copy on the high-quality prison printing press.

The Krays had offered £2,500 for 500 bent licences. Crosbie said he'd do it for £500. That was still a lot of money back then and, he reasoned, it was a sum that was more likely to be paid. He never saw a penny. That was the first and last time he worked with The Twins.

Eventually the pull of Glasgow proved too much and he moved back home. With a few grand from robberies under his belt, he opened up a shop in Ayr Street, Springburn, specialising in fancy metalwork like latches and gates. Crosbie was skilled in that field and was always keen to make a few bob. There was just one problem with it – boredom.

He robbed a major shop in Glasgow's city centre. That was OK but it could've been better. He had overlooked a load of money.

Next he tackled a branch of the Royal Bank of Scotland on Riddrie Road in the shadow of Barlinnie Prison. He recruited a friend and the pair broke in at night. They tried to roll the safe out to their van so that Crosbie could break into it elsewhere but the snag was that the safe was too heavy.

Abandoning the bank job, they decided to hit a nearby post office. It was alarmed and the cops arrived team-handed and fast. The place was crawling with police desperate to catch this big mob who'd rob a bank and a post office in one night, only to find it was just James Crosbie and a pal.

The bank in question had an interesting future. It would go into the Guinness Book of Records as the most robbed bank in Britain. Years later, it was robbed by Paul Ferris's father, Willie, whose team used a school bus as a getaway vehicle.

Meantime, in 1966, James Crosbie got an urgent telegram. It read:

RETURN TO LONDON IMMEDIATELY. URGENT BUSINESS PENDING.

It was from a London pal of his, Jack Whitney, and Crosbie knew exactly what it meant. A big robbery was on and they wanted him in. Usually Crosbie wouldn't have hesitated but he was about to get married so he declined – a lucky move.

Three weeks later, the cops came crashing through his door in the middle of the night. As he tried to get out of bed, they battered him to the ground and cuffed him. Crosbie was used to raids by the cops but this time they were being particularly rough and with good reason – they thought he'd murdered cops.

The big London job had gone ahead. Jack Whitney had recruited team members when Crosbie couldn't make it. One was a guy called John Duddy and the other was someone who would become very notorious – Harry Roberts. After the robbery, the thieves were pulled over by a cop car. Harry Roberts started blasting and all three cops were dead.

The London cops hunting the killer knew that one of them was a 'Jock' and Crosbie's name was top of the list. They made Crosbie sweat but eventually realised it was John Duddy and he was arrested in a house in Gallowgate, Glasgow.

All three killers were sentenced big time. Harry Roberts was given the most – thirty years – and was told he'd serve every one of them. Such was his infamy that his name was used in a football chant in England by fans trying to goad the police:

Harry Roberts,
Harry Roberts,
He kills coppers.

As of writing Roberts has served thirty-eight years and seems no closer to being released.

James Crosbie had had a very close call. That wasn't going to put him off robbing though. He took every chance – like the time he went to a travel agent to book tickets to go and watch Celtic in the European Cup. He noticed the travel agent kept a fortune in travellers' cheques in a filing cabinet so, the next night, he robbed the place.

Yet, like many other robbers, he was always looking for the big one – one so big he could retire. The chance came from very close to home – next door in fact.

A neighbour had financial difficulties and was moaning that he wished he knew someone who would rob a bank. An everyday chat? Not when the neighbour had the inside info on cash deliveries to banks and he was chatting to one of Britain's most wanted robbers.

Very soon, he and his team of one – Crosbie only ever worked alone or in very small groups – had carried out an armed heist at the Clydesdale Bank in Hillington.

Within minutes, cops had sealed off the area and shut down nearby Glasgow Airport. What they didn't know was that Crosbie had already calmly driven in there.

Months before, he had obtained his private pilot's licence and, togged up like a businessman, he had simply driven through the cop cars after waving the ID. And he was off scot-free with £67,500, the biggest haul from a bank robbery to that date. But even with such a large sum, he couldn't stop himself. A short while later, he and the same bloke robbed the Clydesdale Bank at the corner of Dumbarton Road, close to the exit from the Clyde Tunnel but, this time, he didn't fly through the police cordon – he cycled. Crosbie actually used a pushbike as his getaway vehicle, knowing that's the last thing the cops would be looking for.

But not everything had gone right with the job. In the bank, his gun was fired twice though no one was injured. He'd later claim it went off accidentally though the cops would claim otherwise.

Now he wasn't just a robber but a potential killer. James Crosbie had become Scotland's Most Wanted.

That job netted him £87,000 – a fortune in 1974 and once again the biggest haul from a Scottish bank robbery.

With success came problems. Crosbie had a great deal of cash lying around. He convinced his accountant that it had come from his legitimate businesses over the years and arranged to have £40,000 of it invested. These days, we call it laundering.

That £40,000 was being kept in a bag at a safe house. This was a standard arrangement used by street players under which the householder was paid a weekly retainer to store the money.

The householder's daughter had a friend, Margaret Keenan, who was too nosy for her own good. One day, while visiting the house, Margaret looked in some cupboards and found the dosh. She stuffed £27,000 of it into her vanity case and ran round to her boyfriend in Possil.

For all Possil's reputation for crime, the man she was going out with was an honest one. He promptly went to the cops. James Crosbie was in trouble and soon he was in the nick, charged with robbery, attempted murder and possessing firearms relating to the last bank job.

Somehow, his lawyer, Joe Beltrami, convinced a court to grant bail. Beltrami, knowing the cops had warrants on Crosbie for the earlier bank job in Hillington, advised him not to go home. All Beltrami meant was that he should live somewhere else. Crosbie got on his toes. A couple of weeks later, hiding out in Falkirk and with his money fast running out, he picked up a copy of the *Daily Record*. 'CROSBIE! WHERE IS HE NOW?' ran the front page. The whole of Scotland was hunting him. He needed to get out and he could only do that with money. There was only one way he knew to raise a significant amount of cash . . .

Calling in some favours, he got a gun and then cased a bank in Gorgie Road in Edinburgh. Working entirely on his own, he robbed the bank of £20,000 – more than enough to get abroad, buy a house and live comfortably for years.

The next morning, he was having breakfast in a café with the money in a holdall by his side. He had a headache that just wasn't shifting so asked the waitress for an aspirin. They'd run out but there was a chemist just across the road. As Crosbie was making his way back to the cafe, a car suddenly screeched to a halt and three men in suits jumped him. Three Glasgow CID officers had been at the High Court in Edinburgh and were driving back when they spotted him. The cops couldn't believe their luck – neither could Crosbie.

With witnesses and the cash Crosbie was going down. He pled guilty to all the charges, hoping that would mean a lighter sentence than the expected tariff of twenty years, but, at the High Court in Edinburgh, Lord Robertson was in serious mood. 'James Crosbie,' said the judge, 'you are nothing more than a cold, calculating scoundrel whom I consider to be the most dangerous man in Scotland and, indeed, a threat to the very fabric of our society.'

Lord Robertson then sentenced James Crosbie to the full whack, twenty years in the pokey.

In jail, James Crosbie picked up the pen and won four Koestler Awards for his writing but, once he was free again, he just couldn't help himself. In 1996, he was caught trying to smuggle £250,000 worth of dope through Birmingham Airport and jailed for four years. Free again, he was caught at Invergordon in 2000 boarding a cruise ship to Iceland with eighteen bars of cannabis resin stuffed into specially made trousers. He got eight years for that.

Now free again and almost seventy years old, he is writing and being booked as an after-dinner speaker. It's the straight life for him. The question is – for how long?

NO LUCK, NO LOVE

It was a romance made in heaven, they said. But who could have guessed how it would end or how soon?

Friday the thirteenth – some people might think that's an unlucky day, one when it's best to stay in bed. But the young couple were in love, they said, and in a hurry to be wed. So Friday, the thirteenth of October 1972 it was.

Twenty-one-year-old Dutchman Ernest Dumoulin and eighteen-year-old German Helga Konrad had eloped and run away to Edinburgh very much against her parents' wishes. Moving into lodgings run by Herbert Wood at 9 Torphichen Street, Ernest paid three weeks' rent in advance which allowed him to apply to be married in a Scottish registrar's office in those pre-EC days.

A few weeks later, Herbert Wood and his wife witnessed the wedding on 13 October and, after a meal, Ernest and Helga retired to their room. Well, they were honeymooners, after all.

Herbert was a little bit surprised to hear the young couple leave the house only a short time later. He smiled, betting that it wouldn't be too long before they were back and in to bed. How wrong could he be?

Later that night, a seaman dashed up to a couple of cops. He'd been strolling along the foot of Salisbury Crags when he'd come across a woman – a dead woman.

A short while later, they met Ernest Dumoulin who'd gone for help – an ambulance. The dead woman was Helga, his wife of just a few hours. Ernest told the cops a heart-wrenching tale of how he and Helga had gone for a walk up the Crags to chat, kiss and cuddle and watch the beautiful lights of Edinburgh. She slipped and fell, he said – right there next to him. Romance had turned into disaster.

The public were heartbroken for the young man. Herbert Wood was too – one minute he was witnessing their wedding, the next she was dead. Ernest took to his room, playing the theme tune of the film *Love Story* over and over on a Dansette record player.

Tragic – that's what the cops thought till they were approached by Herbert Wood. The man had gone into Ernest's room to tidy up and discovered a letter and receipts for a £412,368 insurance policy that had been taken out on Helga's life the day before she died. In 1972, that sum would have been worth the equivalent of £1.1 million today. Wood took the paperwork straight to the cops.

When the local office of Hambro Life Assurance not only confirmed this but also revealed that Ernest had tried to claim the policy the very morning after Helga died, the cops knew they had a murder inquiry on their patch.

Digging into Dumoulin's past, the cops found he had been a failed financial adviser who'd turned conman over in Germany. He had met Helga through a lonely-hearts advert he had placed in a newspaper. She was a country girl, from a rich family but old-fashioned, sheltered and, obviously, very lonely. He'd known her for only two weeks when he convinced her to draw her life savings of £65 out of the bank and run away with him. Dumoulin denied it all, insisting that Helga had slipped and fallen off the 100ft cliff. He was charged with murder.

At his trial at Edinburgh High Court in 1973, Dumoulin sensationally claimed that it was Helga who had plotted to con an insurance company by faking his death. Then he dropped the bombshell – she had tried to kill him up on Salisbury Crags and had fallen when he put his hands up to save himself. 'God must have saved me then,' he said.

The couple had been alone and she was dead. What was the jury to make of this?

The seaman who had found the body had spoken of someone watching from the top of the cliff. He might have been able to help except he'd disappeared and all efforts to find him failed. Maybe it was because that part of Salisbury Crags was well known as a meeting place for gay men looking for sex – illegal in 1972. That part of the Crags is still to this day a place for drug dealing, underage prostitutes and all sorts of nefarious activities.

As usual, help was on hand from experts in the shape of the post-mortem medics. They noted that there were very few scrapes and bruises on Helga which indicated that she hadn't slipped but had either run and launched herself off the cliff or been pushed very hard indeed.

When Hambro Life Assurance revealed that the insurance policy would have cost Ernest £442 a month to maintain – a fortune he didn't have – the jury were settled. Ernest Dumoulin was found guilty of murdering his wife of only a few hours. In those days of increasing sexual freedom, parents would use the evil Dumoulin as a warning to their teenage daughters about the dangers of men.

Ernest Dumoulin has served his sentence and is now living in Germany. At his trial, he had declared that, when he spotted Helga trying to push him off the cliff, 'God must have saved me then.'

God didn't save him then with his lies but he has saved him since. Dumoulin, now sixty years old, admits that he did murder Helga. He is a Protestant minister tending to his flock in a small German town and conducting marriages. Let's pray they have a happier ending than his own did.

THE ROAD NORTH
TO HELL

A haze of blue cigarette smoke hung low over the bar. It was Friday night – pay night for many – but, in the bustle of drinkers, talking loudly and laughing, someone was quietly planning a little pay day of their own.

The group of friends chatted over drinks in the smoke of the Railway Tavern, Cowlairs, in 1973. Robert Marley had inside information that the wages at the British Engineering Works at Townhead, Glasgow, would be swollen by Christmas bonuses to around £50,000. It was a good haul but, as a novice, he'd need help.

Marley soon recruited Jim Aitken and local hard men Steve Doran and Jim Murphy but some expertise on armed robberies was required. Al Brown and Sid Draper, young men leading major teams in the Kray Twins' London, were contacted.

'Up in the sticks?' they had retorted. 'Easy money!' And soon they were heading northwards and towards infamy.

On 21 December 1973, the team went to work and all hell broke loose.

The yard looked ghostly and unreal on a dark night lit up by the floodlights. From a distance, the workers moving around looked disjointed and unreal but the light was good enough to see what the robbers needed to see.

On Aitken's signal by walkie-talkie from a car park overlooking the yard, Brown, Draper, Marley and Murphy, hefting pistols and sawn-off shotguns, hit the security guards as they were loading the moneyboxes on to a forklift truck.

They squirted ammonia into the driver's eyes and shot both guards in the arm and the back in spite of them being unarmed. It was all going to plan till the gang drove towards the gate – then it went all went pear-shaped.

Gatekeepers aren't meant to be heroes. Checking vehicles in and out, looking at the workers' passes – that was about the stretch of it. If there was a problem, they had to phone someone else – that's it. They weren't paid to be heroes but one man had different ideas.

Gatekeeper Jim Kennedy, forty-two, had heard the commotion and shots. No one robbed anyone on his shift so he was out there at the gate, blocking the gang's escape, right at the last minute – when they were seconds from being out on the road and away to freedom, the money safely stashed in their motor.

'What the fuck?' one robber shouted and then they all sprang to action.

Out of their car and fast, they hit Jim Kennedy twice on the head with the butts of shotguns and he hit the deck. Then a gun went off accidentally, flaring up in the night sky. Panic fizzled in the air. That wasn't meant to happen. It looked as if the gang members might take to their heels and flee. But Al Brown wasn't prepared to do that. Calmly, coldly, the Londoner leaned over and shot Kennedy at point-blank range, killing the man as he struggled to his feet. It was murder now and all for £10,000 – a fraction of their original estimate.

Glasgow police quickly realised they needed help if they were to track down the gang. Voices overheard during the robbery suggested Londoners were involved. Soon, the famous Detective Superintendent Jack Slipper of Scotland Yard was on the case.

After a series of anonymous tip-off calls, the police arrested Robert Marley. The worker-turned-crook then turned Queen's evidence and, before long, the gang had been arrested.

At the eighteen-day trial, then the longest in Scottish criminal history, Brown and Draper were given life with twenty-five years minimum. All the others received less substantial sentences. Marley spent years in solitary confinement for his own protection for turning against his team.

Scotland was horrified. It was a callous murder and Brown and Draper were seen as the leaders.

Brown and Draper didn't take kindly to prison life. In 1985, Al Brown led a breakout from the segregation block at Peterhead Prison, took wardens hostage and managed to get the keys to the jail. All night, he and men like TC Campbell controlled the notoriously strict prison. It was just one incident of many for Al Brown but it was one that was such an embarrassment for the prison service that an official policy of secrecy was adopted on the episode.

Considered a high-security risk, Draper was moved to Gartree Prison, Leicestershire, which, at the time, housed a great many IRA prisoners. In December 1987, he and John Kendall (a member of the Hole in the Wall Gang, infamous in England for years) escaped when gangland friends hijacked a helicopter, landing it in the prison yard. Draper was free for fifteen months. Eventually captured, he was given an additional four years for the escape.

Over the years, he'd been given numerous additional sentences for causing trouble in jail. In 1999, when the parole board refused to consider Brown's release, he promptly escaped. A girlfriend, Fiona Gallacher, boasted of how she had holidayed with Brown in Marbella. Over a year later, he was arrested in a luxury apartment in Brighton in possession of 35,000 amphetamine tablets.

In 1996, Draper managed to have his original sentence of twenty-five years reduced to twenty on appeal and he was duly released. The authorities had somehow forgiven the escapade with the helicopter. But the Scottish system has a longer memory and similar efforts by Brown to get his sentence reduced failed. Everyone knows that the laws in Scotland are different from those in England but there are other differences too.

Had the state not forgiven Al Brown for the night he controlled Peterhead Prison? Or was it by chance the way he coldly killed Jim Kennedy, just an ordinary man who did more than his job?

Either way, Al Brown regretted the day he came north looking for easy pickings.

ONE LONELY MAN

A soft touch.
A bold social experiment.
Failure of the prison system.
The future.

It was many things to many people but all agreed that the Special Unit in Barlinnie Prison, Glasgow, which was set up in 1973, held Scotland's most dangerous prisoners. But who was the most violent man ever to cross the threshold of the Special Unit?

The list of its residents reads like a who's who of Scottish crime. Jimmy Boyle, Hugh Collins, cop-killing ex-cop Howard Wilson, armed robber Big Bill MacPherson and so-called Ice-Cream Wars murderer TC Campbell were among many others. All were fierce fighters – men the system couldn't handle. All have made their mark on society, one way or another, for bad and some for good as well. But who among them was deemed to be the most lethal?

Larry Winters had been a strange, troubled child and, in the mid 1950s, he ended up in St John's Approved School in Glasgow. Run by the De La Salle monks, its regime was one whose brutality has only recently been exposed. Certain staff sexually and physically abused Larry Winters every day, leaving him morose, anti-authority and as likely to cut your throat as buy you a drink – and both for no reason. That's how they left him and that's how he was sent into the world as an adult.

In 1964, aged twenty-one, Winters was wandering around Britain when he found himself in the White Horse, a friendly little pub in Soho, London. It wasn't a place used to trouble. Suddenly, Winters pulled a pistol and demanded that the till be opened. The till jammed. Without waiting Larry Winters shot the barman dead, fleeing the pub empty-handed. It wasn't long after opening time and the till held only about five pounds anyway. That's all he could have stolen had that till not jammed. But that was Larry Winters for you.

Arrested and jailed for life, Winters began to make a reputation for himself in the Scottish prison system. Fashioning knives out of every conceivable object, he slashed warders at every opportunity. Taking on groups of them, he spent years in solitary confinement, where he smeared the walls with his own shit in dirty protests. Winters didn't seem to care.

They built the infamous cages at Porterfield Prison in Inverness for guys like Larry Winters – cages within cells, prisons within prisons, they were policed by baton-carrying warders with big fierce dogs on leashes. There he found himself crossing paths with hard man Jimmy Boyle and cop-killer Howard Wilson. In spite of the deprivations and strict detention, they managed to start a riot during which numerous prison officers were seriously injured and one was blinded.

Enough was enough, the politicians had decided. What they needed was a really secure place where the prison could try out different ways to hold and control these men.

Barlinnie Prison – the BarL – in Glasgow used to hold women as well as men. To ensure segregation, a separate building was erected inside the jail grounds for the women and it was separated from the other wings by security fences. The women had been moved out to other jails and that building now lay empty. That would do.

There they opened the BarL Special Unit and tried a new approach. The prisoners were given a great deal of freedom, they made decisions over the furnishing of their cells and they were encouraged to participate in artistic work. They were also supervised by staff who treated them as human beings.

Most of the prisoners were wary to start with – suspicious that they were going to be tricked in some way. These were violent men who had been thrown into The Cages and treated like rabid dogs. Now they were free to walk around, dress how they liked and even handle sharp knives in the kitchen. There had to be a plot – a catch, so they thought.

When it never came, they settled down and the unit worked for them. At last the system was coping with the prisoners it couldn't previously cope with. The most difficult men had become converts, fully embracing the new freedoms they had been given. All, that is, except Larry Winters who became more depressed, more isolated, more unpredictable.

Ian Stephen, the psychologist who worked at the unit, recalls Winters lifting a pair of scissors and imagining what it would be like to stick the blades through his own throat. It didn't happen but it could have at any time. Staff and prisoners alike knew what Winters was capable of.

Since being admitted to prison Larry Winters had become addicted to drugs. In those days before the universal use of heroin, he took cannabis and pills – anything he could lay his hands on.

'If Larry wasn't out of his head, he was in your face,' said one former con. 'It was as if he was medicating his demons – treating himself.'

The Special Unit had come in for some criticism from the outside. There were too many freedoms, was the claim. Drinking parties and sex with partners during visits were just two of the allegations and they were true to some extent. There's been more than one child conceived in the BarL Special Unit.

Winters wasn't interested in the booze or the sex much. Drugs were his thing and he used the liberty allowed him to have as many drugs smuggled in as he could. Most of the time he would just lie in his bed, staring at the wall, zonked out of his brain. People could see what was going on but they left him there – he was less dangerous in that zombie state.

It was a disaster waiting to happen.

One day in 1977, fellow prisoner John Neeson found Larry Winters sitting on the potty in his cell. He was thirty-seven and dead from an overdose of prescribed tranquillisers – choked on his vomit was the verdict of a Fatal Accident Inquiry. They reckoned it was an accident not suicide as Winters knew too much about drugs. Maybe he knew just enough. Maybe he had finally wearied of those demons.

After his death, it was revealed that Larry Winters had written some remarkable poetry and possessed a genius-level IQ of 160 but he had absolutely no self-control and there were no limits to his behaviour. They made an award-winning film of his life, *Silent Scream*.

Some called him psychopathic. Others say he was an abused child. Whatever else he was, Larry Winters was the most dangerous man in the Special Unit, Barlinnie. Ask any of the ex-inmates. They should know.

WALTER'S ARMY

A huge armed mob was roving round the country at will. Worse, the cops had a secret – they didn't have a clue who the mobsters were.

Over three years in the mid 1970s, this big team drove the police crazy. A battalion of armed raiders was hitting hospital payrolls, wages depots and banks with military precision all over Scotland. Every time some bank was robbed the media would blame the faceless gang. The cops said nothing. Yet the journalists who reported on the crime wave were right and even they didn't know the half of it.

It reached hysterical proportions. Ordinary folk fretted that their wages were going to be stolen or worried that a trip to the shops could land them in the middle of a full-scale shoot-out.

It wasn't as if the folk of Glasgow weren't used to armed robbers. As recently as 1973, Al Brown and Sid Draper had led a raid on the British Engineering Works in Townhead and a poor gatekeeper, whose duties also included acting as night watchman, was shot and killed. That was awful but the lot who had been involved were quickly caught and jailed. This new big mob seemed to be invincible.

The police were under pressure and yet they were clueless about the gang's ID – so clueless they had to invent a name for them. XYY Gang came from the radio code used by the cops. The more dangerous a wanted culprit was, the further through the alphabet would be their code. For this team there was no doubt – XYY, the most lethal criminals in Scotland. There was never a ZZZ.

When the breakthrough came from an informant, many of the gang were found in Maryhill and in the southside of Glasgow, right under police noses, just some hundreds of yards from Orkney Street police station. The cops thought it was the end of the matter but the real trouble was just starting.

Walter Norval, a well-known face from the west side of Glasgow, was the ringleader. Norval was a hard man, a gangster of the old school who ruled with iron yet always according to a code. He had made his name in the gangs, moving on to protection rackets, working pubs, clubs and bookies – and then, of course, to robbery.

Being a tough guy wasn't Norval's only strength – he had brains too. With thirteen men in custody, the cops began to unravel the scale of the operation – there were scores of large robberies, hundreds of foot soldiers, secret weapons arsenals and explosives. Norval's operation was so big that the media came up with another name for the team – Norval's Crime Syndicate.

Walter Norval had run his large outfit with a mixture of discipline and determination – that's why they had survived so long. After their arrest, those same attributes would produce explosive results.

The trial, due to start in November 1977, had to be delayed when the High Court in Glasgow was bombed in an effort to destroy all the paperwork relating to the case. Norval's daughter, Rita Gunn, was charged with conspiring to damage the famous North Court but was acquitted.

Rita's husband, William Gunn, wasn't so lucky, getting five years in jail for threatening to kill one of the leading witnesses. The judges – four in all as the gang were to face separate trials – had to be constantly guarded by armed police. Jurors also came under attack and were provided with police bodyguards for the trial's duration.

A leading prosecution witness, who was in prison at the time, was provided with a constant police escort and kept in solitary confinement. In spite of this, he was scalded with boiling water.

Glasgow was in turmoil. Who exactly was running the city? Had organised teams got so big and powerful the cops were out of their depth? Other problems emerged in court. Though the Crown thought they had good inside information on how the gang worked, Norval had kept everything tight. Only he knew exactly what was going on and who was responsible for what. And he was old school so he wasn't talking.

For a while it looked as if Norval and his crew were going to beat the powers of the state. Eventually, six of the accused were acquitted though seven were found guilty of the armed robbery of a bank and a hospital payroll. Out of many big armed robberies, they could only get two jobs to stick. The cops were furious. They were even angrier when Walter Norval himself only got fourteen years in jail.

The remaining free members of the gang went on to commit more robberies, many surviving for years and becoming major players in organised crime. In the meantime, Norval served his sentence quietly enough. A popular man in jail, he often organised concerts for the cons' entertainment and was never slow to get up on the stage himself. Norval was old school – he wasn't going to let a bit of jail time get him down.

The world had all but forgotten about Walter Norval till June 1999 when a seventy-one-year-old man limped meekly into the dock at Glasgow Sheriff Court and pled not guilty to possessing cannabis. His lawyer said the old man was embarrassed at the charge but claimed he used cannabis to relieve pain caused by chronic arthritis. The Crown believed him and dismissed the case.

Walter Norval, the most feared gang leader of the 1970s was back in court – this time without the bombs.

Now back in his Maryhill community, Norval is seventy-eight years old but as fit and strong as a man twenty years younger. Quick-witted and with an amusing story for every occasion, he has left many a stranger with a smile on their face. Little do they realise that they've just met the man who once brought Glasgow to its knees.

NO HIDING PLACE?

They were young and single and it was Saturday night but little did the two friends know that their evening out would end in tragedy.

Christine Eadie and Helen Scott were seventeen years old and best friends. The year before, they had both moved out of their parents' homes and now they had good jobs with regular wages. They lived in Edinburgh – a city that knew how to do weekends. The young women were going to enjoy themselves – and why not?

Christine and Helen met up with two other friends on Saturday 15 October 1977. The plan was to go to some pub before moving on to a party. They chose The World's End in the High Street, just down from the castle – a good little pub in spite of the cruel irony of its name.

Two young guys chatted up Christine and Helen almost immediately which was not surprising for two pretty young women on a weekend night. The men looked ordinary, safe and, apart from unfashionable short hair, unremarkable. The four hit it off well. When the two other friends announced they were going on to the party, it was hardly surprising that Helen and Christine said they were staying on with the blokes. So they exchanged farewells and that was the last time the women were known to have been seen alive.

The next afternoon around 2 p.m., on the foreshore between Aberlady and Longniddry, East Lothian, a young couple found Christine Eadie. Naked, badly beaten and with her hands trussed behind her back, she had been strangled with her own tights.

Early that same evening, a gardener, walking his dog in a field near stables in Haddington, found Helen Scott's semi-naked body. Helen was also badly beaten and she too had her hands tied behind her back.

The young women's deaths sparked one of the largest manhunts in Scotland's history. Extra police were drafted in to trawl for clues as huge floodlights lit the scenes. Although most of their clothes were found, neither of the girls' handbags was recovered.

All the surrounding roads were blocked and drivers and passengers questioned. Hundreds of cars were traced that had been spotted in key locations but all with no results.

Photofit pictures of the two men were issued to the beat cops and detectives around Edinburgh and to the press. The media appealed for witnesses time and again.

Two look-alike policewomen carried out a re-enactment in The World's End, sending shivers down the spine of any caring person. But still there was no breakthrough.

The men who'd chatted to Christine and Helen that night in the pub had had short hair, which was unusual in 1977, so the police interviewed every male soldier stationed at Redford Barracks in Edinburgh. They got no joy from this line of inquiry either.

Across in Glasgow two women, Agnes Cooney and Hilda McAulay, had been found murdered in similar circumstances. Edinburgh police kept an open mind about whether the same person or people might be responsible.

Some suggested that aspects of the deaths – one of the girls having been strangled with her tights and both handbags being missing – were familiar, as were some details of the Glasgow women's murders. There were perhaps echoes of an earlier time and an infamous spectre – Bible John.

All cops were immediately banned from speculating on the possibility of Bible John being back. He had terrified Scotland's streets for long enough. If the public suspected he was on the prowl again, there would be widespread hysteria. That would be hell for public safety and it would totally scupper the investigation. So no cop speculated aloud but that didn't stop some thinking about Bible John.

Anonymous calls and letters flooded in – as usual in such a murder hunt, many of them were cruel time-wasters. But two letters from the Wishaw area attracted the police's attention. The first said that there were two murderers and they were well-known criminals from Glasgow. The second named the men.

Though the police never released the details, we now know that Arthur Thompson, the Godfather of crime in Glasgow, and his son, 'Fatboy', were interviewed as part of the investigation in the early 1980s. The Thompsons had a holiday caravan at Port Seton, near to where Helen and Christine were found, and they often spent weekends there, going out on pub crawls in Edinburgh. Though fierce criminals, the Thompsons were cleared of any involvement in the murders.

For over twenty-five years, theories on who had killed Helen and Christine grew and grew – soldiers now stationed elsewhere, Edinburgh criminals languishing in jail for other offences, the same men who killed the Glasgow women – but they were all just theories without any proof. For an equally long time, the killer or killers probably thought that they had got off scot-free but they didn't reckon on one thing – DNA.

In 2002, the police took DNA samples from items remaining from the young women's murders. They know it can work. In 2001, a man was convicted for the gruesome killing of a Glasgow woman twenty-one years after her death.

In 2006, a known sexual offender and murderer, Angus Sinclair, was charged with the murders of Christine and Helen twenty-nine years after the tragic event. As this is being written, we await progress in the case.

For so many years, The World's End murders were a sad symbol of how young lives can be wasted and killers can be walking around free. Maybe one day soon their killer will be brought to justice. Maybe it'll send shivers down the spines of all other mindless murderers out there.

DOCTOR SWEET,
DOCTOR SECRET

Beautiful, bright and charming, she had everything to live for. But she led a double life – did it lead to danger and death?

Anxious knocks at her flat door brought sixty-eight-year-old Elizabeth Gordon to answer in a hurry. It was a work colleague of Brenda Page, her neighbour across the landing, and they'd called by arrangement to do some work. The trouble was that Brenda wasn't answering her door.

Brenda's workmate knew that she was friendly with Elizabeth Gordon and, if she'd had to go out unexpectedly, she would've left a message with her. No message.

Elizabeth kept a key to Brenda's flat though. Their tenement, 13 Allan Street in Aberdeen, was the kind of place full of good neighbours you could trust. Besides, Elizabeth and Brenda were very friendly indeed, often sitting together of an evening chatting.

Asking the colleague to wait, Elizabeth slipped into Brenda's home to see if she had slept in. In the flat everything seemed normal and Brenda's three cats purred and waltzed round Elizabeth's familiar ankles. Not wanting to frighten or disturb her pal, Elizabeth edged the bedroom door open gently and peeped in. What she saw was a scene of horror. Brenda Page was in bed all right. Not sleeping. Dead.

'I saw nothing but blood and hair,' the deeply traumatised Elizabeth later recalled. The poor woman was so shocked by her friend's death that she couldn't spend another night in her own home for the rest of her life.

It didn't take long for the cops, pathologists and forensic team to work out the details. Sometime in the evening of 13 July or the early morning of 14 July 1978, someone had broken in through the window of a spare room at the back of the house. Brenda had been battered on the skull and face with a heavy, blunt instrument like a poker or spanner. She was fully clothed and lay across the bed as if she'd fallen there. She hadn't been sexually interfered with in any way.

Nothing had been stolen so the cops' immediate thoughts turned to a burglary gone wrong – a thief being disturbed and lashing out at the person who could identify him. Then, as usual, they considered a relationship soured by jealousy, money or the hundreds of other reasons that drive a once-loving couple to hate. Brenda had been divorced three years before. It had been amicable and she was still on good terms with her former husband, Dr Christopher Harrisson, a biochemist. They checked, of course, but his movements that night were accounted for.

Nor did Brenda have a lover. Her family knew that as did her neighbour and colleagues. She was a friendly open person – she would have told them.

Brenda Page was actually Dr Brenda Page, a gifted genetic scientist at Aberdeen University. At only thirty-two years old, she held a top position, was well known throughout her field and loved her work. With the oil industry just kicking off big time in the North Sea, she had also carried out some breakthrough studies in protecting deep-sea divers from the various risks they ran.

Well off for money, she had a range of hobbies she excelled at. A high-class cook, she was also superb at knitting, crochet, painting and dressmaking. Sporty, she was particularly good at tennis.

It is often said that the poorer you are, the more disorganised your life will be, the more booze you'll drink and the number of lovers you'll take will be greater. You are also more likely to be murdered and this is as true today as it was in 1978. But Dr Brenda Page's life was nothing like this so the cops could see that this case was going to be a difficult one to crack. Worse, the public agreed and quickly came to the view that a mindless killer was on the loose – someone in Aberdeen was killing for kicks.

When a milkman provided a description of a man he'd seen leaving 13 Allan Street in the early hours of 14 July 1978, a photofit was drawn up and distributed widely. Some 50,000 posters marked every street and wall in the city – nothing. The cops searched the area inch by inch and found no clues. Binmen were asked to search for the murder weapon, taxi drivers were quizzed about passengers from the street that night and an intricate search of local railway tracks and roadsides was carried out. All of this produced nothing and the people of Aberdeen were terrified – a killer was on the loose and they could be next.

Then the cops dropped a bombshell – some evenings every week, Dr Brenda Page worked as an escort girl. Everyone assumed that meant she was a high-class call girl and, in a way, this helped to allay the public's fears – surely even expensive prostitutes came into contact with sick and lethal punters? The cops were forced to go public. Dr Brenda Page wasn't a prostitute, they said, but worked for a respectable company that provided good-looking, well-educated females who knew their table manners as dinner guests for lonely businessmen away from home. Tall, beautiful, with lush brown hair, well read and polite, Brenda Page certainly fitted that bill. What was more, she didn't keep her 'hobby', as she called it, a secret from friends, workmates, family, anyone. But then why would she? It was the late 1970s – no HIV, free contraception, sex clubs a-go-go, down and dirty music, all-night clubs, women's liberation. Forget the sixties, the seventies was the true time of sexual and social freedom. This was especially so among the educated middle classes – the class Brenda Page was from.

According to her family, Brenda would openly joke about her hobby. Yet, privately, they believed she worked as an escort because she was lonely. The delightful doctor couldn't get a date even in the liberated seventies.

On the night she was killed, Brenda had been working as an escort and had dined with two businessmen at Aberdeen's plush

Treetops Hotel. Very quickly, cops cleared the businessmen of any suspicion. They were drawing blanks at every turn.

At one point, the search stretched as far away as Edinburgh. Cops were drafted in to search around Waverley Station for a green duffel bag. Though they never revealed the significance of that bag, it was presumably thought to have held the murder weapon or the killer's clothes that would have inevitably been covered with bloodstains. Police even hassled homeless folk and jakies just in case one of them had found it and kept it. No joy.

People in Aberdeen were once again double-locking their doors and windows and lone men being challenged and sometimes even attacked by vigilante-minded citizens if they were seen walking the streets late at night. To counter this, the cops announced that Brenda might well have known her killer. Most of the people murdered in Scotland know the people who kill them very well. Because of this, those killers seldom have to break into their victims' homes – there's no need. So was the police's suggestion that Dr Page had known her killer just a PR exercise designed to calm people?

People calmed down all right but only, as usual, over a period of years – years in which the killing of Dr Brenda Page has remained unsolved and, thankfully, no similar murders have happened – at least not in Aberdeen.

To this day, many people still believe it had something to do with her escort work. Suspicion, like dirt, always sticks but these folk had their reasons. There were those who would reveal – privately, of course – that Brenda wasn't as innocent as she seemed and her life not half as lonely as it was perceived to be. The last time Brenda Page was seen alive was as she was leaving the Treetops Hotel at 2.30 a.m. 'That would be a late dinner, then?' some folk were asking when what they really meant was, 'No, it wasn't.'

It was all speculation and rumour that, of course, can never be proven for one reason – the delightful doctor was dead.

When she was last seen, Brenda Page was happy, contented and enjoying a good night out – except when she was seen by her killer, of course.

Was it personal? A burglary gone wrong? Or had she just fallen foul of a thrill killer?

Whatever the answer, he's still on the loose.

THE STUFF OF NIGHTMARES

Axe-wielding psychos on the loose – not a Hollywood horror flick but real life in the streets of Scotland.

The State Hospital, Carstairs – the very name sends shivers down the spines of decent people. But some of the patients there are just offenders with mental illnesses who pose no danger at all. Then there are the psycho killers.

Slightly built, nineteen-year-old Robert Mone must have looked smart in his Gordon Highlanders uniform as he walked along the Dundee street. Those who knew him would've noticed that he was heading to his old school, St John's RC Secondary, but his purpose was not for a social visit – it was for murder.

Mone carried a long thin object wrapped in paper. When he marched into the needlework class, where teacher Nanette Hanson was in charge of a group of fourteen-year-old girls, the paper was torn off. It was a shotgun.

For the next two hours, Mone terrorised the class, shot through windows and blasted at any cops who came near. A few years before, the Marist Brothers who ran the school had expelled him and he'd ended up in an approved school. It was 1 November 1967 – payback day.

Nanette Hanson was only twenty-six and had moved up from Yorkshire with her husband of a few months. But she was strong-willed, mature and kept her cool throughout, comforting the terrified lassies. Mone amused himself by kissing one girl and sexually interfering with another two. Bored, he started blasting again.

Cops arrived and tried to speak with him but he refused to listen. Eventually, he said there was only one person he'd talk to – Marion Young, an eighteen-year-old nurse he'd met once and who, he said, 'understands me'.

Brave Marion came along when asked to by the cops. She even convinced them – against their better judgement – to allow her to go into that room of hell. Between them Nanette and Marion convinced Mone that he should let the frightened, tearful girls go free – the girls but not the women – which he did. Then he lost the plot entirely. Pointing the gun at Nanette, he pulled the trigger. It failed. He pulled the trigger again. Click. Cursing and swearing, he swivelled, jabbing the gun at Marion, the woman he asked to help him, and fired. Nothing.

Mone had been with the army in Germany. There, he'd gone AWOL and, on his way home, he'd bought the gun in London. Although this mad gunman had been planning this revenge visit for a long time, he hadn't thought to test the shotgun.

Pointing the gun again at Nanette he pulled the trigger. Failed. Pulled. Failed. Pulled. Failed. God knows what was going through the poor woman's head and heart.

Mone pulled the trigger again and this time he shot Nanette at point-blank range. As Marion knelt beside Nanette, giving her whatever comfort and first aid she could, an ambulance crew arrived and Mone let them in. With the crew were two of the Marist Brothers who he hated so much he'd plotted bloody revenge. Mone ignored them, sitting on a desk singing songs to himself – lost in his own hellish world.

As soon as Nanette, Marion, the paramedics and priests had cleared the room, armed cops burst in team-handed, expecting a shoot-out. But Mone sat there smiling, unseeing, humming to himself and was led away with no fight. He had murdered – task accomplished.

Nanette Hanson hung on to life with everything she had till the struggle proved too much. Only after her death did they find out that Nanette was in the early stages of her first pregnancy. A new job, a new husband, a new city, a new home and a new baby on the way – she had everything to live for till Robert Mone snatched it all away.

At his trial, Robert Mone was found to be severely schizophrenic. There was only one place he could be sent to – the State Hospital. One psycho in the pot.

Thomas McCulloch's crime was less dramatic but just as bloody. At the Erskine Bridge Hotel in Renfrewshire, in 1970, he complained that he hadn't been given enough butter with his bread roll. Rather than waiting for more, he shot the chef in the face. Just for good measure, he pulled a second gun and shot the manageress in the shoulder. When caught by the cops he was found to be carrying four shooters.

Thankfully, the two victims survived. McCulloch was found to be murderous and insane so it was the State Hospital for him. Two psychos in the pot.

Brady and Hindley, Fred and Rose West, Huntley and Carr . . . evidence abounds that certain murders only happen when particular relationships have been formed. Mone and McCulloch were about to rear their snarling heads.

It was 30 November 1976, a drizzly, dark, dreich night. But it wasn't just any night. It was the night close friends, maybe lovers, Mone and McCulloch planned to go free. For six months they'd plotted their escape and they were equipped with knives, axes, garrottes, fake IDs, uniforms, false beards, a torch and nurses' hats. Now it was time to go.

They pounced on nursing officer Neil MacLellan and patient Ian Simpson and threw paint stripper in their faces. Mone had planned everything and thought the paint stripper would disable the pair long enough for them to get the keys. Wrong. Side by side, nurse and patient, prison officer and inmate, fought like fury for their lives. Mone and McCulloch hacked them to hell.

McCulloch sat on MacLellan's back and continued chopping at him with a cleaver long after the man was immobilised. As he lay dying, Simpson groaned and Mone grabbed a pitchfork that had been left in the room and speared him with it just to make sure. Satisfied they were both dead, McCulloch leaned down, sliced off both of Simpson's ears and claimed them as a sick trophy.

The high razor-wire perimeter fence was formidable but they'd spent months making a rope ladder and, within minutes, Mone and McCulloch were free.

As planned, Mone lay down on the road near the hospital and pretended to be hurt. McCulloch slipped on a nurse's uniform and false beard and flagged down the first car, saying there had been an accident. The plan was to kill the driver and hijack the vehicle. As the driver went to help, a passing police car pulled in – good news for him but hell for the cops. As soon as they got out of the motor, PC John Gillies and PC George Taylor were hacked with axes and cleavers.

As Mone and McCulloch sped off in the police panda car, Gillies lay in a critical state. He would survive but Taylor died.

McCulloch wasn't a great driver and the roads were icy. When he inevitably crashed the car, the two were unhurt. A passing van slowed down to help and McCulloch pretended to be a cop with his prisoner. As soon as the good Samaritans got out to help, they were hacked and stabbed and thrown into the back of their own van. Lying in the back, barely conscious and in agony from their wounds, the men were off on a journey from hell.

A short while later, thinking he saw a police roadblock up ahead, McCulloch drove into a muddy field and the van got stuck – if only he'd known that the State Hospital staff at that point still didn't realise that the men had escaped and two men had died in the process.

Abandoning the van, McCulloch and Mone made their way to a farmhouse where, after terrorising the shocked family, they stole their car and headed off at speed.

Finally, the escape alarm had gone out from the State Hospital and police forces all over the south of Scotland and north of England were on the alert.

After almost three hours of bloody carnage, the car Mone and McCulloch had nicked from the farmhouse was rammed by a cop car on the A74 just north of Carlisle. Even then, they fought like fury but, eventually, the bravery of the police and their superior numbers won the day.

At the High Court, Edinburgh, Mone pled guilty to killing the policeman and McCulloch admitted he'd killed the nurse and patient. They were ordered to be imprisoned for the rest of their lives – an order that wouldn't last – but other events were to occur first.

It started in January 1979, when an elderly lady, Agnes Waugh, went missing from her home in Kinghorne Road, Dundee. Her front door was open, the gas fire and lights were on – had been for days – and it was as if she had just walked out.

The police were very worried and ordered a door-to-door search of the block. In the ground-floor flat, they found a scene from hell. Two elderly women were bound to chairs. Their faces were bloody and bruised and they had stockings wrapped round their necks. Both were dead. A younger woman lay stretched out on a bed, her face was also bruised and an electric flex and a stocking were tied round her neck. She too was dead.

They didn't have to look far for the killer. Some of the wounds were caused by a heavy, distinctive ring and they eventually tracked that ring to Christopher 'Sony' Mone, the father of Robert Mone. A thief, hard man and drunk, Sony Mone was a detested character. He'd inflict violence on anyone of any age or gender for no reason. He loved tattoos. Some he sported declared how hard he was and others depicted devil worship but the one he was always most willing to flash was on his penis. It read 'TNT'.

Instead of being ashamed of his son's murders, Sony Mone used to boast that he wanted to be more famous than the Carstairs killers. He was to have his day later in 1979, in the High Court in Dundee, when he was sentenced to life for the murders of Agnes Waugh, Jane Simpson and Catherine Miller.

Sony Mone couldn't keep his trap shut in jail and cons don't like those who murder women. In Craiginches Prison, Aberdeen, in 1983, he was knifed to death by another prisoner.

Robert Mone, his son, remains in the State Hospital. Now in his thirty-ninth year of being locked up, he is unlikely to ever be released.

McCulloch, described as 'an incurable psychopath' by Lord Dunpark in the High Court in 1976, when he was ordered to be detained for the rest of his natural life, is, however, a different matter.

In 2005, he used human rights legislation to be moved to a lower-security wing of Saughton Prison, Edinburgh. Now fifty-six, he is preparing for freedom with day release and work experience.

Thomas McCulloch may well be freed in 2007. Let's pray he really is a changed man.

1980 TO 1989

NEW WAVE, OLD WAYS

President Ronald Reagan was wounded in an assassination attempt (1981). The PLO were expelled from Beirut and went out with their guns blazing (1982). Israel withdrew from the Sinai Peninsula (1982) while famine ravaged most of East Africa (1984–85). Iran and Iraq went to war (1980–88) and Argentina and Britain fought over the Falkland Islands (1982). Hundreds died in Tiananmen Square, Beijing as Chinese tanks rolled in to quash demonstrations (1989) and the Berlin Wall was brought crashing down (1989).

The first case of AIDS was reported (1981). Scientists warned about global warming (1983). A hole in the ozone layer was discovered (1986) and the world population surpassed five billion (1987). Mark Chapman killed John Lennon (1980). Bobby Sands and other hunger strikers died in Northern Ireland (1981). Race riots swept through Brixton (1981) and the IRA bombed the Grand Hotel, Brighton, during the Tory Party's annual conference (1984).

Six members of the Doyle family were murdered in an arson attack on their home in Bankend Street, Glasgow, in so-called Ice-Cream Wars (1984). TC Campbell and Joe Steele were convicted of this crime and the longest fight over a miscarriage of justice in Scotland's history started. Campbell and Steele would be found innocent by the Appeal Court in 2005.

A young Paul Ferris went to work with Arthur Thompson, The Last Godfather of crime in Glasgow.

Heroin arrived in Scotland big time.

ILL REPUTE?

She was minding her own business – just getting through the day. Her problem was drink, her business was prostitution and it showed in her dress, her gait and on her face. She needed help. Someone was about to give her hell.

Carol lived with her boyfriend Billy in Barrowfield, a stone's throw from Celtic Park. She was small and frail – tiny even for that part of the east end of Glasgow where poverty rages fiercer than in any other European city. Life was hard for everyone in the east end. For Carol, it was about to become a nightmare.

She was found lying there on the ground, shivering and naked, her face and body covered in blood. By the time the ambulance crew arrived they weren't sure she was alive. Carol might have been small but she was tough. She was alive all right – just.

It was just after 1 a.m. on 1 November 1980 when the ambulance screamed up to the door of the Royal Infirmary. The paramedics hurried to stretcher her into the A&E ward. Even then, in that short journey from London Road, they weren't sure if she would still be alive. The duty doctor that night was a young woman about Carol's age. At the Royal, they very quickly got used to dealing with assaults and knife attacks every night. Yet, when the young medic looked down at her patient, she must've felt like weeping. This was bad – the worst.

The lassie's face had been slashed several times and so deeply that her features weren't discernible. Blade marks ran down her

273

body and her legs were zigzagged by deep wounds as if her attackers had been playing noughts and crosses on her flesh.

The young doctor worked solidly on Carol's wounds for almost twelve hours. She had done a good job but that job wasn't finished, she knew that. If there was to be any chance of her looking normal, the poor woman would need surgery again and again. There was a hard time coming her way. The young doctor couldn't be blamed for not knowing exactly how hard.

Before she ended her shift and went for some well-earned slumber, the doctor wrote case notes on Carol. It was mainly about the extent of her injuries and how they had been made by knife blades. Then she added one word, one question: 'Raped?'

Within a short period of time Carol was able to talk and talk she did. She told the horror story of being dragged into a workmen's hut by three young men who repeatedly raped her. Bored, they played at making zigzag marks on her face, body and legs with blades and then they raped her again.

The cops were called to the Royal. Carol repeated her story and even gave them the names of the rapists. She wasn't alone in her quest for justice.

Glasgow had many areas whose reputations were vile. In a hard city, small schemes stuck out as the hardest, the most violent. There was Blackhill – so bad it didn't need a nickname. Then there was Govan's Wine Alley – a place ordinary citizens daren't enter even in daylight. The Barrowland's Muggers' Alley – a nickname and a warning. Then there was Nightmare Alley – the worst of the worst, some folk thought. Its real name was Barrowfield and that's where Carol lived and suffered her ordeal.

Normally cops could expect nothing but grief from Barrowfield folk but not this time. They came forward in droves and many offered the same names for the rapists as Carol had given. The police now had names, addresses, more forensics than they needed and the young woman herself was willing to stand up and tell an open court what had happened. It was more than enough to secure a conviction for this nasty crime. Then it was decided that no action would be taken.

It wasn't the cops but the Crown who had decided the woman, now known as Carol X to protect her identity, made an unreliable witness because she was a prostitute. The Crown decided that she was of ill repute and no one would believe her but Carol X wasn't having that. She went to the papers, the *Daily Record* ran a campaign and a public outcry ensued. Rape is rape, the paper had said and the public agreed. A major scandal was brewing.

Top lawyer Ross Harper agreed to pursue a private prosecution on Carol X's behalf. Not since 1909 had the Crown allowed a private prosecution covered by ancient Scottish laws. Only two others had been allowed in the previous 300 years. But Ross Harper was determined. So was Carol. They won.

At a private prosecution on 21 January 1982, the three men went on trial. There was a queue of interesting witnesses, one a Glasgow journalist who had approached one of the suspects at the time the case had been dropped. Thinking he was now safe from prosecution the man had said, 'You know I fucking done her.'

One man was found guilty and sentenced to twelve years. It was a victory for public opinion. A victory for women. A moral victory for prostitutes.

Nicholas Fairbairn MP, then Solicitor General for Scotland, was forced to resign in the aftermath. His political career would falter for a while but rise again – too little a price to pay, some people thought.

Poor Carol X took to booze big time and continued as a prostitute. Years later, her looks gone and by then a hopeless drunk, she could be found in east end pubs selling the only thing she could. For the price of a drink she'd lift her skirt and show her scarred thighs.

A sad end to a sad woman. Once a victim and a victim still. Forgotten again by the state that betrayed her.

BEHIND CLOSED DOORS

Beautiful and peaceful – that's rural Scotland but it also has its secrets. Sometimes it's bloody murder.

Dumfries may not have the jagged mountains and rugged landscape of the Highlands but its rolling hills, winding rivers and gentle pace are beautiful nonetheless. Yet, there, in that small town, as in towns everywhere, no one really knew what went on behind closed doors.

David Little was a success by many folk's standards. The thirty-four-year-old made decent money dealing in cars and had a good-looking wife, Veronica, and a lovely little daughter, four-year-old Samantha. Life should have been very happy for them in their home in Lochside, Dumfries. Should have been.

The Littles lived a secret life of violence. David would be OK for ages then something – God knows what – made him snap and he'd lash out at his wife. To start with it was just now and then and she forgave him every time. Besides, it was the late 1970s and admitting your man hit you was like admitting failure.

Veronica was almost constantly bruised and bleeding. She'd cover it all up or, when she couldn't, she would lie to her family and friends. Then there was the rape. It would start with a slap and then he'd go further, stripping her and forcing himself on her, with wee Samantha crying in the next room.

As the years passed, the violence became more frequent and, by 1981, it was almost a daily occurrence. It also became more vicious and, one time, he hurt her so badly that he left her crippled.

Nothing would stop him – not even when Veronica fell pregnant again. David Little would still slap her and even punch her in the stomach so it was no surprise when she miscarried. That very night, as she grieved for the unborn baby she had lost, her insides raw and sore from the miscarriage, he raped her again. How bad could things get?

When, in 1982, outside Dumfries in that wide expanse of rolling countryside, a farmer stumbled across a man's body in a shallow grave, it must have been terrifying. Many farmers are used to death – but of beasts, not humans. And a shallow grave meant only one thing – murder.

Dumfries cops didn't have the daily dose of violence and killings the big city bizzies had to deal with. They did have one major advantage though – intimate local knowledge.

It wasn't long before they found out that David Little had suddenly left the area. Soon after the doctors confirmed that the murdered man, who'd been shot, was indeed the car dealer. Hunt on.

No one knew better than the police that car dealing meant a lot of bobbing and weaving and an occasional underhand bit of business by the less scrupulous. It was easy to make enemies in that business – but serious enough enemies to result in a killing?

As a couple of cops nosed into Little's business contacts, the main effort was invested in looking at the usual first stop in any murder – the spouse. Veronica Little was the least likely suspect in a murder, especially one that involved shooting, but the police's job is to put aside such positive prejudices and poke into all sorts of corners. That's where local knowledge came into play.

Dumfries may be a beautiful part of the world but living there, as in any small community, has its costs – like trying to keep something entirely secret from your neighbours. They'd heard the rows, the screaming, the weeping and it wasn't long before the cops had a vivid picture of the violence David Little had perpetrated on his wife. Although they might be sympathetic to the woman's plight, this was a murder investigation and they now had one essential ingredient – motive.

Not all the neighbours stuck to the point in hand. Some fell into what felt like low-level gossip, commenting on things like the fact that a young lassie by the name of Elaine Haggarty had often been at the Littles' house. A nice girl, Elaine was a regular babysitter for the couple but she had started turning up at other times too until it reached the point where she was hardly away from the house. Then there was that local boy, William McKenzie – he'd been spotted a couple of times. Maybe he'd a wee fancy for Elaine?

That's when the forensic bods came up with a vital clue. David Little had been shot five times. Each of the bullets had been gold washed, a process that made them more lethal – a process only a few people would know about. Had this been a professional hit?

After a couple of intense interviews, the police charged Veronica Little with murder and she wasn't alone. Seventeen-year-old Elaine Haggarty and eighteen-year-old William McKenzie were charged along with her.

At their trial in Edinburgh's High Court in 1982, it all came out and a lurid tale unfolded of events in a small rural town. It hadn't happened in Glasgow, Edinburgh, Dundee or Aberdeen but in gentle Dumfries and that's what would shock the people of Scotland.

David Little had seduced their babysitter, ex-convent girl Elaine Haggarty, when she was only sixteen years old. The man didn't even try very hard to keep it a secret from his wife but maybe that was just another way of torturing her.

One night, Elaine didn't want to make love but you didn't say no to David Little. He promptly slapped her and raped her. Over time, that's what their relationship became like – just the same as his relationship with his wife. It seemed that Little thought he could do whatever he wanted with the women but there was one thing he hadn't thought of – friendship.

One day, Elaine went to Veronica and confessed all. It wasn't long before the women were telling each other about the violence they each suffered and how they both felt trapped. They became close, very close – lesbian lovers, in fact. In afternoons of stolen intimacy at the Littles' home, they'd lie together talking about how to stop the violence both were still suffering at Little's hands. It isn't known which one of them first came up with the idea of murder. It probably started as mere wishful thinking that their tormentor was dead. Gradually, though, the thought took wings and they began to plot.

Elaine had met a young local guy, a part-time soldier by the name of William McKenzie. She knew that McKenzie had taken a real shine to her and he was flattered when she reciprocated his attentions. As a soldier, he had the weapons, the bullets and the training – but did he have the bottle?

The two women used the only tool they had to try to convince McKenzie – sex. Two women – he couldn't believe his luck. Then they started to suggest murder. Eventually, with the promise of endless nights of passion and a paltry £120, William McKenzie shot David Little and buried his body in the shallow grave. Problem over?

Like many killers before them, the three discovered that plotting death was one thing but finding peace of mind after the murder was another matter entirely. They were constantly on edge, tense and suspicious, worried that they hadn't covered their tracks.

As the whole story emerged, supported by sound forensic evidence, there was clearly some sympathy in the court for Veronica Little and Elaine Haggarty. No one was in any doubt that David Little was a cruel and evil man who had brutalised them both. If, one day, as he beat her yet again, Veronica had reached out in desperation for a kitchen knife and stabbed him to death, there might have been a different outcome. But, instead, she had plotted his murder. That wasn't self-defence and, as such, the crime deserved the full weight of the law. Well, that's how it was viewed in 1982.

Found guilty, Elaine Haggarty was sent to a secure childcare institution without limit of time, William McKenzie was sentenced to life and sent off to a Young Offenders' Institution. Veronica Little stood pale-faced and silently weeping as the judge sentenced her to life in prison.

'God help me,' she said, her voice trembling, before she collapsed in the dock.

If someone had helped her years earlier and stopped the abuse, maybe she would have a different, happier story to tell. Maybe she wouldn't be in this book.

RAISED TO KILL?

'Smelly Robbie! Smelly Robbie!' Kids everywhere can be cruel – just as they were in Grangemouth in the 1950s. If only they'd known who they were tormenting.

He was a strange kid – a loner who was prone to aggressive outbursts. Everyone knew that he'd been given up by his mother and fostered by the Tulip family. Kids weren't very kind to 'orphans' in those days – the fact that he didn't stay with his natural mother and father was just another excuse to give him a hard time.

All his childhood, Smelly Robbie would be plagued by other kids but, one day, he was going to wreak his terrible revenge on kids everywhere.

They had long forgotten about Smelly Robbie in Grangemouth when they read their newspapers in autumn 1982. Eleven-year-old Susan Maxwell had disappeared from her home in Coldstream on 31 July and was found 300 miles away. She had suffered great sexual indignities before being killed. Poor lassie, everyone agreed. It was the type of crime that gripped every parent and decent citizen with terror. Someone had abducted young Susan and taken her to a place to rape and slaughter her. It was the kind of dreaded crime that had to be stopped immediately but, in spite of enormous efforts by the cops, they had no leads in Susan's murder.

Almost a full year later, five-year-old Caroline Hogg was abducted from her Portobello home. She was found, having been sexually assaulted and killed, 300 miles away, but the location of her body was only twenty-four miles from where Susan had been found. Alarms bells started screaming.

Posters of the two wee girls swamped Scotland. Every cop force and every parent in Scotland was on the alert. When any young girl was reported missing, the road traffic cops would immediately start checking motors travelling south into England. No joy.

Other young girls all over England had suffered the same fate as Susan and Caroline and almost 250,000 people had been interviewed in the national campaign to nab their killers. But were they linked? To handle all the information being scooped up by different forces, a national database, CATCHEM, was created for the first time. Still no joy.

It took till 1994 for a breakthrough to be made and what a breakthrough it was. English cops had nabbed the guy they believed had sexually assaulted and killed ten-year-old Sarah Harper in Leeds in 1986. The suspect wasn't helping them – he was saying nothing. But the forensic teams got on the case and concluded that he had killed others – maybe many others – including Susan Maxwell and Caroline Hogg for sure.

Another shock awaited Scots – the killer was Scottish. He was a man by the name of Robert Black who, as a kid in Grangemouth, was known as Smelly Robbie.

Robert Black had been put into care by his mother when he was just a baby. A kindly couple called Tulip fostered him through those difficult years of his childhood. He was a loner – shy one minute and violent the next with no reason and no warning. Young Robert liked to play with his shit and he would also stick objects into his anus. Even as a young child he felt that he should've been female despite the fact that, from an early age, girls fascinated him sexually.

When Black was only eleven years old his foster mother died and he was moved to a children's home in Falkirk. Within months, he was caught sexually interfering with younger girls. He was caught and punished but that didn't stop him and he had to be moved to different children's homes several times.

In 1962, having reached the then legal school-leaving age of fifteen, he got a delivery job in Greenock. Later, in custody, Black admitted having sexually abused at least forty children as he did his rounds. Nobody sussed what the delivery boy was up to.

His first conviction was for lewd and libidinous behaviour when he was seventeen. That involved abducting a young girl before sexually interfering with her. The pattern was now set.

All of his adult life Robert Black was an active sex abuser. He had only one serious adult relationship, with a young woman called Pamela Hodgkinson. When she broke that off, he headed to London in 1972 and his career as a sexual predator was about to go big time.

The firm of Poster Dispatch and Storage knew nothing of Black's background when they hired him. They took him on as a driver, after all, not someone who would be working with kids. But, working on his own and travelling all over the UK and the Continent, it was the sexual predator's ideal job.

Cops reckon that Black killed thirteen-year-old April Fabb in Norfolk in 1969 and they have tied him to another five murders of girls before he chanced upon young Susan Maxwell. Yet the decision was made to try him for the killing of Susan, Caroline and Sarah only.

In 1994, he was found guilty at Newcastle Crown Court on all three counts, including charges of abduction and murder. The judge understood who he was dealing with and sentenced Robert Black to ten life sentences. He'll never leave prison alive.

In Newcastle, later that year, there was a secret conference of top cops from all over Europe. There was only one point on the agenda – Robert Black's MO. By the end of the day, they all agreed that Black had been responsible for seventeen murders and one abduction. The locations stretched from Ireland via France to the Netherlands – although most of his killings had been in Scotland and England.

They decided to approach him and see if he'd be willing to speak about these other crimes. He was going to die in jail anyway so what had they got to lose? He said . . . nothing – nothing at all.

Every year since, European cop forces have gathered together and examined other cases from Black's killing years, 1969 to 1993. Every year, they leave the meeting depressed yet convinced that other names should be added to his list. Every year, a delegation is sent to Black in his cell. Every year, they then go back to their hotel rooms and make phone calls to the grieving parents all over Europe and every year they have the same story to tell. They wish they could help. They had hoped they could help. But they can't help – not now and, they think, not ever.

Why? Because Black is not talking. Not a word. Not a murmur. As they give him the details and ask him to confirm them, a smile glimmers slowly into those dead eyes – a smile of pleasure and victory.

Robert Black isn't talking. Smelly Robbie is having his revenge.

NINJA AND NUN

'I'll wait,' said the scary-looking young man with the Scouse accent.

'She's not in,' said the caretaker for the umpteenth time, 'and you can't wait there.'

The young bloke sat down on a chair in the corridor outside the social worker's office door. He looked strange. It wasn't just his shaven head, the big stud in his nose and his earrings – lots of kids dressed that way in 1988 – he seemed manic, half-crazed and was stinking of booze.

The caretaker, Felix Graham, might have been almost seventy years old but he was an ex-boxer and he could still handle himself. However, he knew better than to create a ruckus in that place of peace, the pastoral centre that was there to help people. So he'd leave the young man to cool down and he'd get bored soon enough.

A short while later, Father Colin Stewart returned to the pastoral centre at St Mary's Roman Catholic Cathedral in Huntly Street, Aberdeen. He was busy, as were all his colleagues, so he went directly to his office. The door was stuck. Father Stewart pushed harder and it gave way a little before some force pushed it back, slamming it shut. Someone was holding the door from the other side.

A burglar was what the good priest thought and he rushed to get Mr Graham to help. Downstairs, the two were just in time to see the young man Felix had spoken to earlier clamber down a fire escape, run through the backyard and jump up and over the high wall. If he had looked strange before, he looked positively terrifying now. Naked to the waist, he was carrying clothes in his hands and his chest and face were smeared with blood.

'Sister Josie!' shouted Father Stewart, running towards the office he shared with the nun. 'Is she in?'

Sister Josie lay on her back, crucifixion style, almost naked, covered in dark blue bruises, purple bite marks and blood. She was dead.

The cops were on the scene in a flash. Everyone in the city knew of Sister Josie and her good works. Besides, who would murder a nun in a cathedral apart from a crazed madman? Someone very dangerous was out there and they had to nab him quick.

The fifty-nine-year-old victim's full name was Sister Josephine Ogilvie and there was something special about her that made her stand out even from the other folk who were there to help the flock. She had silver hair, glasses, a twinkle in her eye and a wry sense of humour but, more than that, she was exceptionally gifted in reaching kids no matter how bad their situations were. Early on, the kids dubbed her Sister Josie and it was adopted by everyone – even the Bishop. Sister Josie – the warm, familiar name suited her. Everyone was going to miss her so much – everyone except the killer.

The cops sprang into action, cordoning off the entire area in record time. Thanks to Father Stewart and Felix Graham, they had a reasonable description of the man they were hunting and knew he had a Scouse accent – not something that's very common in the Granite City. Within two hours, they had a breakthrough. A guy of that description had been buying booze from a local licensed grocer. The cops hit a guesthouse at nearby Dee Place and weren't too polite about it – they needed to get the killer off the street. There, they found Mark Reynolds, sitting in his underwear, eating curry leftovers as his clothes sloshed round in the washing machine. His face and chest were still splattered with blood.

Twenty-three-year-old Reynolds was charged with Sister Josie's murder. He wasn't arguing. Instead he was blaming drugs – LSD and dope. But a couple of days later, when he was banged up in Craiginches Prison, he told a warder, 'I got up this morning and realised I was a murderer – that I had strangled someone.' He had done a lot more than that.

The post-mortem on Sister Josie revealed terrible injuries. He'd punched and kicked her all over, trampled on her, jumped on her, stabbed her, bit her, strangled her, cut her with scissors and raped her. Half her ribs were smashed, an ear was sliced off, her spine was fractured and her neck was almost broken. The only saving grace was that Sister Josie had died early in the assault from a heart attack. No grace at all.

Even some of the cops were furious and felt like hurting Mark Reynolds badly for the mindless atrocities he had perpetrated on the nun who loved everyone. The public – regardless of religion – wanted to lynch him. Her good friend and colleague Father Stewart reflected sadly on how Sister Josie was just weeks away from moving to a new position in Edinburgh, the city of her birth. The Bishop of Aberdeen, Mario Conti – now Archbishop of Glasgow – prayed publicly for calm and forgiveness.

At his trial at the High Court in Aberdeen, on 23 August 1988, a series of psychiatrists, including one from the State Hospital, Carstairs, described Mark Reynolds as mentally ill. In fact, he'd been diagnosed as schizophrenic in 1982 and been prescribed heavy-duty antipsychotic tablets since then. The trouble was that he didn't always take his medication but he would often dope himself up on drugs such as LSD or hash.

The night before the killing he had stayed up all night smoking dope, downing handfuls of painkillers and watching sadistic videos. The reason he had gone to St Mary's that dreadful day was to see another nun, Sister Mary McDonald. She was a social worker and he thought she could help him deal with his depression.

Former altar boy Reynolds also had some weird ideas. He considered himself a true follower of the lethal Japanese martial art Ninjitsu and had the black outfit, red headband and weapons.

He often paraded in his rig-out, looking for all the world like a proper Ninja warrior as far he was concerned.

Reynolds' own lawyer admitted that his client was a very ill person indeed. The trial judge, Lord Cullen, didn't hesitate to send him to the State Hospital without limit of time.

Everyone in Scotland had been watching this trial carefully and not just because of the outrage that a gentle nun being killed in such a brutal manner provoked. A few years before, the Tory government had decided that many mentally ill people who would previously be in hospital were to be treated in their own homes. In England, there had been a couple of tragic murders committed by such ill folk. Was this the way of the future? Did we all have to put up with dangerous killers in our midst? If Reynolds had been cared for in hospital, Sister Josie would still be alive. The public were furious as well as scared and wondered when the next murder was going to happen but calm was on its way.

Reynolds hadn't drifted north from Liverpool on his own as had originally been assumed. His mother – a kindly, caring Christian woman – had moved with him up to Aberdeen thinking it would get him away from the bad influences and drug dealers down south. His mother was indeed a regular worshipper at St Mary's which is why Reynolds had gone there for help that day. She'd meant well and had tried her best but it had ended in tragedy.

Bishop Mario Conti went into overdrive talking about and preaching peace and forgiveness. A huge crowd of all religions turned out to pray for Sister Josie and special prayers were said for Mark Reynolds. Sister Josie's own rosary beads were presented to Reynolds' mother. It's what the good nun would have wanted.

The message got through to the world. What happened that day wasn't about murder but about forgiveness. Even after her death, Sister Josie's work went on. She continued to touch so many people.

Touched everyone who knew of her. Except, perhaps, for Mark Reynolds, the Ninja killer.

LICENSED TO KILL?

Just another car crash off a hazardous country road? No – the most intriguing unsolved murder of the last twenty years.

Willie McRae was a larger-than-life character. A prominent Scottish lawyer, he'd fought and won many cases opposing the government. An SNP activist, he'd held national office and come close to becoming an MP. Yet McRae also revelled in his radical anti-nuclear stance – a dangerous position to hold in the 1980s.

On Friday, 5 April 1985, he left his Glasgow office to head to his weekend house in Kintail in the far north. Laden with his usual bulging briefcase and armfuls of legal documents and with a big grin splitting his face, he turned to his office staff and said, without further explanation, 'I've got them! I've got them!' These were to be the last words he was known to have spoken.

Around 10 a.m. the following day, an Australian tourist and his wife pulled their car in at an isolated spot on the A87. A maroon Volvo lay twenty or so yards off the road, straddling a burn, and the couple wanted to check no one was hurt. They found a man slumped in the driver's seat, unconscious, his head smeared with blood.

The next car on the scene was driven by Dr Dorothy Messer, accompanied by her fiancé David Coutts, a Dundee SNP councillor, who was shocked to recognise the injured man as Willie McRae. Dr Messer immediately examined McRae and found he was alive though dilated pupils indicated serious brain damage.

The police had been alerted by another passing motorist and PC Kenny Crawford arrived on the scene from Inverness all on his own. The cops had been told that a prominent Scottish politician, activist and lawyer was lying injured in an isolated spot so what did they do? They sent one lonesome PC. But PC Crawford did his best and he and David Coutts struggled to get McRae's limp body out of the car. With the limited facilities available to her, Dr Messer concluded that McRae had been hurt in a road accident. The doctor had also done her best and there was nothing to contradict that opinion – yet.

Willie McRae was transported by ambulance to Raigmore Hospital, Inverness, and then on to Aberdeen Royal Infirmary – the standard procedure for brain damage treatment. There, six hours after his discovery and God knows how long after he had been hurt, a nurse washed the blood off the patient's head and discovered a bullet hole. An X-ray confirmed that Willie McRae had been shot just above his right ear – the hit man's bull's eye.

Willie McRae died at 3 a.m. on 7 April 1985, at least thirty-six hours after being injured. Already folk were rightly questioning the way in which the whole affair had been handled.

Realising there had been a cock-up, Chief Superintendent Andrew Lester, head of Northern CID, took over the case immediately. Yet McRae's car was promptly removed from the site of what was now a suspicious death. Normally, it would have been cordoned off and stayed put while squads of forensic bods, photographers and scene-of-crime officers did their work.

It was later revealed that the police couldn't even correctly remember where Willie McRae had been found. They'd got it wrong by over a mile in that featureless countryside and only revised the location when their mistake was pointed out by one of the civilians who had been at the scene. The tragic comedy of errors continued.

At the time McRae's body was found, young PC Crawford had discovered a small pyramid of the dead man's personal papers about twenty yards from his car. They'd all been carefully torn up and on top was his smashed wristwatch. The constable had carefully collected everything but who had put them so neatly there? Who knows? Too many people had trampled over the ground, ruining any clues there might be.

A search of the scene the day after McRae's death revealed a Smith & Wesson .45 in the stream about twenty yards from the car. The gun had been fired twice and had no traces of any fingerprints. Twice? Who could shoot themselves twice in the head? McRae wasn't wearing gloves when found. So who wiped the gun of prints? Over twenty yards? Who could throw the hefty gun that distance when they'd just put a bullet in their own brain?

Despite all these unanswerable questions, a post-mortem would deliver an open verdict suggesting suicide. When challenged, the police suggested the heavy gun had been carried downstream by the water of the wee burn. A few questions put by curious journalists soon dismissed that theory. While they were trying to remove McRae from his car, PC Crawford's cap had fallen off and David Coutts had bent to retrieve it, getting a clear view of the stream beside and under the car. There was no sign of any gun.

It also emerged that the pathologist had failed to carry out a basic test on the bullet wound which would have determined how close the gun had been when it was fired. This is a fundamental test for suicide since suicides always press the gun hard into their skull just to be sure. A hit man, on the other hand, might fire from inches or feet away. The closer you get, the messier you get and it's the kind of messy evidence that's difficult to conceal.

McRae had left for Kintail laden with documents, a bulging briefcase, a bottle of whisky and a large pack of cigarettes to feed his chain-smoking habit yet none of these things were found amongst his belongings. At the time of his death, McRae had been working on yet another sensitive case. Having previously legally prevented the UK Atomic Energy Authority in 1980 from dumping nuclear waste in the Ayrshire hills, he intended to have a similar impact on plans to dump waste from Dounreay in the sea.

McRae had hinted to colleagues he had been passed classified government documents – not for the first time – and colleagues knew he was carrying highly sensitive papers on this case. Friends believe it was the Dounreay inquiry he was referring to when, on that last Friday night as he left the office, he said, 'I've got them! I've got them!' But no papers of his relating to Dounreay have ever been located.

Over months before his death, Willie McRae's house was repeatedly burgled and, during these break-ins, his legal papers were disrupted and destroyed. In fact, on the morning of that fateful trip north, there had been a fire in his home. He became cautious and very security conscious and he carried copies of the Dounreay papers with him at all times – as he did on the day he died – but those were never found either. The only other copies of the Dounreay papers were kept in his office. Who'd break into a well-known lawyer's office? But they were stolen when it was burgled. Nothing else was taken.

People began to look for a wider explanation of McRae's death. They didn't have to look too far back. The year before McRae died, a gentle woman called Hilda Murrell was found murdered in her cottage in rural Shrewsbury. Hilda was a rose grower, a pacifist – who could want to kill her? A robber? Yes – but the only things stolen from her home were some papers to do with her other passion – anti-nuclear protesting.

Later it was leaked to the press that Hilda's nephew was a naval intelligence officer involved in the sinking of the *Belgrano* during the Falklands War, then a great controversy since the ship had been heading away from battle when deliberately sunk. But no papers of his were taken – just Hilda's anti-nuclear evidence. It was yet another smokescreen. The question was why?

Retired police officers have revealed that, because of his legal and political work, McRae was on the files of MI5. One of the cars used to trail him was identified as a Triumph, registration number PSJ 136X. Wherever McRae went, that car followed. He had noticed the motor – Willie McRae was nobody's fool – and when he raised the matter with a friendly cop, the policeman had checked the computer. The car came up marked as a 'blocked vehicle'. That's shorthand for belonging to the Special Branch or MI5.

Yet no inquiry was ever held into the death of Willie McRae. Instead, there was a whispering campaign suggesting that McRae was everything from an alcoholic to a homosexual to a man in deep financial trouble. Good enough reasons for why he might be troubled, why he might have killed himself, but absolutely without any substance according to anyone who really knew him.

The post-mortem report has been kept secret. The procurator fiscal in Inverness has refused to comment on the case, citing the Official Secrets Act. *Madame Ecosse*, Winnie Ewing of the SNP, is a qualified lawyer and, when she carried out an investigation for her political party, she was bluntly denied access to the Crown Office papers in spite of giving the customary legal guarantee of confidentiality.

Every independent person who has ever examined the case of Willie McRae has concluded it wasn't suicide. So, if it wasn't suicide, then what? Murder? But by whom and in whose name? Yours?

As this book goes to press, new witnesses have come forward – witnesses who have never spoken out before. They confirm the view that Willie McRae didn't take his own life but was taken out by MI5. Will the government soon reopen his case, then? What do you think?

THE CAMBUSLANG RIPPER

Usually she'd call home from the station for a lift. That night she decided to walk the short distance. It was a fatal decision.

They found Elizabeth Walton the next day, 3 December 1982, in the grounds of West Coats Primary School, Cambuslang – the very school her daughter attended. Attractive and vivacious in life, in death she wasn't a pretty sight.

She had been strangled and savagely beaten. After death, her clothes were stripped off and her body, wrists and legs mutilated with a knife. By her side lay her clothes carefully tied in neat knots laid out in a line. This wasn't just a brutal murder – it was a ritualistic killing. An extremely dangerous man was on the loose. For ritualistic read potential serial killer. All the patterns were there. This was a murderer who wasn't going to stop.

Local cops pulled out all the stops. Early on, they called in the Serious Crime Squad to help. The biggest team of cops Lanarkshire had seen in many years started knocking on doors and an incident HQ was set up near the scene of crime.

It took only three days for their first breakthrough. A man arrived at the caravan saying he had some information that may help. He'd been near the scene around 11 p.m. on 2 December, the time of the killing, when he'd noticed a suspicious-looking man hanging around some bushes. He gave the cops as much of a description as he could remember.

Murder investigations are always peppered by sad time-wasters making up stories but this bloke seemed reliable enough.

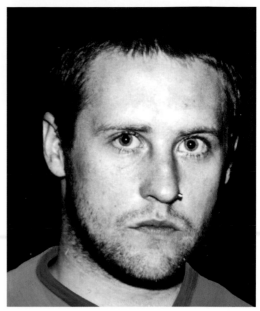

From an early age in his hometown of Falkirk Robert Black had been in trouble for sexually abusing young girls. He then began abducting and killing them. The police reckon he's responsible for the deaths of seventeen girls and the abduction of one. ('Raised to Kill?')

In 1988, former altar boy Mark Reynolds replaced the drugs he used to control his mental illness with LSD and cannabis before heading to Aberdeen's St Mary's Roman Catholic Cathedral where he brutally attacked, raped and murdered one of the nuns. ('Ninja and Nun')

When solicitor and SNP activist Willie McRae left his Glasgow office for Kintail one Friday in 1985, his parting shot was an enigmatic one – 'I've got them!' he shouted. Willie never made it to Kintail – his body was found in his car. Did 'they' get him first?

Hilda Murrell who, the year before Willie died, was murdered in her home in what the police said was a burglary. But only documents relating to the anti-nuclear protests Hilda was involved in were stolen. Willie had hinted that he was in possession of secret documents relating to the Dounreay nuclear plant . . . ('Licensed to Kill?')

Jean Keay was one of three elderly people attacked in their home. George Scott and Jean's sister, Hazel Smith, survived the ordeal but Jean died of horrific injuries.

The house in Prestwick's Ardayre Road where the three pensioners were assaulted in 1992. The level of brutality led police to believe a vicious gang must have been involved.

Thomas Moore was found guilty of the robbery and murder at Ardayre Road. However, further police inquiries and Moore's own testimony led to his girlfriend, charity worker Brenda Horsburgh, being jailed for life for killing Jean Keay.

Chief Inspector Stuart Kernohan, one of the cops investigating the Ardayre Road murder. It later transpired that he'd been having an affair with one of the chief witnesses for the prosecution, Kerry Bristol, the girlfriend of Thomas Moore's brother. ('Beauty the Beast')

In 1987, committed Christian Andrew Hunter and his Samaritan wife Lynda were expecting their first baby when he reported her missing from their Carnoustie home.

Police suspected Hunter was involved in his wife's disappearance. The TV programme *Crimewacth UK* featured the case of missing Lynda and here medium Anne Anderson seeks paranormal guidance in the search for her body.

In an elaborate effort to cover his tracks and establish an alibi for himself, Hunter drove Lynda's car to Manchester, left it parked on yellow lines to ensure it attracted police attention and then got the train home. He even made sure he had a timed receipt from a shop to try to bolster his claims that he'd never left Tayside – all to no avail. ('Beware the Deceiver')

It was said that Gordonstoun School old boy Paul Macklin (left) had always been a bit weird but, when he got in tow with the equally strange Robert Cadiz in Aberdeen in 1994 and the pair got their mitts on some firearms, there was bound to be trouble.
('Walter Mitty Gets a Shooter')

A self-confessed nymphomaniac, Nawal Nichol was accused of paying two men to murder her husband but she never faced trial. Instead, she became very wealthy from the payout on her husband's life insurance policy.

Once a patron of all the best clubs, Nawal quickly spent the money and soon had to make a living as a lap dancer. The seedy lifestyle would seem to have taken its toll on her looks. ('The Black Widow')

You certainly wouldn't think that academic Paul Agutter was a mass murderer yet that's exactly what his attempt to murder his wife would have turned him into had he been more successful.

Carole Bonsall, Agutter's mistress. The Agutters had an open relationship but trouble started when Agutter fell for Bonsall in a big way and wanted to be with her. Most folk in this position would seek a divorce but Agutter had other ideas . . .

After serving seven years for his crime, Paul Agutter got a job at the University of Manchester, teaching ethics in science. Once the university discovered his background, his contract was not renewed. Let's hope it was something as innocuous as vitamin pills he was shopping for on the day this picture was taken. ('Vitriol and Venom')

Brian Doran

Ken Togher

Arthur 'The Godfather' Thompson

Joe Hanlon

Bobby Glover

Some of the big names that hit the Scottish headlines in the 1990s for the wrong reasons.

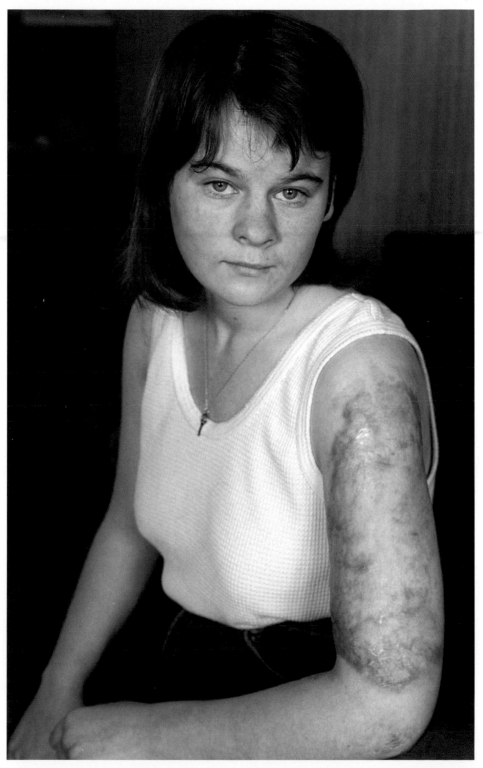

Barbara Gillen. Over a period of days, five young women kept Barbara prisoner and brutally tortured her. The reason? She owed them £40. After her ordeal Barbara said, 'The nightmares haunt me every night. Will they ever end?' ('The Bitches from Hell')

Kim and Ian Galbraith had moved from England to the peaceful rural setting of Loch Fyne in the mid 1990s. He worked as a policeman so it was doubly distressing for his colleagues who found him dead in his bed with his brains blown out. Kim can be seen being led from court during her trial for the murder of her husband. ('Till Death . . .')

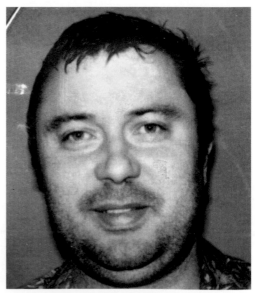

In 1999, after discovering a severed arm in Loch Lomond, police divers search the loch to see if they can find any more body parts. Then a head washed up on an Ayrshire beach. It belonged to young Barry Wallace whose parents had reported him missing.

Evil William Beggs had already escaped conviction for a sexually motivated murder the police were confident he'd committed. Beggs claimed to be innocent of young Barry's murder but his impeccably clean flat was to yield a crucial piece of evidence.
('Limbs, Lochs and a Lethal Lust')

Iain Scoular was twenty-four years old. Politely spoken and from a good family, he lived in a very nice house near the scene with his well-to-do parents. The cops would follow up the lead.

Yet the more detectives inquired into Scoular's sighting of the mysterious man, the more intrigued they became about Scoular himself. To put it politely, he was a bit of an oddball.

From a well-off, high-achieving family, Iain Scoular had been a failure at school. More than that, he was an outsider, a loner who was prone to making up stories, and, at other times, he became depressed. His despairing parents had sought help and he'd been treated by a psychiatrist at one point. But that was the extent of it – there was nothing extreme to worry about. He was just a bit of an oddball but being an oddball didn't make him a murderer, did it?

Then cracks began to appear in Scoular's version of events. He had said to cops that he'd been home by 11 p.m. on the night Elizabeth Walton was killed, contradicting his previous statement. Scoular was adamant he was now telling the truth but he hadn't reckoned on the cops speaking to his overprotective mother – or, more to the point, on her talking to them.

Jean Scoular kept a tight leash on Iain in spite of him being twenty-four years old. When he went out, she sat up waiting for him and, if he wasn't back at a decent hour, she would go out in her car scouring the streets till she found him.

Jean and her husband were concerned by how often the cops were interviewing their son. Probably they knew him as a not very bright, naive guy and worried he might get implicated in a very serious matter they believed he had nothing to do with.

His father wrote to the chief constable to complain. It had no effect. After all there was a potential serial killer stalking the streets. His mother went round to the cops' incident caravan to take issue with the murder squad.

That's when she revealed that Iain hadn't come home till 1 a.m. on the night Elizabeth Walton was killed – two hours later than he'd told the cops. Mother had inadvertently put son if not in the frame then at least under suspicion.

Iain Scoular was interviewed again and changed his story twice, lying both times. Then witnesses ID-ed him as having been seen running fast past the shopping centre in Cambuslang shortly after Elizabeth Walton's murder. Now he was in the frame.

Jean Scoular visited the cops again arguing for her son's innocence. While there she said, 'The next thing you know, you'll be charging him for that taxi driver.'

The cops hadn't thought of that but now they would look into it.

A couple of months before, on 1 October 1982, the body of taxi driver Catherine McChord was found crammed into the boot of her cab in Braeside Place, Cambuslang. She had died violently and deep stab wounds had been found on her chest and the back of her head. The cops had carried out a huge exercise interviewing taxi customers and drivers, especially female drivers, but it was all to no avail. Then they found out that Catherine had spent three years in jail for a £143,500 scam of a spot-the-ball competition. Had she still been active? Connected to gangsters? Was this a hit? But Catherine wasn't active or connected and it wasn't a hit – she was just an innocent woman going about her job when some crazy man decided to kill her.

The cops had got nowhere close to catching Catherine's killer but now Jean Scoular had given them a task – to compare Catherine and Elizabeth's murders for similarities.

There were a few. Both had died violently. In both cases, a knife was used by a left-handed person, just like Iain Scoular. Neither had been sexually assaulted. Both died a short distance from each other, close to Iain Scoular's home. But there was something even more uncanny. Inside Catherine's taxi, a cigarette lighter, an inhaler and her car keys had been carefully positioned in a straight line on the driver's seat. Was that the small start of the type of ritual many serial killers develop? A ritual that would grow with each killing? Like Elizabeth Walton's clothes being carefully knotted and left neatly beside her body?

As a theory it was interesting but they needed more than that. They got help again from Jean Scoular.

When she had gone to them to complain, she had said that Iain had been at home with her and her husband on the night Catherine McChord was killed. Checking their notebooks, they soon realised that someone was lying. Iain Scoular had given a completely different account of his whereabouts on that night. So where had he really been? But there was more. All the police activity had stirred up people's memories. The public were cooperating fully in trying to get this thrill killer off the streets. Two separate witnesses both Scoular as running away from a taxi the night Catherine was killed.

Then the forensic team made a breakthrough. Two hairs from the jacket Catherine McChord had been wearing were found on Scoular's trousers. They had enough. Iain Scoular was charged with double murder.

The trial at the High Court, Glasgow, in May 1983 was a harrowing experience for the jury as the details of the murders were revealed and graphic photographs of the victims shown. In contrast, Scoular sat in the dock unmoved as if the whole proceedings had nothing to do with him. Even when psychiatrists described him as a psychopath, he didn't show a flicker of interest. However, when the same doctors described him as sexually impotent he looked up, anger and protest in his eyes. It was the closest Iain Scoular came to showing any reaction during his fourteen-day trial.

The jury found him guilty and, in sentencing him to twenty years in prison, Lord Allanbridge said, 'I consider you an extremely dangerous young man.'

As Iain Scoular stood impassively staring at the judge, his only movement was his jaw working on a sweet.

Few people in Scotland disagreed with Lord Allanbridge. In fact, the cops and psychiatrists thought he had shown remarkable restraint in his comments.

The question remains, if Scoular hadn't gone into the police caravan that day of his own free will, would he still be free and might he have gone on to become one of Scotland's most notorious serial killers? Let us all be grateful we'll never find out.

BEWARE THE DECEIVER

All afternoon the two sisters had talked. One had marriage problems but nothing serious. Or was it?

Watching her sister drive away, Sandra hoped it would all blow over. After all Lynda had everything – a great job, good money and she'd just married her lover, Andrew. Better still, she was pregnant. What more could she wish for?

But Lynda was having bad morning sickness and she and Andrew were arguing. Like that day, 13 August 1987, when Lynda travelled down from her home in Carnoustie to tell Sandra she was pregnant. It should've been a celebration but turned into a moan.

Lynda was upset that Andrew was going to a work party the following week instead of spending time with her on her day off. Just wee niggles that get to couples some time. They'd had worse things to deal with before.

Andrew had been married before. He'd met his first wife, Christine, through the Salvation Army in his hometown of Paisley. They had a son and, in 1977, the family had moved up to Broughty Ferry in Dundee just across from where Lynda stayed with her partner, lecturer Dr Ian Glover.

Andrew had done voluntary work through the Salvation Army and now had a job in a children's home while studying part-time for a qualification in social work. Lynda had been a Samaritan for years and was now qualified in social work with a good job. Once she'd got to know her new neighbours a bit, she offered Andrew help with his studies. This was typical of the attractive twenty-six-year-old woman's giving nature, her friends and family would say.

With Andrew and Lynda having so much in common it was no surprise when their friendship turned into an affair – no surprise to anyone apart from Christine, Andrew's wife.

Yet Andrew and Lynda had another shared interest that was their secret – for the moment. The devout Christian Salvationist and gentle, caring Samaritan both loved sex – torrid, passionate, adventurous love-making as often as they could. To put it simply, they couldn't get enough of each other.

Lynda moved out of her Broughty Ferry home and bought a house in Carnoustie, expecting Andrew Hunter to move in with her. It's not a step he took lightly, moving between Lynda and Christine a couple of times and enjoying both in bed. At the same time, Hunter had embarked on an affair with another woman. Neither Christine nor Lynda knew this, of course – perhaps if they had known, there would be no story to tell.

Hunter eventually settled down with Lynda but he kept in regular contact with his son who lived with his mother. One day, shortly before Christmas 1984, Christine dropped the boy off at the children's home where Hunter worked. After finishing his shift, he took the lad to the cinema and then back to Broughty Ferry.

In spite of heavy knocks and shouting, he couldn't get anyone to answer the door. Hunter went to the house of Lynda's ex-lover, Dr Ian Glover. He explained the problem and asked to use the phone to call Christine. No answer.

Visibly panicking and anxious, Hunter ran across the street to another neighbour who kept a spare key for Christine's house. By now, Hunter was accompanied by equally concerned neighbours. He opened the door and strode in and there was Christine, dangling from the hatch to the loft. Hanging by her neck from a noose, she was clearly dead. A depressed woman, desperately unhappy at the failure of her marriage? The authorities thought so and easily and understandably accepted a verdict of death by suicide.

Tragic as Christine's death was, some might think that would have pushed Hunter and Lynda closer together – quite the opposite. Andrew Hunter became angry and resentful towards his partner and even resorted to assaulting her, often in public. The pair spiralled into an unparalleled period of unhappiness and he'd often move out of the Carnoustie home and go back to the house he'd shared with Christine.

Every argument, fight and separation was followed by reconciliation and long sessions of passionate sex. Not that Hunter was going short in that area. During this time, he took up again with a gay lover he'd met back in Paisley while visiting a local sauna. If only the Salvation Army had known . . .

He also began to use working girls, becoming well known to almost every prostitute in Dundee. Not satisfied with that, he seduced a twenty-two-year-old drug addict he'd met through his work. If only his social work bosses had known . . .

No one in authority knew about his sex games, of course. Not even the neighbours in Broughty Ferry seemed to notice in spite of him often taking the young female junky there and her staying the night.

During one of their happier periods, Lynda and Hunter decided to get married. The wedding took place on 1 November 1986 and some wedding it was. They would honeymoon at posh Fernie Castle in Fife and then on to Israel. But pride of place must have gone to the wedding album. Sitting in the back of a horse-drawn carriage, Lynda looked beautiful and Hunter, in full Highland dress, carried a Bible in his hand – just as all clean living, good Christians do.

For a few months, everything between the couple was sweetness, light and passion. Then the old problems began to re-emerge. Hunter was back visiting the prostitutes and seeing a lot of his young junky ex-client. Things had to get better or the newlyweds were heading for trouble. That's when Lynda announced she was pregnant. She was delighted, of course, having always wanted babies. At first, so was Hunter – or so he said – then it was back to his old ways. Things even got worse as it seemed as if he resented the unborn child.

That's when Lynda visited her sister Sandra to break the good news then share with her how bad her marriage was. The following Friday was the day Lynda had taken off but Hunter was going out with work mates. No problem – Sandra would come up to Carnoustie and spend time with her. What else are close sisters for?

On the day, 21 August 1987, Sandra arrived at the house as planned only to be met by Hunter and no Lynda. According to Hunter, she'd gone off to her parents' house that morning, taking her old dog Shep as usual, and hadn't returned. Maybe she'd forgotten her arrangement with Sandra?

Hunter sat with his sister-in-law in the sunny garden and then they drove downtown where he took her for tea at a local hotel. There was still no sign of Lynda so Sandra left about 7 p.m. at night. She was worried – this wasn't like Lynda.

The next day Andrew Hunter reported his wife missing – so were her car and the old dog, Shep.

The cops had a major mystery on their hands. They didn't believe that a newly married, pregnant young woman would simply walk out on her life – unconvinced cops equals investigation.

Within a day they discovered that Lynda's car, a white Vauxhall, had been found the day before in Manchester. Sitting on double yellow lines, it had been broken into. It had been found on the day she was meant to have met Sandra. Why Manchester? It didn't make sense.

Early on, they had checked out Hunter, of course, but, on the day she went missing, he had been at work. He was then given a lift to and from his work night out by a neighbour. The next day, he had bought a pair of trainers in a Dundee shop before going on to a meeting with his boss. It was a foolproof alibi. Or was it?

Quietly, the cops started testing whether Andrew Hunter could have killed his wife, driven her car to Manchester and still had time to shop and work in Dundee. The answer was yes but they needed more than that.

Lynda Hunter's mysterious disappearance became the first Scottish case to feature on BBC's *Crimewatch UK*. It was a good move by the Tayside cops as, when new information flooded in, it all pointed at Andrew Hunter.

However, they still needed a body. They'd had reports that Hunter and Lynda had been seen in her car on the day she disappeared. People spotting the couple had also said that Lynda had looked upset so the cops got a large team mobilised, together with body dogs that were specially trained to sniff out corpses. They checked a particular wood. No joy.

Then another dog did them a favour. In a wood close to where the cops had searched, a dog walker found Lynda's decayed corpse seven months after she'd disappeared. The cause of death was obvious – Shep's lead was still wound tightly around her neck.

When arresting Andrew Hunter for murder, the cops found him in the company of his young junky girlfriend. Poor soul that she was, a short while later she died of a heroin overdose. Close pals say she committed suicide as she blamed herself for Lynda's death.

The man who was to blame, Andrew Hunter, was at the High Court in Dundee later in 1988. The *Crimewatch UK* appeal had generated so much public interest that people crowded outside jostling for seats in the public gallery every day.

The Crown's case painted the whole story. Hunter had driven Lynda to get some medicine for her morning sickness. The couple had argued, he'd grabbed Shep's lead and strangled her, killing his unborn child as well. After he had dumped her body in nearby woods, he took Shep's collar off and abandoned him on the road. Poor Shep had apparently been found and, with no collar or ID, he was destroyed as a stray.

Hunter had then gone to work and come home. He'd sat with Sandra and then calmly had tea with her even though he'd just murdered her sister. That night, he'd gone out with his colleagues and was driven home late. Instead of going to bed, he put on a long blonde wig and drove the car to Manchester, deliberately parking it on double yellow lines to attract the cops.

Catching a train home, he went straight out to buy the training shoes, keeping the timed and dated receipt, had a haircut and went about his business as usual.

Compelling enough as that was, there was one final nail for his coffin. Shep's collar was found at his home. Being concerned that the old dog might get lost, Lynda never let him go without that collar and ID tags. It was absolute proof that Hunter had been there at the time Lynda was murdered. It was old Shep's revenge.

Found guilty by a majority verdict, an expressionless Hunter stood to be sentenced by Lord Brand. 'You are an evil man of exceptional depravity,' said the judge, before sending Hunter down for life.

Andrew Hunter, the Salvationist who'd fallen from grace, murdered Lynda, the beautiful good Samaritan, but what of his first wife, Christine? Did she really hang herself? And his young junky girlfriend? She could have revealed so much about his murky life – was there more to her death than there appeared? We'll never know. In Perth Prison, Andrew Hunter died of a heart attack on 19 July 1993.

He was still a young man and in seemingly good health. Vengeance is mine, said the Lord?

1990 TO 1999

NASTY NINETIES

Margaret Thatcher resigned as Prime Minister (1990). Nelson Mandela was released from prison (1990) and became President of South Africa (1994). Boris Yeltsin became President of Russia and invaded Chechnya (1994). Saddam Hussein denied Iraq had nuclear capacity (1990).

Bill Clinton became US President (1993). 'I did not have sexual relations with that woman, Ms Lewinsky,' said Clinton (1998). He was impeached and charged with perjury over this denial but cleared later that year.

Princess Diana was killed in a car crash in Paris (1997).

Tony Blair became British Prime Minister after a historic landslide victory at the polls (1997). There was the first meeting of a Scottish Parliament since 1709 (1999).

Glasgow was the City of Culture (1990). Mel Gibson's *Braveheart* won five Oscars (1996).

Arthur 'Fatboy' Thompson was gunned down and killed outside the Glasgow home of his father, Arthur 'The Godfather' Thompson (1991). Joe Hanlon and Bobby Glover were killed in reprisal for Fatboy's death (1991). In the longest trial in Scottish criminal history, Paul Ferris was found not guilty of killing Fatboy (1992). Glasgow's Last Godfather, Arthur Thompson, died in his bed of natural causes (1994).

Nabbed with £34 million worth of coke, Scots Brian Doran and Ken Togher became the world's biggest drug traffickers (1995). Thomas Hamilton slaughtered the innocents of Dunblane (1996).

BEAUTY THE BEAST

Elderly, sure, but George Scott wasn't scared of anything. If he had known what was to happen one dark night, maybe he would have hesitated – or maybe not.

There was a noise downstairs. George, seventy-four, was sure someone had broken into the house and was heading his way. George stood behind his bedroom door, listening and tense. He was going to do something about this.

Scott was in Ardayre Road, Prestwick, where he lodged with his elderly friend, Hazel Smith. Also in the house was his landlady's younger sister, Jean Keay, sixty-nine. They were a happy group, comfortable with each other's company, but terror was about to walk into their lives.

All the residents might have been above pension age but Scott didn't think that mattered. He was brave and angry when he heard someone break into the house one night and sprang to challenge the burglars.

Soon, the house would lie in blood-splattered chaos. Hazel Smith was slashed with a chisel and permanently disfigured. George Scott was tied up on the ground with his skull shattered. But, worse, poor Jean Keay would die a horrible death. Who could be so vicious and cruel to a group of old folks?

Within hours, Strathclyde Police had launched a murder inquiry. Such was the level of violence that had been used, they reckoned the killers must be a gang of men well accustomed to dishing out the brutality. They were going to be surprised on several counts.

George Scott and Hazel Smith were badly affected by their injuries. At first, the medics feared they might not survive. Game elderly folk they might have been but their injuries were severe and would have poleaxed folk half their ages. They were just too frail to help the cops.

At first, the investigation moved slowly with few clues. Both surviving victims wanted to help but they were too badly shaken to identify their assailants. The motive appeared to be theft as Scott had been robbed of £1,000 and the keys to the bookmaker's where he was manager. But this involved a horror killing and the assaults on elderly people sickened everyone. The police played on public anger and sympathy to the hilt.

Repeated radio and TV appeals for witnesses were augmented by a £5,000 reward. Everybody wanted to help and the phone lines were busy. Most of the calls in such a situation are well meaning but trivial or irrelevant. It's the cops' jobs to try to sift through the rubble and catch the gems.

One caller, an anonymous female voice, seemed genuine but nervous. She said she thought she knew who the killers were but hesitated and didn't give enough info. The cops had no name and no number. They were entirely in her hands. Then she called back, still frightened, saying her life would be at risk if she gave them the information. Promptly she was offered police protection. At last the case started to move.

Attractive Kerry Bristol, twenty-nine, was that anonymous caller and she had information on her boyfriend's brother, thirty-one-year-old Thomas Moore. Before long, the police visited Moore's home in Greenan Grove in Greenfoot, a prosperous area of Ayr. This was most unusual – the cops thought they'd be investigating a team of robbers from some rundown Glasgow scheme or the clutch of similar desperados and junkies from down in Ayrshire. They didn't expect to be visiting a nice part of Ayr or targeting the kind of folk they were about to investigate.

Thomas Moore had no record and nor did the people he shared his home with – his girlfriend, Brenda Horsburgh, twenty-four, and her sister, Sylvia. Not only had these folk lived within the law as far as the cops were concerned, they were also respectable. Beautiful Brenda had even at one time been a fundraiser for the charity, Save the Children.

Young, attractive and trendy, Moore and Brenda lived a fast and luxurious lifestyle. They were most unlikely robbers and even less likely murderers. But, in August 1992, Moore and Brenda Horsburgh were arrested and charged with robbery, assault and the murder of Jean Keay.

A comedy of errors that was far from funny unfolded. Moore blamed Horsburgh and she blamed him. She said that he had run short of money and had taken to robbery. He had broken into the house in question with the intention of robbing it and, when the old folk put up a struggle, it had erupted into violence – or so she said.

Moore said that Brenda had been with him that night and she had been the one who'd dished out the battering that killed elderly Jean Keay. Cops are trained to expect the unexpected but Brenda Horsburgh looked and sounded like the most unlikely of violent murderers.

Finally, Moore went on trial alone and Brenda was released on bail. In February 1993, Thomas Moore was found guilty of murder and sentenced to life. But the action was far from over. If Horsburgh thought she had been let off the hook, she was in for a shock.

The cops and forensic people were painstakingly piecing together evidence, not just from the murder house but also from scenes of other crimes. They also had inside help – from inside jail – as one bitter man, Thomas Moore, gave them as much information as he could.

Almost nine months later, Brenda Horsburgh too faced trial for murder, robbery and assault. In evidence, Moore said he had been facing financial difficulties and had resorted to robbery to pay his mortgage. So, rather than move from their nice house in prosperous Greenfoot, the pair had taken to theft, violence and murder.

The prosecution alleged that Moore and Horsburgh had carried out many burglaries, always preying on elderly and vulnerable victims. On this occasion, they had trailed George Scott to his lodgings, planning to steal his keys to the bookmaker's shop he managed. Waiting till they thought the house was empty, they broke in – only to be surprised by George Scott charging at them out of a bedroom. Moore admitted hitting Scott with a baseball bat and sending him tumbling down the stairs. But Moore wasn't responsible for most of the violence – far from it.

Brenda Horsburgh had been alone in a bedroom with Jean Keay. Upset and anxious, Jean wouldn't stop shouting so Horsburgh repeatedly smashed her on the skull with a baseball bat. If that wasn't bad enough, the former charity worker then pushed a pair of rolled up tights into the badly injured woman's mouth. A final indignity – a lethal indignity – that caused the old lady to suffocate and die.

Later, it was Brenda Horsburgh who'd struck Hazel Smith with a sharp chisel, causing the old woman severe injury and permanent disfigurement. Why this vicious assault took place was never made clear. There didn't seem to be reasons for any of the attractive young woman's bloody and terrible actions.

The jury at Kilmarnock High Court took less than two hours to find Horsburgh guilty of all charges.

In mitigation, Horsburgh claimed she had tried to help Jean Keay by putting her in the recovery position as she lay unconscious on the floor. Clearly the judge took the view that this had only been necessary because Horsburgh had smashed in the woman's skull. Too little too late. Horsburgh was sentenced to life imprisonment

In another twist after the trial, one of the leading cops in the case, Chief Inspector Stuart Kernohan, suddenly abandoned his wife and their two young children in Spain during their first ever holiday abroad. Later they found out why. The cop had been having an affair with a witness – the beautiful key witness Kerry Bristol. They moved south and set up home together. In 2005,

Kernohan became Commissioner of Police for the sun-kissed Cayman Islands.

Meanwhile, Brenda Horsburgh started her life sentence. No one in Ayrshire cared how the former voluntary worker would cope. As in her crimes, there's little charity in jail.

IN PRAISE OF
OLDER WOMEN

Cheery Helen Torbet loved to walk the Scottish hills. But, when she ventured to a favourite spot in Wester Ross, little did she know she would never be going home.

Retired doctor's wife Helen, sixty-two, always stayed at the Grianan House B&B in Inverinate, owned by Mrs Jessie McMillan, to spend time wandering the hills around Loch Duich, Wester Ross. Leaving her husband at home, Helen had been to the guesthouse for six years running and had become good friends with Mrs McMillan and her thirty-one-year-old son Donald. It was a home from home.

On her last visit in July 1993, Helen Torbet disappeared. At first, the police suspected she had fallen on one of her walks in the treacherous hills and a massive search was launched. But Donald McMillan revealed that he had seen Helen leaving in a car with a stranger, a man. Since her bag and clothes had been cleared from her room, the police turned their enquiries to her male companion.

After months of fruitless investigation, the police began to side with local rumours that Helen had been having an affair and had run off with her lover. When her husband, Dr Thomas Torbet, a retired gynaecologist at Glasgow's Southern General Hospital and a district court magistrate, sold their marital home in Busby only months after his wife's disappearance, tongues started wagging again.

In Wester Ross, former soldier Donald McMillan complained to the media about police harassment as they returned to question him in his caravan next to his mother's guesthouse. Local police were baffled until ten months after Helen Torbet's disappearance, when and a vital clue was unearthed.

In spring 1994, a holidaymaker discovered Helen's handbag and purse in some undergrowth only 200 yards from the guesthouse. The police immediately searched the McMillans' home and found Helen's holdall under the floorboards. In the bag was Helen's diary with one final entry in her own handwriting. It read, 'Strange letter awaited me from Donald McMillan. Embarrassing to cope with.'

McMillan was immediately arrested. After rifling through his caravan, police found pornographic magazines with his personal scoring system. The young women scored up to ten but older women were given marks as high as 400. The suspect admitted being sexually fascinated with older women and indulging in a range of habits like wearing women's underwear. Finally, McMillan confessed to murder and directed police to his victim's corpse. Helen was found wrapped in bandages and tape in a shallow grave near the guesthouse. For all the times the cops had been back to that house, the vital clues had been lying practically under their noses.

A post-mortem found that McMillan had suffocated Helen Torbet before cutting off her nightdress with intent to rape her. At his trial, McMillan argued he had killed Helen accidentally while he was trying to calm her down after an argument. The court disagreed, concluding it had been a sexually motivated murder. After only one hour, the jury found McMillan guilty and he was sentenced to life.

Returning to court in 2003 to have a minimum jail sentence set under the new human rights rules, McMillan again argued that he had killed Helen accidentally. Lord Cullen rejected the plea and said, 'It was a sexually motivated assault and you must have subjected the victim to a terrifying ordeal.' This time, McMillan was told he must serve at least fifteen years in prison.

To this day, one vital piece of evidence remains missing – the letter from McMillan which upset Helen Torbet so much. Donald

McMillan knows what was written in the letter and he's not saying and never will. On 12 February 2007, Donald McMillan was found dead in his cell.

WALTER MITTY GETS A SHOOTER

'I've got to go on a mission.' He was at it again – fantasising about being a secret agent.

'Yeah right,' sneered his companion for the hundredth time that week. 'You're all talk and no action.'

'We'll see. I'll prove you wrong.' But would he?

Paul Macklin had always been a strange guy, even as a child. A loner who was awkward and restless, he did have one thing in his favour – privilege. But was it going to be enough to keep him out of trouble?

Gordonstoun, near Elgin, is one of Britain's top public schools – it's where Prince Charles was sent as a kid. That would knock him into shape, Macklin's folks thought. Gordonstoun had a reputation not for producing scholars but for building character. A few years of cold showers, hard exercise and tough masters would make a man out of Paul Macklin. But what type of man?

The other kids at Gordonstoun didn't like Macklin much so he did what he always did and lived in his own wee world of make-believe. No harm in that? There is when you tell the world it's all true – when you believe it.

Macklin's tales weren't just little white lies but intricate webs of deceit – all starring Paul Macklin, of course. His favourites were about being signed up in the army, having guns at his disposal and training to be a secret agent – James Bond, licensed to kill.

No one believed him but that didn't stop him constantly inventing the stories and telling the world, insisting every word

313

was true. A real Walter Mitty character, most people avoided him. At best they simply tolerated him.

When he left school, he went to live in a flat in Aberdeen, sharing it with other young men. Adulthood didn't change Macklin's ways. In fact he got worse. Now he claimed he was a secret agent for MI6 and would regale his flatmates about being followed, having been on mysterious business abroad, hit jobs against paramilitary leaders in Ireland and so on.

By 1994, now twenty-one years old, Macklin had met someone who listened to him. A former public school boy, Robert Cadiz was the son of two millionaires, made rich from the North Sea oil industry. He had a lot in common with Macklin, in other words, but there was more. He called Macklin's bluff.

The pair sat and discussed what fun it would be to live beyond the law. If uneducated, barely literate men from slum tenements could do it, surely, with all their schooling and advantages, they could? How easy it would be. All they needed were the tools and a plan.

A short while later, they had the tools – a sawn-off shotgun and a pump-action shotgun with a bundle of cartridges. Walter Mitty had a shooter and now he was going to use it.

The pair planned to rob Aberdeen District Council's Contract Services Department. It sounds an unlikely target but they had inside information that, at a certain time of the month, around £300,000 could be had there. Off they set with their shooters and balaclavas. Macklin's fantasies were about to become deadly reality.

The raid went wrong almost from the off. The men were spotted and a chase was on. They shoved a gun into a motorist's face and hijacked his car. The cops were on their tail and cornered them. A stand-off followed with Macklin waving his shooter and screaming at the cops that, if they took one step closer, they were dead men. It was a bloodbath in the making.

Maybe reality finally kicked in with Paul Macklin or maybe it was plain fear but he and Cadiz gave up with a whimper, not a bang.

The court only dealt with the reality, not the fantasy. In front of them were two privileged, spoiled adrenalin junkies arrogantly risking the lives of others to get high.

The two men were jailed for a total of seventeen years. It should've ended there. It would have for most people who had a better life waiting for them when they came out of jail. But Paul Macklin wasn't everybody.

In 2000, Cadiz was jailed for two years at the High Court in Glasgow for dealing in coke, ecstasy and speed. But his pal was going to outdo him in the crime stakes.

In 2003, Macklin was back in court again. After an incident in a flat in the Printfield area of Aberdeen during which masked men, armed with guns, baseball bats, axes, knives and hockey sticks, broke into a flat, tied a guy up and threatened to shoot him, Macklin met the cops in the street yet again.

In the High Court Macklin was cleared of threatening to shoot the man in the flat but there was the other not so small matter of having a shooter and threatening the cops.

When the police arrived at the incident scene, they spotted Macklin and took after him. Three times he had turned, aimed a handgun and threatened to blast them. Walter Mitty had got a shooter yet again.

Found guilty, Macklin was sentenced to fifteen years in jail and described by the judge as 'a dangerous individual' and 'a considerable threat to the community'.

No one in Aberdeen disagreed. They had learned that Walter Mitty was serious – deadly serious.

THE BLACK WIDOW

When Nawal Nicol walked down the street men's heads turned. She knew it and enjoyed their attention but she did more than that – although little did her husband know.

Dark-skinned, with high cheekbones and almond-shaped eyes, it was no wonder Stuart Nicol fell in love with Nawal. They were married and lived together in the small town of Ellon, close to Aberdeen. Both twenty-nine years old, they appeared the ideal young couple with a golden future ahead of them but Nawal had a secret that would have fatal consequences.

One night in June 1994, Stuart and Nawal went to a local club with some young friends, Jason Simpson and Muir Middler. It was a jolly night with a lot of drinking, joking and dancing. As the last slow dance was played, Stuart and Nawal took to the floor, a happy young couple very much in love – or so it seemed.

The four friends wandered back to the Nicols' home for a nightcap. A short while later, when Nawal excused herself and went to bed, Simpson and Middler wished Stuart Nicol goodnight and left.

Thirty minutes later, Stuart heard a knock at his front door and went to answer it. There stood his friends, Simpson and Middler. Did Stuart think they had forgotten something? We'll never know. Simpson grabbed Stuart, gripping his arms behind his back. Middler pulled out a fierce hunting knife and stabbed Stuart repeatedly in the chest. Four times the chib's blade sliced into his body. One blow pierced his heart, killing him instantly.

It was bloody betrayal by people Stuart Nicol considered friends. The two murderers panicked and hid the knife and their blood-drenched clothes in nearby woods. It took the cops next to no time to find the evidence and Simpson and Middler were arrested.

In September 1994, Simpson and Middler were found guilty of murder and sentenced to life imprisonment. But the police weren't finished. In June 1995, Nawal Nicol stood accused of murder and the whole seedy story emerged.

Nawal had an insatiable appetite for sex and took lovers everywhere. Later she would say that she had had fifty lovers in one year but the courtroom echoed with gasps of shock when it was revealed she had been having affairs with her husband's murderers.

The prosecution alleged that she had sex with young Simpson only days before he turned killer. They also suggested that she had offered the young men £25,000 each if they 'got rid of' Stuart Nicol.

Simpson took the witness stand and claimed that Nawal had worked out different ways of murdering her husband and escaping. She'd spoken of dissecting his body and throwing it off the cliffs at nearby Slains Castle, possibly the inspiration for the original Dracula story, tampering with his car brakes and faking a break-in to their home that would result in his death. She'd considered the lot – or so it was claimed.

It looked like Nawal Nicol was going down for murder in spite of the best work of her lawyer, Donald Findlay QC. Then, on the second day, there was an astonishing turn of events when the Crown dropped all charges against Nawal Nicol. It's a decision they have never explained – they don't have to.

So the woman the press had dubbed 'The Black Widow', after the spider of that name which eats its mate, was to walk free, an innocent person in the eyes of the law, and she could never be charged with her husband's murder again. She was to make the most of her freedom.

With the sale of the marital home, a fortune in insurance payouts and £10,000 from the Criminal Injuries Compensation

Board for the loss of her husband, Nawal Nicol was a wealthy young woman. She enjoyed every penny. Some called her shameless.

Already beautiful, the widow had her breasts enlarged and liposuction on her thighs. Dressed in micro skirts and low-cut tops, she was seen in all the top clubs almost every night, usually with a different young man on her arm.

Her behaviour angered and upset Stuart Nicol's grieving parents who had won custody of Nawal and Stuart's only child. But there was nothing they could do – as Nawal never tired of telling the press, 'I have nothing to be ashamed of. Sure I got the money after Stuart died but I was entitled to it. Remember I had nothing to do with his killing.'

Although she'd been found not guilty in the eyes of the law, not everyone was convinced of Nawal's innocence. If anyone was looking to take some revenge against her, it wasn't long in happening and it was all her own fault.

Within three years, Nawal Nicol had spent her fortune. Broke, she moved to Spain where she worked as a stripper first in top holiday venues and then in a sleazy brothel in Ibiza where she peeled off for the punters.

Nawal returned to Scotland and all she could afford was a rundown rented flat in Ayr. She then became a lap dancer in the Fantasy Bar in Edinburgh but she didn't prove to be a success, the customers preferring her lithe younger colleagues. Desperate for money, she stooped to making hardcore porn films.

Stuart Nicol's father, Frank, had got a strange offer from Perth Prison. For only £400 each, Simpson and Middler would be killed. He declined the offer, saying, 'I want them to rot in jail. I want them to serve every minute of their sentences.'

Most people understand his response as the anger of a father grieving for his dead son. And most people wouldn't blame Frank Nicol for harbouring some anger against Nawal Nicol, his son's widow – The Black Widow, some would say.

VITRIOL AND VENOM

Illness in the family is always a worry. Sudden, unexplained illness was hitting the citizens of Edinburgh. Was there a mass murderer at large?

Elizabeth Sharwood-Smith and her oldest son Andrew had been rushed to hospital with terrible stomach cramps and sickness. Back in their Edinburgh home, they were fine again until, two days later, the symptoms returned. Something wasn't right.

Elizabeth's husband Geoffrey was worried but he knew more than most. Geoffrey was a consultant anaesthetist and knew all about medical symptoms. He knew a fair bit about poisons too and that's what he reckoned had happened to his wife and son. By a process of elimination, Geoffrey Sharwood-Smith worked out that tonic water bought from the Hunters Tryst branch of Safeway could well be the culprit. He didn't have long to wait for confirmation.

Alexandra Agutter became dreadfully ill and her husband, biochemistry lecturer Paul, was on the phone calling the emergency doctor. There was no reply but thankfully a locum picked up Paul's message and made a prompt visit. He agreed that Alexandra was very ill and arranged for an ambulance to rush her to hospital. When the paramedics arrived, one asked Paul what his wife had had to eat or drink last.

'A gin and tonic,' he replied and handed over a bottle of Safeway tonic water. Earlier that evening, Alexandra had asked Paul to make her a G&T which he did but he hadn't taken one himself, explaining that he had promised to give their gardener a lift home.

Sure enough, Geoffrey Sharwood-Smith's suspicions were confirmed when the tonic water was found to be laced with atropine, a poisonous compound obtained from the aptly-named plant, deadly nightshade. Safeway had already removed thousands of bottles from their shelves under pressure from Geoffrey Sharwood-Smith.

The publicity would be terrible for their business – all the more so because they had received no threat and no demand for money. Someone seemed intent on killing for killing's sake.

Paul Agutter made contact with Geoffrey Sharwood-Smith. The two were well-educated men with a great deal in common. Sharwood-Smith was impressed by Agutter's knowledge, particularly of various poisons and their effects but, then again, he was a biochemist.

Looking for a poisoner is one of the most difficult tasks for cops – it always has been. It is one of the most secretive ways to kill. Poisoning supermarket goods also suggested a warped mind – someone whose only motive is the power of killing and who doesn't care who their victims might be. Trawling through the usual suspects was unlikely to help the cops in this instance. Then they had a breakthrough.

Twenty-six-year-old Wayne Smith confessed to poisoning the tonic water. The man was certainly odd enough and he hated the world. The cops grilled him and soon learned that he didn't know the fine details of the case, such as the fact that seven bottles had been poisoned. He was just yet another time-waster – or so the cops thought.

The public in Edinburgh were determined to help – after all they were the ones at risk. Eight people had been poisoned so far and, although no one had died, that had been a matter of luck and quick medical care. This time it was tonic water but a poisoner could poison any drink, any food. Any one of them could be next and not be so lucky.

All the Safeway workers at Hunters Tryst were interviewed. One recalled a man who he thought had been hanging around the store in a suspicious manner just a few hours before the

Sharwood-Smiths had bought their contaminated tonic. Trawling through the store's CCTV footage took a long time but eventually the worker was certain he had spotted the man – Paul Agutter. Was it a usual suspect after all?

Agutter was arrested and interviewed. What the cops then learned about him would have immediately put him in the frame in any other kind of attempted murder of his wife. Paul and Alexandra Agutter had an open marriage and both were free to pursue affairs with other people. But he had fallen big time for his mistress, beautiful Carole Bonsall, and wanted to marry her. So why not simply get a divorce? Why not, indeed?

Agutter pled not guilty throughout and so never explained why murder and not divorce. However, he was known to have had financial troubles and he was depressed. Did he want to kill his wife for insurance payouts?

At his trial at Edinburgh's High Court in 1995, the Crown presented the case that Agutter had laced seven bottles of tonic water and returned all bar one to the shelves. He did so knowing that other people would fall ill and perhaps die. His reasoning behind doing this was that the cops would be more likely to look for a mass murderer than an aggrieved spouse. It was a clever plan befitting Agutter's academic brilliance and, if it hadn't been for an observant supermarket worker, the cops' suspicions might never have been directed towards Agutter, especially since his wife Alexandra defended him throughout, even when confronted with the evidence.

But you have to wonder why he didn't get rid of the poisoned tonic water after his wife took ill. If he really wanted her dead, why did he hand the bottle to the paramedics? Who knows? But it is certain that that slip-up saved lives.

Paul Agutter was found guilty and sentenced to twelve years in jail. In prison, he ended up with an interesting cellmate – Wayne Smith, the man who had falsely confessed to poisoning the tonic water. Smith had admitted putting weedkiller in cartons of fruit juice at another Safeway store after his false confession. God had told him to kill cops, apparently.

Alexandra Agutter finally accepted that her husband had tried to kill her and divorced him while he was in jail. Carole Bonsall, the lover for whom he was willing to kill, ditched him.

Agutter was released from prison in 2002 after only seven years of his sentence. A sad and lonely man, he was, by then, fifty-eight years old. Since Alexandra had taken out a court order prohibiting him from approaching her, he headed south to live with his parents.

Remarkably, he got a job at the University of Manchester lecturing young students on topics that would include ethics. When the university discovered that they had a convicted poisoner on their staff, they decided not to renew his contract.

Paul Agutter had a good job, an understanding wife, a beautiful mistress and he lost them all. But it could have been worse.

Eight people and more might have died at his hands. Agutter was one slip-up away from being famous – as one of Scotland's biggest mass murderers.

THE BITCHES FROM HELL

Christmas – a time of goodwill and peace to all people. But, for someone, it was about to turn into hell.

It was three days before Christmas 1995 and the last thing twenty-one-year-old Barbara Gillen needed was debt collectors at her door. But that's what her best friends, Joanne McCulloch and Marion Davis, were that day. Barbara owed them £40 and they wanted it pronto.

Young Barbara was skint. Out of work and on state benefits, she was struggling to keep her flat on. She was a generous young woman but she wouldn't be able to afford much of a Christmas that year – never mind suddenly repaying £40.

McCulloch and Davis, called 'The Fat Slags' in their hometown of Greenock, weren't pleased. No, they weren't pleased at all and, in case Barbara hadn't understood how displeased they were, they trashed her flat. That would have been bad enough but the young woman's ordeal had only started.

They took her prisoner and then led her forcibly into the street. Young Barbara had seen them in action before – they'd beat up women and men and think nothing of taking on teams of guys, often using blades. Once angry, they were capable of anything and they were furious with her now.

She screamed and kicked, pulled and pled. They ignored her and easily held on to her as they marched her through the streets. Other passers-by turned and looked but, when they saw that it was The Fat Slags, they moved on, minding their own business. So no one came to tiny brunette Barbara's aid as they led her to McCulloch's flat in the town's Banff Road. There, they were joined by Louise Campbell (sixteen), Julie Duffy (seventeen), Claire Gilmour, then a fifteen-year-old schoolgirl, and Kenneth Woods (twenty-seven). Locally, Woods was known as 'The Beast' but, despite this soubriquet, he was no match for McCulloch and the rest. The women were in charge that day.

Barbara regarded all these people as her friends. At one time, she had even shared a flat with McCulloch and Davis – that's how she had come to owe them £40 – yet now she was frightened of them and she was right to be.

As Kenneth Woods watched, all the young women set about brutally beating their petite prisoner, blackening her eyes and breaking her nose. They rubbed her face in dog dirt and ripped her jacket from her body, setting it on fire. It was a taste of things to come. The women then forced Barbara out into the freezing snow. It was Greenock in December and bitterly cold. Without her jacket and with the shock of the assault, Barbara Gillen shivered and shook in the street.

The female gang were giggling and laughing – playing games with her now. On the threat of another beating, they forced her to sing Christmas carols and ask for money from people on the busy Greenock streets. Some folk actually gave her money. One friend approached, showing concern at the tiny woman's state.

'Get away!' Barbara shouted. 'Go before they do the same to you.'

She fled.

No one else asked her if she was OK – who would with that gang standing around her? But no one called the cops either. The public abandoned Barbara Gillen to her fate.

Back at McCulloch's flat, the ladies from Hades locked Barbara in a freezing, tiny kitchen cabinet that was so cramped her knees were tucked under her chin. They left her there while they binged on booze, cannabis and temazepam, known as Jellies.

Hours later, their captive's legs had gone numb, her feet twitched with cramps and her whole body was chilled to the bone.

Eventually, it all got too much and the weeping, terrified Barbara cried out, begging to be let free. Almost instantly, she wished she hadn't.

Now drunk and stoned, the women were in the mood for more of what they thought of as fun. They yanked Barbara out of the cupboard and dumped her in the middle of the living room floor. Stripping off most of her clothes, they held her down and sexually assaulted her. Stubbing lit cigarettes out on her skin, they then forced her to carry out obscene acts on them. She was raped by women.

At some point, they decided to hurt her some more, stabbing her leg with a blade, setting fire to her hair and shaving off her eyebrows. Louise Campbell and schoolgirl Claire Gilmour twice forced her to drink their urine – on one occasion, it was mixed with cigarette butts, turpentine, old fish fingers and grease. All the while, her tormentors laughed, drank and smoked joints.

Bored with their human toy, they shoved the weakened and sick Barbara back into the freezing cupboard. She crouched on the floor, in pain, cold, terrified.

Suddenly the door opened. Maybe they were going to let her go free? Barbara looked up with hope. They poured boiling water down on her. Time and again, the door sprung open and kettles of boiling water were poured over her naked flesh. She was in agony.

By the second day, the women taunted Barbara they were going to kill her as they continued their sadistic and sexual games. She was helpless and had learned to meet their demands unquestioningly, no matter how revolting those demands were. Hesitating or protesting only resulted in more torture and greater pain.

They owned her now, body and soul. She had become more than their human toy. She was now their slave. Or so they thought.

Barbara asked to go to the bathroom. They were resting, catching their breath and getting more energy for their next onslaught. Of course she could go to the bathroom. Confident she wouldn't dare turn against them now, they let Barbara got to the toilet alone. In the small bathroom, Barbara listened to her tormentors in the living room laughing and shouting that they were going to give her more.

She knew, if she returned to the living room, she could be going back to face her own execution. With each attack, the women were getting crazier and more vicious. Where would it stop? Would it stop? If it did, could they allow her to walk out alive? To go to the police? Barbara knew this was her one chance to live. She had to be quiet and she had to be quick.

There was one tiny window. Hoisting herself up on the sink, almost slipping and falling, she scrambled through and dropped down on the ground, landing with a winding thump. Half naked, barefoot and exhausted, she staggered though the slush and snow to bang on a neighbour's door, the first house with lights on. The woman who answered the door swooned and almost fainted because the sight on her doorstep was so horrific.

Taking Barbara in and covering her burned, skinned, scalded, bleeding and bruised body, the woman telephoned the cops. Greenock has one of the highest crime rates in Britain. In 1995, more people were jailed there per capita than in places like Turkey. The cops were used to crime but this was one that sickened even them – what made it worse still was that it had been carried out by women. It was a sad sign of the new times, the 1990s.

With her torturers locked up in custody, Barbara began to relax. But it would be a long time before she recovered, if ever.

Hospitalised for weeks, a doctor compared Barbara to a victim of a Nazi concentration camp. She hadn't known it but she had been six weeks pregnant at the time of the assault. Of course, she had lost the baby during her ordeal.

In spite of plastic surgery and counselling, she will always carry some physical scars and who knows what the depth of the emotional damage she has suffered might be?

Brave Barbara took to the witness box at the trial in Glasgow High Court in May 1996. As she tearfully recounted all the atrocities she had suffered, her six torturers giggled and laughed in the dock, tormenting her still.

The female gang and Kenneth Woods were charged with various offences concerning Barbara's assault and abduction and all were charged with her attempted murder. However, although Woods had been present throughout, he was deemed to be a bit-part player who had mostly acted as an onlooker. It was the women who stood accused of the most horrific crimes – a catalogue of evil that amounted to sustained torture over a period of two whole days.

Sickened by fifteen days of harrowing evidence, the jury had no hesitation in finding them all guilty. Marion Davis was the luckiest. She was found guilty of abduction and assault and got only two years. The others didn't escape so lightly. Sentencing them to a total of sixty-one years in prison, ranging from eight years to twelve, Judge John Horsburgh branded them 'bitches from hell'. All decent people agreed.

Two days after they were sent to Cornton Vale jail, another female prisoner threw boiling water mixed with sugar over Julie Duffy and Joanne McCulloch. Kenneth Woods was stabbed in the leg in prison. Even the cons didn't like the evil torturers.

Some time later, looking back on her two days of torture, Barbara Gillen could only wonder about what had happened to her. 'They were once my pals but they became monsters. How could they do it?' she asked. How indeed?

Later, in 1996, Barbara had got her life together well enough to marry her boyfriend, George Balfour. Like any new bride she was full of joy and hope and looking forward to their own home and babies. But unlike most new brides she had a shadow hanging over her.

'The nightmares haunt me every night,' she said. 'Will they ever end?'

Let us all hope so – for her sake.

TILL DEATH . . .

It was a scene to turn the strongest stomach – never mind those of rural cops who were more used to sheep on the road than murder. One of their colleagues lay dead on the bed, his skull smashed open with a bullet.

Ian Galbraith, thirty-seven, had moved north from England to be a bobby in Argyll only a few years before. He and his wife Kim, twenty-nine, were looking for a better quality of life in a quiet rural idyll for themselves and the family they had started to build with two-year-old Lauren. Their dream had turned sour – fatally sour.

At the crime scene at their cottage in Furnace, on the banks of Loch Fyne, Kim Galbraith was talking. She gibbered on about a break-in to their home by men she couldn't describe. They had shot Ian and then raped her and looted the house. Before they left, they had torched the place and she had fled.

The cops didn't like this at all. It all sounded like something out of a bad film plot – a Hollywood director's lurid notion of murder and rape in the Highlands. There were enough holiday cottages in the area to rob at will. Why choose one with a family in it and a big, strong policeman as well? Only desperate or crazy people killed cops.

Before long Kim Galbraith had changed her story. She confessed to murdering her husband with his own hunting rifle, shooting him through the back of his head as he lay sleeping. She had been driven to it – or so she claimed.

Galbraith was charged with her husband's bloody murder and, at her trial in 1999, she spun a tale of torture and sexual depravity.

According to the small, pretty, frail-looking woman, her tall, beefy husband wasn't the pillar of the community he appeared to be. She claimed he had demanded kinky sex in a dog's kennel or three-way sessions with prostitutes and, when she wasn't compliant, he beat and raped her, often at knifepoint.

This horror continued through their whole marriage, according to the accused, and she had cracked that night in Argyll. It had been too much and she had shot her tormentor as he lay asleep.

Kim Galbraith painted a picture of her husband that no one else recognised – there hadn't even been a hint of what she was describing. But still she claimed she had been acting under diminished responsibility. The jury was treated to a definition of diminished responsibility – 'a state of mind bordering on but not amounting to insanity'. They rejected it and found her guilty of murder. She was sentenced to life.

Galbraith wasn't finished there. She fought tooth and nail through the legal system. The next year a bench of five judges decided that she had acted under duress, accepted her plea of culpable homicide and reduced her sentence to ten years.

In 2002, almost four years after she was jailed, a subsequent appeal, taking into account she had been a 'model' prisoner, reduced her sentence to eight years. A few months later, Kim Galbraith was freed. The prison service said at the time, 'Her prison record has been exemplary.'

She had served four years and one month for shooting her husband in the head. Yet, from early on in her time in jail, very soon after she had killed her man, Kim Galbraith had maintained sexy, lurid correspondence with male prisoners in other jails. One con, in a top-security jail in England, said:

> I'm a man of the world and love women but what she wrote was obscene, scary given the claims she made at her trial. Seemed to me she loved kinky sex. I dropped the letters after a short while. I mean would you hook up with her after what happened to her husband?

After her release, it was revealed that, while on day release from prison, preparing for freedom, she had been taking comfort breaks. After she went to her work placement, she would be picked up by a private detective and driven to his flat for romps in his bed. Does that sound like a victim of a sex maniac?

Before his tragic death, Ian Galbraith had approached a counselling agency for help – for help with his wife. He claimed she was sexually demanding and perverse and she would fly into tempers when she didn't get her way and, as diminutive as she was compared with his bulky frame, she would abuse and beat him. Ian Galbraith was killed before the counselling agency could help.

When she was last heard of, Kim Galbraith was living in the south of England near her daughter Lauren. The young girl is set to inherit a small fortune through her father's death. It's the least the wee soul deserves. However, she'll never meet her dad's parents who have been banned from seeing her.

A solicitor has been appointed to make sure that Kim Galbraith never gets near the money. Let's hope he is alert. The first jury were right to find she wasn't insane – some would claim she never has been.

LIMBS, LOCHS AND
A LETHAL LUST

The loch waters were dark and freezing, just perfect for the police divers' training. But the training was about to turn into reality. One cop was going to make a grisly find.

It was December 1999. The days were ticking away before the new millennium and the massive celebrations planned every-where. Cops up and down the country would be on duty, making sure the crowds were safe, but not this crew of specialist divers – they were going to be involved in a sensational murder hunt.

It's not recorded how the police diver felt when he grasped the plastic bag floating in the water and discovered a severed human arm. But how would anyone feel? Disgust? Fear? Revulsion? That's how this murder case would make the public feel.

It was just off Rowardennan on the quiet side of Loch Lomond in fifteen feet of water. The cop diving team from Stirling always trained there. When they found the arm, then another, then the legs, the case quickly became known as the 'Limbs in the Loch' case.

Severed limbs always give the cops particular problems. Even if the mutilation happened after death, it's not everyone who could carry out such a gross act. Having the ability to do so suggests a callous, brutal murderer capable of great evil. But severed limbs dumped in a loch meant something else. The killer had tried very hard to conceal the evidence, had tried hard to stay free – perhaps in order to target other victims?

The cops had to move fast and their first task was to identify the victim. With no national databank of DNA, blood and so on, this was no easy task. Even when a head was washed up on Barassie Beach, Troon, and was forensically matched to the limbs, they still needed more. They got it from the best possible source – a loving family.

Barry Wallace had gone out to a Christmas party on 5 December with his colleagues from Tesco in Kilmarnock where he worked. Barry was a young, fit, handsome young man who never gave his parents a minute's worry. So, when he didn't come back that night and they hadn't heard from him for days, his folks were frantic with worry. They knew something terrible must have happened. It had.

As the medics and forensic bods worked on the body parts, Barry's dad, Ian, had the heartbreaking task of going to view the severed head. It's the stuff of nightmares to gaze on your beautiful boy's face when the rest of him is gone. But the good man did his duty to the state and his son. It was Barry. That poor father.

A short while later, eighteen-year-old Barry was forensically confirmed as the victim and the cops immediately targeted the likely suspects. They knew Barry had left the party late and was heading home. OK, he'd had a few drinks but he was old enough and, besides, it was Christmas. They reckoned it had to be someone local in Kilmarnock.

Even places the size of Kilmarnock harbour a good few sexually sadistic psychos and the Ayrshire town was no different. There was one person the cops were instantly interested in – someone they had unfinished business with. The neighbours wouldn't have suspected anything of thirty-six-year-old William Beggs. He kept his house in OK nick, didn't have loud parties, worked regularly and was pleasant though not overly friendly when they passed him in the street. A good, quiet neighbour, they thought. If only they'd known.

Twelve years earlier, the same good neighbour had been convicted of murder in Middlesbrough. Ulster-born Beggs was a sadistic gay and he'd picked up a man called Barry Oldham, taken him back to his place, killed him and then tried to decapitate him. Convicted and set to spend life in jail, Beggs appealed. The conviction was overturned on a technicality and he was freed.

Four years later, in 1991, Beggs had picked up a man called Brian McQuillan at a gay disco in Glasgow. Back at his flat while they were having sex, Beggs set about McQuillan, slashing his legs with a razor. The terrified man had to escape for his life by jumping naked out of a first-floor window. It got Beggs six years in jail.

Ever since this incident, the Strathclyde cops had kept a close eye on Beggs, believing that he still trawled bars with the intention of picking up men and then hurting them. He specialised in picking up drunk straight men. Often they'd be married or have female partners. If he had sex with them and then hurt them, the men would be faced with the dilemma of whether or not to admit to their partners what had happened – most wouldn't.

The cops were sure that Beggs would kill again. They went straight to his door in Doon Place, Kilmarnock only to find they were too late – Beggs had flown.

The house looked neat and tidy and, outside, there were bags of rubbish all lined up. It looked like he had been decorating recently. Then one eagle-eyed cop spotted something – a carrier bag full of rubbish had the Scandinavian Seaways logo on it – it was just like the one that a limb had been wrapped up in, when it was found in the deep, murky waters of Loch Lomond. That was enough – armed with a warrant, the cops broke down the door.

The forensic people went through the place inch by inch. One room had been recently decorated and the fresh, new paint smell still filled the air but, there on a bed, they found blood. When samples of the blood were DNA-tested, they were an exact match with young Barry Wallace's DNA. And, because of Beggs's earlier convictions, samples of his DNA and blood were already on file and they matched semen samples that the forensic bods had lifted from the same bed.

William Beggs had cleaned the house from top to bottom and had even gone to the trouble of redecorating a room. Neighbours reported that, shortly after 5 December, they had noticed him working at it into the early hours of the morning. He could clean all he liked but he could never clean enough. All in all, they found twenty-two samples of Barry's blood in that flat.

One of the flat's cupboards had been stuffed full of carrier bags. Sifting through them, they found other bags marked Scandinavian Seaways. In those pre-9/11 days, movement between European countries was as easy as catching the local bus. Beggs had been travelling around a bit. Why? The cops didn't think it was for sightseeing.

Pathologists had other grim findings to relate. The wrists on Barry's severed arms both showed a similar type of deep bruising. After long, careful tests, they confirmed that the poor lad had been handcuffed against his will and had struggled and fought till his last.

An examination of his other body parts revealed that he had been brutally raped, severely punched in the face and jabbed in the arm with some sort of needle. Whether this was a hypo with drugs couldn't be confirmed but, if not, what was that needle about?

As information crept into the public domain, rumours circulated that Barry Wallace must have secretly been gay. The folk speculating about that got it completely wrong. Some of Beggs's former one-night stands came forward and revealed he loved nothing more than targeting an unsuspecting straight guy, getting him drunk or drugging him and then using him. They thought the abuse was sexual but obviously Beggs had even darker lusts to fulfil.

The cops had a victim, stacks of forensic evidence, a record of offences and even a good idea of how the killing had happened. What they still lacked was an accused person in their custody.

Shortly after Barry's murder, Beggs had gone to Ireland and then, when he'd heard that the cops were searching his home, he'd gone on to the Netherlands. The Scottish cops called in Interpol and soon he was arrested and held in custody by the Dutch cops but there was to be yet another hitch. Beggs had legal rights and, as he had proven before, he was going to use every one of them to avoid being sent back to Scotland to face justice.

Beggs appeared at various court hearings in the Netherlands, always swearing he was not guilty of murdering Barry Wallace. His lawyer tried to persuade the Dutch justice system that Beggs couldn't be given a fair trial in Scotland because of all the negative coverage in the media. He had a point. The media and the public were horrified by the murder of young Barry. Yet sent back he was.

At first, the jury in the High Court, Edinburgh, were probably delighted they had been called upon to sit through such an important trial but soon most would regret it. The detail was horrific. The delays were onerous and repetitive as the lawyers and judge debated different legal points.

Beggs had hired top man Donald Findlay QC. Under the principle of Scots Law that everyone deserves the best possible representation, Findlay fought hard. He didn't call any defence witnesses but utilised a strategy of attacking the prosecution at every turn.

After fifteen days, the trial was over and the lawyers made their closing addresses. Allan Turnbull QC, acting for the Crown, reminded the jury that Beggs had caught a ferry to Ireland on 6 December and the expert evidence indicated that Barry's severed head had been thrown off that same ferry. What sort of man did that? A cold killer, that's what kind.

The jury agreed and found William Beggs guilty of murdering Barry Wallace. Beggs didn't blink as the verdict was spelled out and the court adjourned for lunch before reconvening for his sentencing. However, downstairs in the cells another William Beggs emerged. He threw his food against the walls, cursed the jury, judge and all and battered his fist against the brick walls of the cell. It was to be all to no avail.

Showing great restraint, Lord Osborne sentenced William Beggs to a minimum of twenty years in jail and then warned him that he might never be released.

Dumped in the sexual offenders unit at Peterhead Prison, Beggs instantly attracted more media attention. Other cons were moved from their cells to allow him single occupancy. This was not for a

335

treat – the Prison Service believed he was so dangerous that they simply couldn't allow him to be near other men. And that was in a unit which houses the worst sex offenders in Scotland, many of whom are also murderers.

As this goes to press, Beggs is working as the prison barber – his haircuts must be the most dangerous since Sweeney Todd's. He is also lodging appeals on every ground possible and, given the number of legal debates at his trial, these are sure to be numerous. And don't forget this is a man who walked free from a murder conviction before. So don't be surprised if, sometime soon, William Beggs is living near you. For pity's sake, lock your sons up securely.

THE MURDERING CHEF

The cops were dumbfounded. The young woman had lived quietly and decently but now there she was lying in her bedsit with her throat cut to the bone.

Melanie Sturton, twenty-two, was the daughter any parent would be proud of. While she was studying at a college in Aberdeen, she also worked part-time in an old folks' home. Friends would say how she had loved her work and described her as one of the kindest people they knew. So why did she come to such a bloody end?

It was 11 October 1999 and Melanie's blood-soaked body had lain in her Great Western Road flat in Aberdeen for a few days before it was found. There were no obvious motives or clues so, as the forensics team started to check the scene thoroughly, the police began the job of footslogging round her neighbours and friends.

Early on, the neighbours were interviewed as possible witnesses and to eliminate them from inquiries and they all cooperated fully – including Pamela Gourlay, a twenty-year-old chef who lived upstairs from Melanie.

According to the cops, Gourlay remained pleasant and cooperative even when she was asked to go to the police station to have a DNA sample taken. But maybe, at that stage, she didn't realise what a dead certain trap DNA can be. When the sample she gave matched some evidence from Melanie's flat, Gourlay's mood changed from pleasant and helpful to silent and brooding. No wonder. In her flat were a number of Melanie's possessions.

As if that hadn't been enough, they also found rubber gloves and a razor-sharp boning knife covered in Melanie's blood.

Pamela Gourlay was arrested immediately. Now, when she was interviewed, she wept and wailed but she talked all right. Though Gourlay worked as a chef, all her money went on a substantial drugs habit – so much so that she was reduced to dealing drugs and even begging at times. She was to stoop even lower than that in her search for drugs money.

A few nights before Melanie's body was found, Gourlay and her boyfriend, Kris Taylor, had been at another flat smoking dope and downing temazepam. On their way home, they tried to get money from some cashline machines but failed. They were broke and Gourlay needed her fix.

Back at home, Gourlay didn't sleep a wink so, in the early hours, she headed downstairs. She was wearing a sunhat and two pairs of rubber gloves and she was armed with a knife.

Melanie Sturton was just out of bed, getting ready for work at the old folks' home. According to Gourlay, the young woman sensed something sinister was afoot and tried to stop Gourlay getting in. But Gourlay barged her way into Melanie's bedsit and slashed her across the throat with a razor-sharp boning knife. The young victim screamed, begging her to stop, but Gourlay slashed again and again.

Without a care whether Melanie was dead or alive, she threw a duvet and a rug over her body and proceeded to ransack her flat. She didn't get much – just two bank cards, a CD player, gift vouchers, a purse and some jewellery. Not a vast haul and certainly not worth an innocent life.

If the murder was callous, how Gourlay behaved next revealed her as a cold-hearted woman. That same day, she was acting 'her usual cheery self' according to her boyfriend. They went into Aberdeen city centre where she withdrew £10 from Melanie's account and cashed in the gift vouchers before calmly meeting her parents and treating them to lunch. Nobody noticed a twinge of nervousness about Pamela Gourlay that day.

Gourlay confessed all to the police and she did so not only on audiotape but also on video. However, that didn't stop her trying to change her story at her trial at Aberdeen High Court in March 2000. There she blamed her boyfriend, claiming a sense of loyalty had made her take the blame. The prosecution argued that she freely confessed and, besides, her DNA was all over Melanie's flat and the murder weapon.

The prosecution had some additional help from an unexpected source. Pamela Gourlay's mother took the stand and told of a phone conversation she'd had with her daughter from prison. Gourlay, crying and upset, had said, 'It was me. I am sorry, Mum.' Like any loving mother, Mrs Gourlay couldn't believe her own child having committed such an atrocity and tried to explore the possibility of anyone else having been involved. Through her tears, Gourlay denied this, insisting, 'I'm telling the truth.'

Like any decent human being, Mrs Gourlay was outraged at the crime and showed great bravery in giving evidence against her own child.

The jury of ten women and five men believed Mrs Gourlay and the cops and found Pamela Gourlay guilty of murder. The judge, Lord Marnoch, described her crime as being 'of almost unimaginable depravity' and ordered that she serve a minimum of fourteen years.

Because the judge had interrupted her evidence 186 times, Pamela Gourlay fought to prove she had been a victim of a miscarriage of justice. She failed. She did, however, succeed in getting her sentence reduced to a normal life sentence, which would mean that she would be free far earlier than the trial judge had intended.

Melanie's family were outraged by this but not for long. New laws were introduced in Scotland under which a minimum sentence would have to be imposed in all cases. Gourlay found herself in front of Lord Marnoch again and he saw no reason to change his original view that she should serve at least fourteen years.

Gourlay didn't mend her ways in prison. In 2003, she was found guilty of dealing in substantial quantities of drugs in Cornton Vale and a further four years were added to her sentence. She'll be lucky to taste freedom before 2018. Let's hope that, by then, she *will* have changed.

INDEX